INTERLOCKING DIRECTORATES

*Origins and Consequences
of Connections Among
Organizations' Boards of Directors*

Johannes M. Pennings

INTERLOCKING DIRECTORATES

 Jossey-Bass Publishers
San Francisco • Washington • London • 1980

INTERLOCKING DIRECTORATES
*Origins and Consequences of Connections
Among Organizations' Boards of Directors*
by Johannes M. Pennings

Copyright © 1980 by: Jossey-Bass Inc., Publishers
433 California Street
San Francisco, California 94104
&
Jossey-Bass Limited
28 Banner Street
London EC1Y 8QE

Library of Congress Cataloging in Publication Data

Pennings, Johannes M
  Interlocking directorates.

  Bibliography: p. 199
  Includes index.
  1. Trusts, Industrial—United States. 2. Directors
of corporations—United States. I. Title.
HD2791.P38   338.8'7   80-8001
ISBN 0-87589-469-0

Manufactured in the United States of America

FIRST EDITION

Code 8029

The Jossey-Bass
Social and Behavioral Science Series

Preface

~~~~~~

This book describes a study of the connections among the boards of directors of the largest corporations in the United States. The board of directors is the ultimate source of formal power in a corporation and performs an important role in corporate governance. Directors are entrusted with protecting the stockholders' interests by monitoring the corporate management's decisions and policies. Among government officials, academic researchers, and financial journalists, however, there exists a diversity of opinions regarding the actual functioning of boards of directors. Do directors effectively monitor management's behavior or merely rubber stamp management's decisions? How much actual power do the directors of large corporations have, and do they abuse that power?

Interlocking directorates are a specific concern of public policy makers. An interlock exists when one individual sits on the board of two or more corporations, thus linking these corporations. Multiple directorships may be presumed to increase an individual's power and the power of the firm he or she is affiliated with, since interlocks allow directors access to resources and information. Some public policy makers have suggested that interlocks be prohibited because they threaten free and healthy competition in the marketplace. Others, however, have dismissed such assumptions as unfounded.

A connection between interlocking directorates and the consolidation of power—and the potential for abuse of that power—has been believed to exist, but this hypothesis has rarely been tested. One may assume that a large corporation exerts considerable power because some of the directors sit on the boards of other firms. However, research has not shown that large corporations use their interlocks to exert undue influence or to unfairly restrain competition.

In view of the conflicting opinions about interlocks and the lack of empirical research on their effects, the present study was undertaken to answer the crucial question about interlocks: Do they provide organizations with an unfair economic advantage in the marketplace? By examining the relationship between interlocking and economic performance, we can contribute to the national debate about the need for legislation to weaken or prohibit interlocking directorates.

In Chapter One, I present a framework for describing strategically interdependent organizations and the motivations for interlocking directorates among them. The focus is primarily on individual organizations and their attempts to develop interfirm connections to manage their dependence on other firms. Several types of interlockings—horizontal, vertical, and financial—are considered as strategies for the management of an organization's dependence on other organizations. Chapter Two provides a comprehensive review of the literature on interlocking directorates, and several approaches to the phenomenon are compared. After the evaluation of previous research, the methodology and assumptions of this study are explained.

In Chapter Three, I report the results of a national survey of the largest American corporations on the nature and extent of their interlocking. The main findings concern interlocks between financial and nonfinancial organizations and interlocks between firms belonging to the same market or industry.

Chapters Four and Five explain how interorganizational interdependence affects the propensity of firms to form interlocking directorates. The fourth chapter discusses the relevance of a market's structure to the frequency of interlocking among competitively interdependent organizations in that market. I determine whether interfirm ties are more likely in industries that are comparatively more oligopolistic. The fifth chapter examines interlocks between financial and nonfinancial organizations. The way in which a firm finances its operations is assumed to reveal its dependence on providers of debt, such as banks and insurance firms, and relates financial interlocks to the capital structure of nonfinancial firms.

Chapter Six, a logical extension of the two preceding chapters, examines the relationships between interlocking and an organization's economic effectiveness. First, I explore whether interlocks in themselves are related to effectiveness. I then determine whether interlocking is conducive to economic effectiveness for organizations whose interdependence on other organizations is high. I conclude by discussing whether the relationship between interdependence and interlocking is contingent upon the degree of economic effectiveness.

Chapter Seven examines the implications of the results, including the implications of these results for antitrust policy. This chapter also discusses several new issues that emerged in the course of this study and identifies new avenues of research.

The research of this book was partly supported by a grant from the Office of Naval Research (No. NR 170–801) and by financial assistance from the Graduate School of Business at Columbia University. Indirectly support was also provided by the National Science Foundation in its funding of a research project at the State University of New York at Stony Brook. Michael Schwartz was the principal investigator there and his team created a large machine-readable data set on the board membership of approximately 800 U.S. corporations. I am grateful to Michael Schwartz and Beth Mintz for providing me access to their files.

The data management of this study often acquired a high level of complexity. I received help from Richard Diettrich, Martin Charns, Sunil Kumar, and Kishore Pasumarty in coping with many of the data management problems. Several colleagues at Columbia took the time to read the whole manuscript and provided valuable comments. Nina Hatvany, Raymond Horton, Donald Hambrick, and Michael Tushman pointed to problems of composition. Ian MacMillan and John O'Shaugnessey took issue with some of the interpretations and methodological procedures. Joel Berk was an ideal consultant for issues in accounting research. Several other colleagues—including Janice Beyer, Philip Birnbaum, Udo Staber, Andrew van de Ven, and David Whetten—acted as constructive critics and eliminated some of the tunnel vision in my interpretation of results. Although I did not always concur with their views, they were instrumental in removing deficiencies in style and content. Of course, they are not responsible for any flaws or errors. Finally, I thank Barbara Valentine, Leung Lee, and Thomas O'Brien for their skillful typing and editing.

I would like to dedicate the book to my children, Barend, Saskia, and Niels, whose first initials formed the password of my computer account. This password symbolizes in more than one way the interlocking between my professional and personal life.

New York, New York   JOHANNES M. PENNINGS
June 1980

Contents

ᔪᔪᔪᔪᔪᔪᔪᔪᔪᔪᔪᔪᔪᔪᔪᔪᔪᔪᔪᔪᔪᔪᔪᔪᔪᔪᔪᔪᔪᔪᔪᔪᔪ

xiii

The Author

〰〰〰〰〰〰〰〰〰〰〰〰〰〰〰〰〰〰

JOHANNES M. PENNINGS is associate professor in the Graduate School of Business, Columbia University. He was awarded his bachelor's and master's degrees in sociology at the State University of Utrecht, the Netherlands (1965 and 1968, respectively). He received his doctoral degree in organizational psychology at the University of Michigan (1973). Prior to joining the faculty at Columbia, he taught at the University of Alberta, Canada, and Carnegie-Mellon University.

Pennings is coauthor of *New Perspectives on Organizational Effectiveness* (with P. S. Goodman and associates, 1977) and has contributed chapters to the *Handbook of Organizational Design* (1980) and *The Organizational Life Cycle* (1980). His articles have appeared in such journals as *Human Relations, American Journal of Sociology,* and *Administrative Science Quarterly.* He has served on the editorial board of *Organization and Administrative Sciences* (1976-1978) and *Administrative Science Quarterly* (1977-1980). Pennings is currently researching organizational birth rates, the use of archival data in organizational investigations, and strategic decision making.

INTERLOCKING DIRECTORATES

*Origins and Consequences
of Connections Among
Organizations' Boards of Directors*

ONE

Types of Connections Among Boards of Directors

More than sixty years ago, U.S. Supreme Court Justice Louis Brandeis expressed his concern and annoyance about connections between firms that were based on interlocking directorates. Such connections exist when an individual is a member of two boards of directors, thus forming a bond between the respective organizations. Brandeis fulminated against these connections, alleging that they were contrary to the public interest: "The practice of interlocking directorates is the practice of many evils. It offends laws, human and divine. Applied to rival corporations, it tends to the suppression of competition and the violation of the Sherman law. Applied to corporations which deal with each other, it tends to disloyalty and to violation of the fundamental law that no man can serve two masters. In either event, it tends

1

to inefficiency for it removes incentives and destroys soundness of judgment. It is undemocratic for it rejects the platform: A fair field and no favors—substituting the pull of privilege for the push of manhood" (1913, p. 13).

Brandeis' condemnation was unequivocal: Interlocking directorates amount to corporate conspiracy; they are a collusive practice that strengthens the cohesiveness among well-connected organizations. Presumably, the individual who sits on two corporate boards provides a connection by which the firms can communicate, establish a common body of information, and develop a uniform structure for superior organizational intelligence. The Pujo committee's report (U.S. House of Representatives, 1913), which prompted Brandeis' commentary, resulted in legislative reform designed to undo these invisible connections, with the hope that the severance of these ties would arrest the flow of interorganizational communication and enhance the efficiency of the market place.

Section 8 of the Clayton Act of 1914 was the direct result of the Pujo committee's deliberations. It expressly forbids an individual to be a director of two organizations that are competitors. However, the enforcement of the Clayton Act has been weak. Several recent studies have shown that between 10 and 20 percent of all interlocking directorates are between competing organizations (Warner and Unwalla, 1967; Dooley, 1969). Interlocking directorates between banks and their industrial customers or between law firms and their manufacturing clients are also very common (U.S. Congress, 1967; U.S. House of Representatives, 1965; U.S. Senate, 1978). Such interlocking directorates can be contrasted with more "innocent" ones, such as those between firms that are unrelated economically—such as a business school dean who sits on the boards of Sears Roebuck and Trans World Airlines or a retired army general who is a director of Rockwell International and United Artists. Although many such interlocks are also prohibited under the Clayton Act, they appear "innocent" because the corporations involved are unrelated strategically, that is they operate in different markets, or are transactionally independent. For example, Sears Roebuck belongs to the merchandising market, while Trans World Airlines provides transportation.

The enforcement of Section 8 of the Clayton Act has been spotty. Occasionally one reads a note in the *Wall Street Journal* about an attempt to block a director's appointment (for example, "Evading an Edict...," 1979; "FTC Official...," 1978; "Minority Banks...," 1976). The Federal Trade Commission has jurisdiction to enforce Section 8, yet this agency does not have the resources to detect interlocking directorates among competitors (U.S. Senate, 1978). A report by the House Antitrust Subcommittee, in 1965, strongly reiterated Brandeis' concern about the antitrust character of interlocks when investigations revealed that 1,206 individuals held a total of 1,449 directorships, and 182 persons held 425 directorships (U.S. House of Representatives, 1965). Attempts by Congress to mandate greater regulation have often been frustrated. Proposed regulations were recently shelved, presumably because they were "not thought to be worth the cost and effort" (Commerce Clearing House, 1977, pp. 55, 782). Some legislators continue to be disturbed by such inertia. Perhaps one source of the disagreement between policy makers and those who implement policy lies in their uncertainty about the significance of interlocking directorates. Are they really the basis of a corporate conspiracy? Are they devices by which competing firms plot to establish and enforce price fixing? Are they vehicles through which financial organizations influence decision making in industrial firms? Such questions become even more difficult to answer when we consider *indirect* interlocks. An indirect interlocking directorate exists if A is on Ford's board and B is on Dupont's and A and B are both on Intel's board; the relationship between Ford and Dupont is an indirect interlock. The most recent U.S. Senate study (1978) of 130 of the country's largest companies found 530 direct (two firms sharing a director) and 12,193 indirect (two firms each having a director on the board of a third organization) interlocking directorates. Although the existence of indirect interlocks is easy to document, their significance and effect on public policy are difficult to determine.

The government and the press have not been alone in their concern about interlocking directorates. Political scientists, sociologists, and economists, among others, have been intrigued by this phenomenon. Because data on directors and their board memberships are widely available, there has been a flurry of research on the social and economic implications of interlocking directorates. Some of these contributions have a *macroscopic* social focus (for example, Domhoff, 1967; Levine, 1972; Porter, 1965; Wallace, 1975); others have a more *regional* focus (for example, those dealing with community power structure, such as Perrucci and Pilisuk, 1970); still others take an explicit *organizational* perspective that regards interlocks as a device for managing relationships between organizations and their environment (Pfeffer, 1972; Allen, 1974; Gogel, Koenig, and Sonquist, 1976; Burt, 1980). The *macroscopic* and *regional* studies discuss phenomena that pertain to a national or regional economy, culture, or society, particularly the social organization of large territorially bounded entities. Examples are class structure, civic culture (Almond and Verba, 1965), structure of higher education (Lupton and Wilson, 1959), and the developmental stage of economic growth. In contrast, *organizational* studies consider the aspects of an organization and the groups and organizations it interacts with. Let us briefly review these three groups of studies.

Among the first two types of studies, it is not uncommon to detect an emphasis on elite theory. Porter (1965) and Wallace (1975), for example, have tried to identify a cohesive, well-bounded elite in Canada that is comprised of individuals who, by virtue of their multiple memberships, link organizations. In the United States and Europe, there have been analogous attempts to trace the existence of a small group of influential decision makers by examining patterns of interlocking directorates. Books with colorful titles, such as *Who Rules America* (Domhoff, 1967) and *Digging for Power* (Helmers and others, 1975), hold that interlocking directorates bind monolithic corporate power structures, and their authors reveal the existence of an economical, political elite that dominates political and economic decision making (see also Mills, 1965; Lundberg, 1969; Lieberson, 1971; Useem, 1979). Often, reporters and researchers offer data without any explicit analysis of decision making or exercise of power, but with the implication that something illegal and not in the public interest is taking place in these elites and the firms they represent. Although it is tempting to draw inferences about networks of individuals or organizations, many of these studies satisfy themselves with identifying clusters of individuals or organizations without examining the social, economic, or political implications of certain patterns of interlocking directorates. The study by Useem (1979) is typical, but unlike many other authors (Domhoff, 1967; Zeitlin, 1974, for example) he acknowledges the possibility of having to discredit his position. One should concur with his conclusion that "Even if the corporate directors in the present study do exercise considerable power over the institutions in whose governance they participate, it remains to be demonstrated that their power is exercised on behalf of anything but the interest of the subject institution. . . . It remains to be shown that the corporate directors studied here do forcefully represent the interest of their class, or at least a major fraction of it, when they participate in the governance of other institutions" (1979, p. 568).

In order to determine which interests the interlocking directors promote, one would have to gain access to communications between individuals who are interlocking directors or to obtain information on interorganizational decision making that has been mediated by interlocks. Because it is virtually impossible to collect such information, most researchers satisfy themselves with detecting networks or clusters of organizations and making speculative assumptions about their socioeconomic power. For example, Levine (1972) depicted a universe of interlocked organizations by a multidimensional representation based on distances derived from the density of interlocking directorates. Some organizations are very closely connected, others are loosely connected; from these connections, Levine constructed a "sphere of *influence*" (italics added) in which some firms are united and others are peripheral. Levine, however, did not provide any evidence on the relative influence of central and peripheral firms.

Presumably, these researchers believe that power and influence are exercised in the interlocking clusters of organizations, but they are unable to explain how these clusters function. Such researchers are like students of black boxes who find the equipment housed in the box so complicated that, rather than attempt to understand the internal mechanism, it is more expedient to study its inputs and outputs. Because it is very difficult, if not impossible, to gain access to interorganizational communication or private conversations and documents, many researchers on interlocking directorates have disregarded the activities inside the black box and shifted their attention to the social and economic effects of those activities. For example, they ask whether well-interlocked organizations have a greater effect than other organizations on political decision making or if they enjoy more leverage in affecting the behavior of the market in which they operate. Yet among the voluminous body of debate and research on interlocking directorates, one finds virtually no concern for testing the positive or negative consequences of such directorates. Interlock research on the macroscopic or regional level has not advanced our understanding of business organizations' influence on political or economic decision making.

Even studies that attempt to examine the interlock connections between industry and government (for example, Freitag, 1975; Lieberson, 1971; Mokken and Stokman, 1978; Zeitlin, Neuman, and Ratcliff, 1976) fail to empirically trace the political implications of linkages. The presumed implications, however, have appeared substantial and have prompted additional regulations—such as the recent attempts to eradicate the revolving-door syndrome, which occurs when government officials resign and join agencies that are the government's clients or serve as liaisons between the government and other organizations. This situation occurred when William Ruckelshaus, former administrator of the Environmental Protection Agency, joined a Washington, D.C. law firm that specialized in environmental matters. Such movement by individuals can be construed as successive, or dynamic, interlocking as compared to the simultaneous, or static, interlocking that is based on overlapping membership. Like the static interlocks, these dynamic interlocks are frequently viewed as compromising the formulation and implementation of public policy. However, no substantive research has demonstrated the implications of static or dynamic interlocking on political decision making (Freitag, 1975).

A related and frequently discussed issue that underlies the controversy about the presumed effects of interlocking is the distinction between *potential* power and *actual* power. Those who hold potential power (whether it is on the basis of interlocking or on the bases of other sources) may choose to use it only sparingly and then with perhaps only minor effects. For example, firms well-interlocked with regulatory agencies have the potential to exploit governmental control for their self-interest, or they might demonstrate their exercise of power by actually preventing a newcomer from joining their industry. Much research and debate has been based on the assumption that because an organization is interlocked with other organizations, it can draw on more resources, has better access to relevant information, and, by inference, has greater potential power. Sometimes the degree of interlocking is even equated with the degree of potential power, as illustrated by Levine (1972). Little is known about the conversion of potential into actual power. Surely we do not know how the possession of potential power manifests itself into specific decision-making processes.

Although we do not want to pursue the debate on potential and actual power, we want to clarify that our primary interest is in identifying demonstrable correlates of interlocking. Even without access to interorganizational communication and the associated decision-making processes, the accumulated effects of those processes can be traced to the frequency of interlocking directorates. Such effects, compounded over time, may translate into differences in effectiveness and other benefits. Our approach contrasts rather sharply with those of others who chose to avoid the difficulty of studying something that is generally hidden. Levine (1972) and others have relied on assumptions of potential power as implied by the metaphorical sphere of influence without examining the effects emanating from that sphere.

The literature on interlocking directorates and social elites, on the military-industrial complex, on the bond between corporations and government, and on the cohesiveness of corporate class segments suggests that such relationships might have all kinds of demonstrable effects. The identification of these effects is essential to our understanding of the full significance of their existence. One category of effects pertains to the very organizations involved. For example, do well-interlocked firms have a hegemony in their industry beyond that which their market share would suggest? Do they enjoy higher returns or superior industrial intelligence? Such intriguing thoughts remain only thoughts unless empirical results are presented to sustain their validity. There is a distinct need to replace myths by veridical statements on interlocking directorates.

This Book's Focus

The main objective of this book is to investigate whether differences in interlocking directorates can be explained from patterns of interorganizational relationships. A second objective is to determine whether interlocking directorates have consequences for organization effectiveness. We are interested in dealing with the con-

cerns of Justice Brandeis by investigating interlocking among interdependent organizations. Some basic questions need to be asked. For
example, what types of interdependencies exist among organizations?
Can different kinds of interlocking directorates be distinguished, and,
if so, can those different classes of interlocks be mapped onto different
patterns of interdependence? Do interdependent and well-interlocked
firms enjoy more benefits? Finally, what is the rationale for imputing
effectiveness benefits to interdependent organizations with comparatively higher levels of interlocking directorates?

This study is one of the first attempts to peek into the black
box, at least indirectly, by formulating hypothetical answers to these
questions and then supplementing them with empirical investigations. By dealing with these questions, we hope to resolve some
ambiguities about the origins and consequences of interlocking
directorates.

First, we must identify a conceptual framework for delineating interorganizational relationships and describing the various degrees of dependence an organization may have on other organizations
in its environment, including its suppliers, customers, competitors,
and other types of organizations. From the conceptual framework, we
can better understand why some organizations are more inclined than
others to develop interlocking directorates. Throughout this preliminary conceptualization, our focus is on interlocking between
interdependent organizations rather than on interlocking as a manifestation of social elites or as an expression of the internal structure of
a corporate class segment. If it can be shown, however, that interlocking has demonstrable effects on organizational effectiveness, then
interlocking, as a somewhat invisible manifestation of interfirm
structures, may have antitrust implications. Whether or not demonstrable effects of interlocking on organizational effects should elicit
antitrust measures depends to some extent on the form that organizational effectiveness takes. Are the outcomes consistent with the public
interest? If well-interlocked firms would manufacture safer products
and maintain stricter pollution standards, their interfirm ties might
not be so objectionable. If they were to enjoy, however, higher profitability through predatory pricing opportunities and comparatively
lower wage levels, undoing the concealed manifestations of interfirm structure would be justified. Thus, if we can show that interlock-

ing tends to promote monopolistic policies that harm the public interest, then indeed the antitrust agencies should heed the Congress' warnings and undo those invisible interfirm structures. This issue will be reviewed after the results on the origins and consequences of interlocking directorates have been examined.

Strategically Interdependent Organizations

Since the focus of this book is on interlocking directorates among strategically interdependent organizations, it is necessary to first define interdependence. Organizations do not operate in a socio-economic vacuum; they have to consider continuously the probable reactions of other firms when they engage in certain activities. For example, one firm may modify its advertising targets and thus trigger a new wave of advertising actions. Another firm may conclude long-term contracts with a supplier, thereby eliminating transactional vicissitudes and uncertainty of supply. Such behaviors indicate that the well-being of a firm is contingent on its own behavior as well as that of others. Its ability to conduct the "art of war," as the *Oxford English Dictionary* defines *strategy*, hinges on the quality of information and of control with respect to interdependent actors. In this book, the term *strategic* refers to the long-term implications of an organization's posture towards other organizations, such as competitors, suppliers, customers, regulatory agencies, and governmental bureaucracies. The choice and implementation of this posture has important consequences for the effectiveness of the organization. We assume that organizations will not remain idle but rather will actively manage their dependence on other organizations in order to safeguard their self-interests and to minimize disruptive influences from the environment by establishing external control.

The unit of study may thus be construed as an individual organization—sometimes called the *focal* organization (for example, Evan, 1973)—and the patterns of behavior it displays toward other organizations on which it is dependent. One could also move to a broader field of analysis and examine clusters or groups of organizations and their shared patterns of interfirm behavior. Debate about the proper unit of analysis has been quite pervasive. Hirsch (1975) suggests that researchers studying organizational environments have to consider the supraorganizational, or *institutional*, context; they must observe not only how organizations relate to their environment but also how collectivities of organizations—an entire industry, for example—reveal phenomena that are not evident from the investigation of a single unit. Thus research on an organization's management of its relationships with organizations in its environment often must consider characteristics of both the organization and the interorganizational context. In the present study, this means that the independent variable might describe the firms' industry and the dependent variable aspects of individual firms.

In the literature on organizational environments, two dominant perspectives prevail. Researchers using an ecological perspective view organizations as selected and reinforced by their environment (Hannan and Freeman, 1977a; J. W. Meyer, 1978). Organizations are reactive systems whose attributes are shaped and altered by environmental conditions. An organization's survival or effectiveness is a function of the match between the characteristics of the environment and those of the organization. Other researchers posit a theory of resource dependence; they view organizations as active and outgoing agents that enter into exchange relationships with other organizations to procure the resources that they themselves cannot generate internally. An organization's survival is contingent upon the success of its exchanges and transactions (for example, see Aldrich, 1979). This latter perspective, adopted in this book, imputes a much greater importance to the active posture of an organization's behavior; that is, organizations are viewed as actively manipulating and controlling their environment to secure a steady supply of resources; they employ a large array of strategic devices to better manage this resource supply. Interlocking directorates are one such strategic device.

All organizations are aware that their procurement of resources is dependent upon their relationships with other organizations. At least three types of interdependence can be distinguished: horizontal, vertical, and symbiotic (Pennings, 1980a).

Horizontal interdependence exists between organizations that compete with each other in obtaining similar resources and marketing similar goods and service; for example, firms belonging to the same industry (food, steel, ordnance) or a set of agencies belonging to a community chest are horizontally interdependent. Typically the interdependence is mediated by third parties—for example, suppliers, customers, and contributors. In the competition for suppliers or customers, firms realize their reliance on other organizations and become aware of their strategic interdependence.

Vertical interdependence exists among organizations located in adjacent stages of production or service. Examples can be found in industrial economics, but also include chains of educational organizations, such as grade schools, high schools, and colleges. The succession of stages of the justice system—police, courts, correctional institutions, rehabilitation centers—provides another example.

Symbiotic interdependence exists among organizations that complement each other in the rendering of services to clients. Such organizations have a functional relationship analogous to that of the cooperating subunits of a firm. For example, various engineering firms may each produce specific components for a nuclear power plant, and two social service agencies can provide complementary services, such as family and legal counsel in adoption cases. Although all interorganizational relationships may entail some strategic relevance, symbiotic interdependence has relatively little strategic relevance. Although the interactions among organizations that offer complementary products or services may enhance the dissemination of new ideas and information, such relationships are often not permanent nor consequential. Elsewhere (Pennings, 1980b) I have explained further why symbiotic interdependence is less important in defining an organization's mission and long-range objectives.

The strategic nature of horizontal and vertical interdependence is more striking. Horizontal interdependence is most salient in an oligopoly in which the firms are necessarily extremely aware of the others' presence. The degree of horizontal interdependence is a function of the number of competing organizations and the similarity of the raw materials and finished products for which they compete. Horizontal interdependence also seems to increase when the market is most inefficient, that is, when prices are no longer an accurate condensation of market information. Then, different firms have the ability to distort or to withhold essential information so that they have an undue advantage over others. This situation invites lack of candor, opportunism, false claims, and bluffing on the part of competing firms (Williamson, 1975). Strategic interdependence is particularly high in markets that have a small number of firms and a high inequality of information.

Economists use the degree of concentration of a market as an indicator of horizontal interdependence. A concentration index indicates which portion of an industry or market's total sales, or value, is controlled by the four largest (or the eight or twenty largest) firms. If this index is greater than 50 percent, organizations are very likely to recognize their horizontal interdependence. This condition does not always hold, however. For example, the petroleum industry is relatively nonconcentrated, yet there exists within it great awareness of mutual dependence. Its firms exhibit high degrees of uniformity of competitive behavior in such areas as pricing, distribution, and advertising. Generally, higher levels of concentration lead to higher entry barriers, higher capital requirements for operating at a minimal efficient size, and product differentiation. These correlates of concentration often augment the awareness of interdependence even further (Pennings, 1980a).

The strategic interdependence is highest in markets whose concentration is intermediate; that is, the relationship between concentration and strategic interdependence is U-shaped. If the number of competing organizations is large enough that pure competition exists, the parameters of the market become constant and the firms' behavior acquires a stochastic character. In contrast, if the market is very heavily concentrated, such as in the U.S. automobile industry, strategic interdependence is relatively insignificant because opportunities for withholding information diminish and departures from standard behavior can easily be decoded by other firms (Scherer, 1970). The behavior of firms is more difficult to decode, to predict, and to understand in industries of intermediate concentration. Therefore, in those industries, the incentive for interfirm strategic coordination and communication will be greatest.

Vertical interdependence is not mediated by third parties but is a direct result of the relationships between a buyer and a seller. However, the characteristics of the industry or market to which a buyer or seller belongs have serious implications for the exchange relationship between an organization and its customers or suppliers. This is clearly illustrated by the theories and research on *bilateral* oligopoly, in which both the firm and its supplier or customer belong to relatively concentrated industries. If the size of their exchange is large, their interdependence is high—especially if the size is large relative to other transactional relationships (Mindlin and Aldrich, 1975). Size might be measured in dollars of purchases or volume of shipments. The magnitude of vertical interdependence, however, is a function not only of the volume of the transaction but also of the substitutability and criticality of the resources provided by customers or suppliers. *Substitutability* refers to a firm's ability to replace a customer or supplier. *Criticality* refers to the importance of exchanges involved; an exchange is critical if a discontinuation of the relationship would quickly or severely impede the focal organization's functioning. For example, for firms that are capital intensive, long-term capital is a critical resource and often a large one, but the substitutability is considerable because a number of financial organizations could provide the necessary financing. To mention other examples, consider a utility firm that derives its energy from a single coal mine; that coal mine is a resource of high substitutability and high criticality. But the well-known Colorado brewery that relies on one particular source for its water supply considers that water a resource of low substitutability, unless it can tap other wells. Substitutability, criticality, and volume probably have a multiplicative effect on the focal organization: they have to be present simultaneously to increase vertical interdependence. If a resource is extensive, critical, and irreplaceable, a firm's dependence on organizations that supply that resource is increased.

The same market uncertainties discussed earlier can aggravate vertical interdependencies. The effects of market conditions are particularly striking in the case of a bilateral oligopoly, a market in which there are few buyers and few sellers. When a firm relies on a supplier whose market is oligopolistic, that firm is dependent not only on a particular supplier but also on the uncertainties of the market in which the supplier operates. Conversely, the buyer is not a passive and anonymous third party who is at the mercy of his oligopolistic supplier. He has some leverage or countervailing power in transactions with his supplier, while he is also highly dependent on his ubiquitous, but few, competitors. For example, A&P, Kroger, and Safeway have some leverage with respect to the manufacturers of food products and face important strategic options in developing long-term exchange relationships with them. They are restrained in their strategic behavior by the presence of their competitors. The small grocer, however, does not have any influence on his suppliers and has to tolerate whatever they dictate. The small business is much more vulnerable than the large supermarket chain and does not have the strategic discretion to reduce its vertical interdependence.

Interorganizational Coordination

Horizontal and vertical interdependence are major antecedents to the more or less synchronized behavior of the organizations involved. This synchronized behavior is reflected in the prevalent patterns of interorganizational coordination and communication; it can be construed as the organizations' way of coping with the uncertainty that is associated with horizontal and vertical interdependence. Interfirm coordination and communication arise because organizations behave in reference to other organizations on which they are dependent. Interorganizational coordination is a means of reducing environmental uncertainty (Aldrich, 1979; Hickson and others, 1971; M. W. Meyer, 1978; Pfeffer and Salancik, 1978; Williamson, 1975).

The persons chiefly responsible for a firm's management of its interorganizational interdependence are the senior officers. Certain sections of the organization are assigned to devise strategies for responding to uncertainty in the market leaving the "core" section (Thompson, 1967) to operate under conditions of certainty or near certainty. Organizations establish boundary-spanning positions to manage interorganizational interdependence so that the core can operate as if the supply of resources were stable.

The senior management of organizations is the most important class of boundary-spanning individuals. Top managers are the organization's representatives in the interorganizational domain; they are the liaison in any major act that involves interorganizational coordination. Supported by other classes of employees, they manage strategic interdependence. In many oligopolistic industries, for example, a firm's senior management is associated with the strategic planning units, long-range planning departments, and industrial intelligence units. Such units complement management's understanding of day-to-day internal operations by reporting on external activities relevant to strategic planning. Such activities are distant from the concerns of the greater part of the internal organization. This isolation is particularly acute in divisional firms, whose divisions are self-contained profit centers that are not coordinated by a central management, unlike functionally integrated organizations (Rumelt, 1974; Williamson, 1975).

In innovative, fast growing, technological industries with organizations of small, efficient size, a large part of the organization may be engaged in the management of interorganizational relationships. Such organizations often show a tendency toward decentralization of interfirm policy. Each functional unit (for example, sales, production, and finance) may deal with its subset of interdependent organizations and absorb or buffer whatever problems it encounters rather than leave such contingencies to other departments.

The markets or industries of young, innovative firms are usually fragmented and consist of many small firms. It is likely, however, that when industries mature and move toward greater degrees of concentration, their organizations become routinized, develop oligarchical decision arrangement, acquire a divisional structure, and the senior management will become increasingly involved in developing and establishing social connections with other firms. Centralized responsibility for these linkages facilitates the coordination and communication between strategic decision makers. Naturally, various decentralized activities may provide support for the formulation and implementation of strategy. A firm's research and development unit, for example, may be highly autonomous and provide important information that will determine the firm's planning. Other supportive boundary-spanning positions at lower levels in the hierarchy include public relations, marketing, and service; all contribute to the management of interorganizational affairs. Under conditions of increasing strategic interorganizational interdependence, the role of such units is likely to diminish in importance while the top decision makers establish social arrangements that expedite the prediction and interpretation of their competitors' behavior and the safeguarding of the supply of critical resources. Decentralization tends to inhibit a firm's adroit responsiveness to the strategic activities of other organizations, and information that has been filtered several times before reaching the top decision makers is apt to be distorted (Wilensky, 1969). Furthermore, intelligence between strategically interdependent organizations is confidential and sensitive. The need for confidentiality and the risk of distortion or disclosure reinforce the trend toward centralization.

These considerations make it plausible to argue that the senior management of such organizations will develop boundary-spanning systems between organizations. At the core of such a system are the boundary spanners of the two organizations who develop their own personal way of monitoring the flow of information. As members of this interfirm core, they develop a set of norms and expectations to maintain stable and regular relationships. In such boundary subsystems as schematized in Figure 1, a boundary person in organization A interacts both with various groups and individuals in his own organization and with a boundary person of organization B who, in turn, interacts with people in his organization (see Adams, 1976). As a result of their interactions, the two boundary persons establish a boundary transaction system that transmits information between organizations A and B.

For example, the person from organization A might meet the person from B at regular intervals, informally and infrequently or at formal meetings, which the representative from B attends with or without other members of B. During such encounters, aspects relevant to interorganizational transactions might be discussed. The medium of communication might also be nonverbal. Many possible scenarios can be envisioned to depict the mutual exposure of boundary spanners. The transmission of information can occur under variable conditions of trust, openness, conflict, and ambiguity.

The quality and quantity of the information that flows between organizations A and B depends on attributes of boundary subsystems and the location of the boundary persons within their organizations. In other words, the efficacy of information transmission hinges on their relationships with other members in the organizations. If the individual from organization A has poor exposure to local sources of information and is peripheral to crucial internal developments, he or she is likely to be ineffective in conveying information to the other organizations. In contrast, if internal exposure provides this person with rich, timely, and accurate information, he

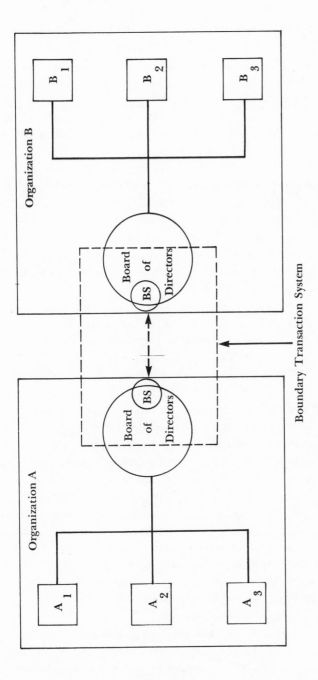

Figure 1. A Structural Model of an Organization Boundary System Illustrated by Two Organizations and Their Boards of Directors

or she is likely to be a central person in the boundary subsystem. Conversely, the quality of exposure to outsiders will enhance information transmission to the individual's own organization. Also, as I have implied, if boundary spanning individuals are senior and influential members (compare waiters versus hotel executives, bank tellers versus chairmen of the board), they are likely to reinforce their exclusive access to influential decision makers of other organizations and to make themselves almost indispensable.

Applying this model to interlocking directorates, we can envision a senior executive in organization A who sits on the board of B and interacts with one or more members of B. The boundary subsystem is not necessarily limited to two individuals but might include several interlocks. Some of the interlocking directors might be "neutral" to the two organizations they interconnect. They are "neutral" if they have no strong affiliation with any of the two firms—for example, if they are not employed by either.

Note that these neutral directors are not nearly as crucial in the boundary subsystem as are the directors who have a primary affiliation such as the senior executive who represents organization A on the board of organization B. Such interlocks can be viewed as directional or one-way. They could be especially crucial in the case of vertically interdependent organizations. The bidirectional, reflexive directors are neutral and will not perform important liaison duties in the management of transactional relationships. Perhaps, they are more conducive to sharing information among horizontally interdependent organizations. Compared to officer-directors, such unaffiliated directors face little role conflict since the pressures from the two firms they connect are not likely to clash, especially because their involvement in the two organizations is often segregated into separate times and places. In contrast, the officer-directors who form linkages with other organizations are subject to two simultaneous influences: pressures from their own organization and pressures from the other organization. As boundary spanners they represent their own organization but also maintain a permanent relationship with their fellow board members in other organizations.

Many organizations develop interlock-based boundary subsystems with other organizations, whether they are competitors or suppliers and buyers. The aggregate set of boundary subsystems of the focal organization can be described as its "institutional level" (Parsons, 1960), the part of an organization that functions to sanction and to legitimize its existence in the larger system.

A complex set of interlocks with other organizations can be depicted. Figure 2 presents a fictitious example of B. F. Goodrich, a member of the U.S. tire industry. B. F. Goodrich is the focal organization; it has established a number of imaginary interlocks with horizontally and vertically interdependent organizations. The first type includes three of the remaining tire manufacturers; the latter types include, on the supply side, providers of capital, steel and plastics and, on the buying side, automobile manufacturers and retail firms.

The figure shows that B. F. Goodrich has eight interlocks, some one-way, or directional, and some reflexive. (This is indicated by the linkage showing one or two arrows, respectively.) The interlock with Citibank is one-way going from the bank to the focal organization while the interlock with the National Bank of Cleveland is reflexive. The connection with Chase Manhattan is also one-way but it goes from B. F. Goodrich to the financial institution. For brevity's sake, I label this interlock a to-financial interlock; the tie with Citibank is a from-financial interlock. Like the reflexive tie with the Cleveland bank, both are financial interlocks. Directional interlocks are much more crucial for the management of vertical interdependence than are the reflexive interlocks.

The illustration also shows two other reflexive interlocks, one with General Electric (a) and one with Firestone (b). General Electric is not a significant supplier or customer and is in a different industry. The interlocking director has little relevance within the context of strategic interdependence. Although all linkages in this graph are interlocks in general, this particular interlock cannot be classified into one of the more specific categories, such as horizontal or vertical. However, the linkage with Firestone is a potential communication channel for disseminating or sharing market information. Sometimes this horizontal interlock is formed by someone originating from a vertically interdependent organization. For example, a senior vice-president of Citibank might be a board member of both B. F. Goodrich and Firestone, thus effectively establishing a horizontal interlock.

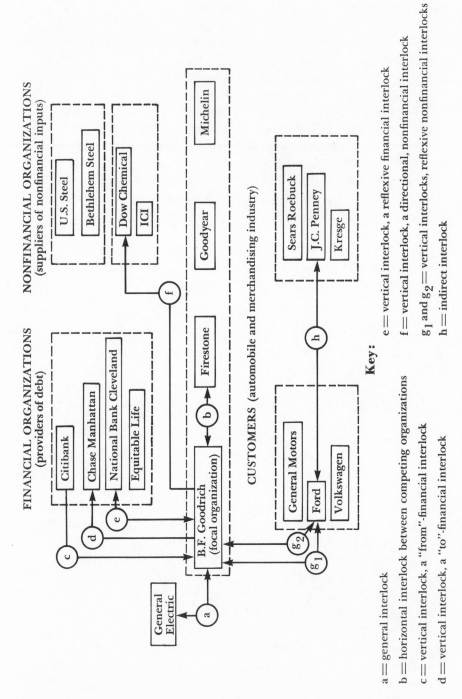

FINANCIAL ORGANIZATIONS
(providers of debt)

NONFINANCIAL ORGANIZATIONS
(suppliers of nonfinancial inputs)

CUSTOMERS (automobile and merchandising industry)

Key:

a = general interlock

b = horizontal interlock between competing organizations

c = vertical interlock, a "from"-financial interlock

d = vertical interlock, a "to"-financial interlock

e = vertical interlock, a reflexive financial interlock

f = vertical interlock, a directional, nonfinancial interlock

g_1 and g_2 = vertical interlocks, reflexive nonfinancial interlocks

h = indirect interlock

Figure 2. Several Types of Interlocks with a Fictitious Example of the Tire Industry

Three interlocks between B. F. Goodrich and nonfinancial, vertically related organizations are also illustrated in Figure 2: a directional tie with the chemical industry (f) and two interlocks with the Ford Motor Company (g_1 and g_2). Two interlocks cause a more intensive interfirm connection as there are two linking pins in the boundary subsystem between B. F. Goodrich and Ford. Finally, there is an indirect interlock between B. F. Goodrich and J. C. Penney (h), which establishes a communication link with one step removed. In Chapter Two, the indirect interlocks wil be discussed in greater detail. Here it is sufficient to note that they have little or no relevance for the presumed management of interfirm relationships because they are too distant from the relevant boundary subsystems.

This aggregate set of interlocks can be construed as one of the components of the institutional level of complex organizations. It has been depicted from the perspective of a focal organization (B. F. Goodrich). Some of these interlocks might have been created for the management of horizontal or vertical interdependence. This book seeks to empirically test this speculation by examining whether interlocking can be predicted from the horizontal and vertical relationships. For example, are B. F. Goodrich and Firestone more likely to develop an interlock if their industry has an intermediate concentration level? Is B. F. Goodrich more inclined to establish financial interlocks if it is dependent on the procurement of external debt financing? Interlocking directors could play an important role in these matters.

Within the context of strategic interdependence, interlocks might have functions resembling those of mergers and joint ventures although they are more covert, less radical, and less consequential in reducing a firm's autonomy regarding other organizations (Williamson, 1975; Pennings, 1980b). Both mergers and interlocks can be construed as attempts to disperse influence, to disseminate or acquire information, and to reduce environmental control. Vertical integration—for example, if B. F. Goodrich acquired a supplier of plastic products—would diminish the control of suppliers on the focal organization. Likewise, B. F. Goodrich might integrate forwardly by setting up its own retail outlets, thus dissipating dependence on merchandising firms. Horizontal mergers—for example, one between B. F. Goodrich and Firestone—can also be construed as a means for coping with environmental uncertainty (Pennings, 1980a).

However, when vertical integration or horizontal mergers are undesirable or not feasible, there may be greater incentive to establish interlocking directorates. The formation of interlocking directorates is therefore assumed to be an important coordination device and a salient component of the Parsonian notion of the institutional level of management. It will facilitate information sharing, it will create commitments, and it will contribute to a stable supply of resources and disposal of outputs.

Cooptation, Persuasion, and Communication

The assumption that boards of directors and interlocking directorates are primarily a device for interorganizational coordination contrasts sharply with the traditional administrative role that many researchers have attributed to boards (for example, Brown and Smith, 1957; Koontz, 1967; McDougal, 1969; Brown, 1976; Zald, 1969; and Mueller; 1978). Their attributions rest on the legal foundations of corporate governance. Publicly held firms are required to hold annual meetings at which the shareholders elect a board of at least three members. This board is delegated to monitor the senior management's decisions and to appoint and dismiss the managers so as to ensure the protection of the shareholders' interest. Some writers have suggested that the board, as the firm's ultimate legal authority, has the opportunity to show concern for corporate social responsibility (for example, see Brown, 1976).

In reality, very few organizations operate under such conditions. Many members of the board, if not the majority, are recruited from the ranks of senior management. These inside directors have considerable control over the board's functioning. Those members who are recruited from outside the organization could suffer from what Williamson (1975) calls *information impactedness;* that is, they are comparatively poorly informed about the organization and its operations and are dependent on senior management for their information. Because these outside directors, who might be selected and appointed by the chief executive officer, could often find themselves dependent on management for information, they might find it difficult to monitor and control management.

The administrative functions of boards of directors are not considered here unless the boards' possible role as coordinator and communicator between organizations is viewed as part of their administrative function. The members of the board who are officers—the inside directors—may also sit on the board of other organizations and the outside directors may have been recruited from strategically interdependent organizations. The fundamental hypothesis of this study is that under conditions of high vertical and horizontal interdependence, organizations will seek out other organizations with which to establish interlocking directorates. The function of interlocking directorates is rather different in these cases, however. Interlocking directorates among vertically interdependent firms can be construed as *cooptation* or *persuasion,* among horizontally interdependent firms as the establishment of *common messengers.* Next I will depict some scenarios to show the potential advantages and disadvantages of these classes of interfirm connections.

Cooptation is a term coined by Selznick (1949), who noted in his study of the Tennessee Valley Authority that the TVA avoided conflicts with local voluntary organizations by appointing their representatives to positions in the TVA. Cooptation is the absorption of new elements into the leadership or policy-determining structure of an organization to avert threats to its stability or existence. As Selznick noted, this cooptation initially gained the TVA support from organizations and interest groups hostile to its objectives; however, in the process of cooptation, the TVA's objectives and corresponding allocation of resources were modified by the newly absorbed groups, and their parochial interests began to displace the TVA's original goals and missions.

In the case of interlocking directorates, cooptation refers to a firm's appointment of an outside director who is employed by a vertically interdependent organization. By creating the appearance of shared decision making, the focal organization neutralizes the firms it has coopted. For example, by permitting a financial firm such as Citibank on its board, B. F. Goodrich may reduce the bank's discretion in lending credit to the tire manufacturer; if coopted, the bank may lose some of its freedom. Also, as Salancik (1977) has suggested, the appointment of such outside directors instills in them a commitment to the focal organization. They are publicly recognized as associated with that organization and are seen as responsible for its actions. Their contact with members of the focal organization en-

courages them to conform to these members' norms, to become loyal
to the organization's policies. The organization that donated the
director has been coopted because the focal organization's interests
have become entwined with the donor's interests. Cooptation ex-
ploits the role conflict that characterizes the interlocking director,
and the interlocking director may not always yield to the pressures of
the focal organization. One must examine whether the interlock was
initiated by the recipient organization or by the donor to determine
which organization benefits most by the connection.

The question of the linkage direction thus seems to be of the
utmost importance. When the direction of an interlocking directorate
originates from the donor organization, the linkage may be an attempt at coercion. The employment status of the interlocking
director—that is, whether his primary affiliation is with the donor
organization or the recipient organization—will suggest whether the
recipient organization is allowing an influential outsider into its
decision-making structure or whether the donor organization is pene-
trating into the decision-making structure of the recipient organization with which it is vertically related. If an interlocking director is
employed by the donor organization, one may speculate that, in cases
of conflict of interest, his or her loyalty will favor the donor organization, on the grounds that he who pays the piper calls the tune.
Although we assume that the main loyalty lies with the employee's
organization, both cooptation and persuasion are a two-way process.
All cooptive interlocks are agents of their employers and sources of
information and control for the recipient organization. All persuasive interlocks may likewise serve as vehicles of information and
control over other organizations but at the same time permit those
organizations to secure information stored in the focal organization.

Regardless of the bias in loyalty, it seems plausible that many
vertical interlocks constrain the behavior of both the donor organization and the recipient. By placing a member on the board of a
commercial bank, a manufacturing organization may succeed in
obtaining favorable treatment from the bank, but such treatment also
helps the bank to place loans. Likewise, the two organizations might
benefit if the bank provides an officer for the firm's board of directors.
In either case, the interlocking directorate simultaneously serves the
interests of the two organizations and diminishes transactional difficulties between them.

Vertical interlocks may also reflect attempts by the focal organization to promote social connections with other organizations in order to become better informed about the environment of its critical suppliers or buyers. By institutionalizing such connections, that organization may achieve better access to remote domains. This type of interlock is analogous to forward or backward integration, that is, when firms merge with their suppliers or buyers. Through such mergers, the resulting unified organization is less dependent on other organizations. Williamson (1975) has asserted that such mergers are the response of specialized firms that encounter transactional difficulties.

In addition to replacing external transactions by internal coordination systems, vertical integration provides intelligence benefits. By becoming a partner in the market of our suppliers or customers, we gain superior know-how and experience; thus we reduce the previously existing inequality of information. Similarly many interlocking directorates between vertically interdependent organizations may not entail a sharing of decision making but rather represent a means for organizations to acquire superior intelligence in the domains of their suppliers or buyers. These advantages can alleviate certain transactional difficulties, which, as Williamson (1975) asserts, are primarily the result of one of the two partners in the exchange relationship having inferior information. By becoming better informed, the interlocking organization promotes its ability to negotiate and to persuade in those domains.

Vertical interlocks also create the opportunity for a firm's executives to socialize in areas beyond their immediate provinces. For example, a manufacturing organization whose officers sit on the boards of financial institutions acquires an entry into the capital markets, possibly establishing trust, legitimacy, and acceptance. To continue a hypothetical case, B. F. Goodrich has established a foothold in the capital market by having one of its key officers on the board of a major supplier of capital, Chase Manhattan Bank. Likewise, donor organizations contribute expertise about their industry to recipient organizations; this process is instrumental in the dissemination of strategically relevant information. Such connections might create frequent and legitimate interactions between the organizations and provide opportunities for the sharing of information. Such information enables a firm to better negotiate its position with representatives of industries on which it is dependent.

Summarizing these conjectures, we can state that vertical interlocking directorates have a dual function. On the one hand, they may entail a coopted firm's loss of organizational autonomy and a coopting firm's increase in control over other organizations. On the other hand, such interlocks might perform an intelligence function by expediting the dissemination of information among transactionally interdependent organizations.

The interlocking directorates between horizontally interdependent organizations are hypothesized to have primarily this intelligence function. The term *common messenger* denotes this function well. The earlier example of B. F. Goodrich showed that some common messengers may be affiliated with vertical organizations, but this is not exclusively so. Some common messengers may be associated with organizations far beyond the focal organization's domain. As a common messenger, the interlock transmits information that alerts the competing organizations to one another's otherwise unforeseen and possibly disruptive actions; firms can reduce their competitive uncertainty by establishing such linkages. They could also enhance the normative uniformity of competitive behavior among them. The need to reduce uncertainty is greatest in industries in which a sufficient number of large firms influence the others' behavior. In industries in which only a few firms compete, each firm can easily decode the behavior of other firms and there is no need for linkages that will provide information. Conversely, in industries in which a great many firms compete, their behavior develops a random regularity so that the sharing of information is not needed. Such a market is often identified with the term *pure competition*. In industries with an intermediate degree of concentration, however, the firms' behavior might be erratic or unintelligible, and horizontal interlocks could aid firms in decoding signals from their competitors. Those signals are then incorporated in each firm's strategic anticipation of its competitors' behaviors and influence the firm's formulation of its strategy.

Horizontal interlocks might also reinforce the propensity of oligopolies to establish norms of market behavior and to impose greater uniformity of action. This uniformity forestalls what otherwise might have been erratic and uncertain activities. Interlocks could help establish norms about prices, costs, and innovations so that departures from the norm are easily decoded. Horizontal interlocks thus could contribute to the creation of *focal points*—standards of behavior that have a normative character (Scherer, 1970). Such standards emerge when firms are increasingly exposed to the behavior of other firms and establish a uniformity of behavior. When all firms behave in a uniform way, they appear to be subject to the same norms. This parallelism of behavior, in itself, does not imply the existence of norms because firms may merely be responding in similar ways to common competitive realities. That norms exist becomes manifest when a firm decides, for example, to cut prices or increase advertising to increase its market share. The firms have abandoned their norms about market behavior.

As an illustration, advertising expenditures are clearly a norm in the cereal industry but not in the cracker industry. Stern and Morgenroth (1968) compared these two industries and found that advertising expenditures varied a great deal among cracker bakeries but fall within a rather limited range in the cereal industry— particularly among the larger members of the industry. One might say that cereal advertising was subject to a focal point, a norm of competitive behavior. In the cracker industry, organizations behave rather erratically; the advertising expenditures of one firm have little bearing on the expenditures of other firms. Somehow these firms did not manifest a sense of conformity and failed to recognize that mutual adaptation to some advertising norm might eventually be more advantageous for them. Focal points are unambiguous, easy to decode and are highly salient when a maverick deviates from such norms in order to acquire a competitive advantage. Horizontal interlocks contribute to the development of focal points and facilitate the monitoring of behavior that is subject to those norms. It is therefore plausible to hypothesize that firms belonging to well-interlocked industries enjoy superior intelligence, greater parallelism of behavior, and fewer opportunities for cheating and opportunism. If this statement were correct, it would support Justice Brandeis' opinion that interlocking directorates promote diminution of competition.

A major difficulty in discussing horizontal interlocking directorates is the proper delineation of groups of competitors. Some firms operate in more than one industry, having multiple product or service lines. Others are vertically integrated. For example, many tire manufacturers have integrated in reverse, moving into the plastics industry, so that the distinctions between the tire industry and the plastics industry become blurred. The tire manufacturers may even compete with their own suppliers or customers. Other firms might be dissimilar from a technological or manufacturing point of view but similar in the disposal of outputs. Compare in this case the manufacturers of paper cups and plastic cups. Other firms have diversified into product lines totally unrelated. This point is particularly salient in the emergence of conglomerates in which the different components, or subsidiaries, are unrelated technologically or commercially. Conglomerates have frequently been the subject of antitrust litigation because their diversification strategies are viewed as harmful to free competition (see Williamson, 1975). Conglomerates, however, have to be considered as organizations that were created as a response to the inefficiencies of the capital market. Therefore, they are not in the same category as more or less specialized firms that have developed multiple product lines in order to gain an advantage in one specific category of business (for example, see Rumelt, 1974). Although interlocking directorates involving conglomerates represent an interesting case, they are beyond the scope of this study (on this point, see Daems, 1977).

Interlocking and Organizational Effectiveness

It would be rather futile to demonstrate merely that interlocking is most prevalent in competitive industries and among highly transactionally interdependent organizations. Implicit in all the preceding conjectures about the motivations for interlocking is the notion that interlocking enables superior intelligence, better control over the acquisition of resources, and more effective marketing of products. It is therefore plausible to hypothesize that well-interlocked firms perform better than poorly interlocked firms in the same market structure and facing the same sources of uncertainty.

Interlocking is one of the many factors that might contribute to an organization's success and survival. Other important factors include internal efficiency and competitive selection by the market. Organizational effectiveness is also affected by extraeconomic factors that we can label *political*, which, in this context, refers to behavior that articulates and aggregates interests to resolve conflict between the focal organization and various interest groups. As a political factor, rather than an economic one, it may enjoy benefits that cannot be accounted for by its market behavior.

We might also say that organizations compete both in the economic marketplace and in the political marketplace. This difficulty is often overlooked in discussions of directors and their overlapping membership (for example, Zald, 1969; Juran and Louden, 1966) and their significance in the economic-political mixture of a firm's behavior. Whenever the political part of that mix becomes sufficiently large (as we hypothesize it does when firms become strategically interdependent), it alters fundamentally the competition in the marketplace, increasing the relative importance of political as distinct from economic competition.

The significance of political factors is apparent in antitrust cases that involve integration and horizontal merger, suits that seek to prevent firms from obtaining economic advantages due to market imperfections. These antitrust suits often argue that a particular merger will increase market failures among the remaining competitors; they seek to prevent any one firm from acquiring invincible market power. Market power denotes a firm's ability to manipulate market parameters, including the setting of price and quantity. OPEC's market power, for example, enables the oil-exporting countries to fix both the price and supply of crude oil.

Interlocking, too, is a political device that could provide a firm with greater potential market power. A well-controlled flow of information results in greater amounts of "political effectiveness" (Katz and Kahn, 1978). Conceivably interlocking allows firms to better understand the market (in the case of horizontal interlocking) and to enjoy a greater degree of information parity (in the case of vertical interlocking). In this respect, interlocking—unlike merger—belongs to a class of relatively surreptitious interfirm behaviors that includes lobbying, interfirm exchange of executive talents, covert pricing agreements, self-regulation, and industrial espionage. Interlocking, however, is not completely surreptitious; for example, all firms listed on U.S. stock exchanges are required to reveal the primary organizational affiliation of newly nominated directors. Although less radical and less abrupt than merger, interlocking does allow firms greater external control and superior political effectiveness. The crucial issue is whether interlocking correlates with effectiveness. In the case of horizontal interlocking, effectiveness benefits could accrue to those firms with horizontal interlocks that are confronted with the greatest number of competitive market conditions. In the situation of vertical interlocking, effectiveness benefits could accrue to those transactionally interdependent firms that have more frequent ties with suppliers or customers.

The benefits of vertical interlocking, however, may be difficult to isolate. Persuasive interlocks, reflecting a firm's active movement into the domain of its suppliers and customers, could yield relatively obvious benefits. Assessing the benefits of cooptive interlocks is more complex. Although they may ensure a steadier supply of critical resources, they may also impede a firm's aggressive maneuvering in its environment. A recent U.S. Senate study illustrates this possibility when it states that major financial institutions "may be able to control [an interlocked] company's competitors by assuring adequate credit and capital to the favored company and withholding financial assistance to disfavored competitors" (U.S. Senate, 1978, p. 128). In such a case, the financial institution can constrain an organization's competitive posture by selectively withholding capital, a critical and nonsubstitutable resource.

Thus horizontal and vertical interlocks present different benefits and constraints, and we must separately examine their effectiveness correlates. It is even desirable to determine whether cooptive interlocks have a different relationship to effectiveness than do persuasive interlocks.

A remaining methodological decision is the choice of measures that constitute effectiveness. The choice of variables is dependent on the definition of effectiveness that one adopts, for organizational effectiveness is a multidimensional concept (Pennings and Goodman, 1977). One's choice reflects issues of values and preferences regarding the criteria and comparison standards to be employed. In addition, one must consider which constituencies' interests are relevant to an examination of the effectiveness correlates of interlocking. An antitrust jury might focus on different criteria than the Food and Drug Administration, labor unions, consumer groups, or an association of disgruntled employees. Some authors have argued that even if one were to limit oneself to a narrow set of criteria, such as return on investment, there remain problems in evaluating interorganizational utilities (see Hannan and Freeman, 1977b). For example, the shareholders of a regulated telephone company might prefer steady returns, while the investors in an innovative electronics firm prefer speculative investment opportunities. Such problems aggravate difficulties in determining whether well-interlocked firms enjoy superior effectiveness. As described later, we employed a limited set of effectiveness measures in our analysis of the relationship between interlocking and performance.

Summary

Our preliminary hypothesis is that interlocking promotes effectiveness. The benefits of interlocking for organizational effectiveness are highest when an organization faces a competitive environment and when it is highly dependent on critical and nonsubstitutable resources. In other words, interdependence and interlocking have an interactive effect on organizational effectiveness, and the advantages of interlocking are strongest when interdependence is most pronounced.

Of the two steps in my argument, the first is to relate interlocking to interdependence. The second step relates effectiveness to the interdependence relationship. Interlocking may relate to effectiveness directly or interdependence and interlocking may have a multiplicative impact on effectiveness. The interlock-performance relationship will be stronger if dependence is higher. The relationship can be stated separately for horizontal and vertical interdependence and their commensurate types of interlocking directorates:

- Horizontal interdependence: *Common Messengers* (reflexive interlocks acting as conduits among competing organizations)
- Vertical interdependence (1): *Cooptive interlocks* (directional, one-way interlocks from external actors onto board of focal organization)
- Vertical interdependence (2): *Persuasive interlocks* (directional, one-way interlocks, from focal organization to external actors)

Firms that behave in accordance with this hypothesized relationship are then expected to be more effective.

This book focuses on the interorganizational motivations for interlocks and the consequences of interlocks. Horizontal and vertical interlocks develop from the strategic interdependence among competing organizations and transactionally related organizations, respectively. The decision to establish interlocks is motivated by a desire to secure information and control over the organizational environment. If interlocking promotes external intelligence and interfirm coordination, it should follow that interlocked firms enjoy higher degrees of organizational effectiveness. The interorganizational model presented in this chapter provides the framework for the subsequent chapters.

This orientation contrasts sharply with historical, Marxist, or elite theoretical approaches to interlocking. This book does not address macroscopic socioeconomic issues. We are not concerned with such questions as what historic conditions preserve and reinforce the power of corporations and the well-connected individuals who are associated with them (compare Coleman, 1974). We will not discuss theories of elitism in which complex patterns of entangled connections among elite members contribute to the integration and cohesion of elites. Nor will we deal with political theories (compare Perrucci and Pilisuk, 1970; Useem, 1979) that purport to show interlocking directorates to be a decisive factor for sustaining the political hegemony of the contemporary "coalesced bourgeoisie" (Marx and Engels, 1971).

As acknowledged earlier, interlocking directorates might have emerged as a result of conditions that are explained by theories of elites or some other macroscopic framework. It is possible that some interlocking directorates have consequences for interfirm relationships, even though their existence cannot be accounted for by the interdependence among the firms. Some organizations might enjoy benefits from interlocks based on social class or elite cohesion.

An example of interlocks that might have been developed from nonstrategic, elite-derived factors and have benefitted the organizations involved is provided by Knowles (1974). He shows that some petroleum and chemical firms were tied by virtue of their sharing an affiliation with the "Rockefeller financial group," a set of individuals who are connected with Rockefeller-related organizations (for example, Chase Manhattan Bank, Rockefeller Foundation, and Rockefeller University). Knowles indicates that Rockefeller-tied firms showed more collusion than the untied firms. It is difficult, if not impossible, to isolate elite-derived interlocks from those that might have arisen from horizontal interdependence or to discern their separate and joined effects on market control and effectiveness. This book is restricted to the explanation of interlocks and their effects as they originate from the patterns of interorganizational interdependence. We bypass the questions of whether wealthy families, elites, owners of large blocks of shares, the "military-industrial complex" and other possible interest groups account for interlocking and benefit from it.

While recognizing such limits, this book is unprecedented in the scope and depth of interlock research. Much previous interlock research was descriptive and void of hypothesis testing, while the investigation reported here is grounded in interorganizational relationships. Also this study is based on comprehensive data incorporating interlocking, industrial, and financial data on approximately 800 U.S. corporations. The conceptualization of interlocks as multiattribute phenomena—for example, directionality, directness, and horizontal versus vertical—is unusual and permits more precise conclusions about their effects on organizational effectiveness. Such effects might not be detectable if one was restricted to interlocking in general even with access to a huge data set, such as the one forming the foundation of this book.

This interorganizational focus does not preclude a concern for public policy; rather, it allows us to investigate whether interlocking has antitrust implications. By examining organizational benefits correlated with interlocking, we can determine whether interlocked firms have discernible advantages. Only once we have explored this topic can we discuss whether interlocks must be eradicated to maintain parity in the market. In the last chapter, I address this issue in detail and indicate to what degree the antecedents and consequences of interlocks dictate a stronger enforcement of the antitrust regulations.

This book intends to resolve part of the controversy about interlocks by scrutinizing some of the myths and stereotypes about them and testing those images against empirical data. In order to do

this, we should first review the methodologies for analyzing interlocking directorates, and present an overview of the research to date.
Such a background will enable the reader to put this study in proper
perspective.

TWO

Investigating
Multiple Directorships

~~~~~~~~~~~~~~~~~~~~~~~~~~~~~~~~~~~

The discussion thus far has suggested that interlocking directorates do not merely establish a social connection between firms, that interlocks may promote a variety of connections, the attributes of which need to be distinguished. The delineation of these varied characteristics bears directly on our understanding of the function of interlocks in the management of organizational relationships. It is therefore useful to reflect further on the differences between various types of interlocks. It is also desirable to complement this discussion with a review of the composition of boards of directors. Interlocking directorates and composition of boards of directors are often mentioned in one breath, but it is important to distinguish between these institutions.

This chapter, therefore, presents a more detailed conceptualization of interlocking directorates and boards of directors and reviews the empirical literature on the nature of interlocking directorates. This will meet at least two needs. It will help integrating and contrasting this study, with its emphasis on strategic interdependent organizations, with the main traditions of interlock research, which include the network-based studies and studies of organizational theory. It will also enrich and sharpen the aspects of interlocking to which we briefly alluded within the context of strategically interdependent organizations. This chapter puts the present study in proper perspective by discussing the current state of the art and by showing how this study differs from previous investigations by adopting or discarding some of their contributions.

Multidimensionality of Interlocking Directorates

The discussion of interlocking directorates has often been plagued by a methodological question: Should the researcher treat them as linkages between a pair of organizations—the position of this study—or the edges (spokes) in a network of organizations? The data on interlocking directorates have enabled many researchers to construct nationwide networks of organizations in which some organizations are central and others peripheral (for example, Bearden and others, 1975; Levine, 1972). However, at the level of interorganizational relationships, we could likewise use the data on interlocking directorates to construct elaborate networks of relationships among buyers and sellers or among competitors. We could examine some plausible hypothesis to explain the formation of such networks. For example, does a well-connected bank in a network of organizations derive its many connections from its debtor and borrower relationships? Even though Bearden and others' (1975) study was of national scope, their results have some "local" significance because they did detect regional webs of organizations in which local banks were comparatively well connected. Similarly, one could investigate a number of competing organizations—for example, all the firms belonging to the paper industry—and examine the multitude of their connections and the location of each organization in this network of connections. Perhaps well-connected organizations enjoy superior intelligence about market conditions. We can distinguish two approaches to the study of networks. The first examines the location of an individual organization in a network of organizations; the second uses the network as the unit of analysis and examines its attributes, such as overall connectedness. These two approaches are highly intertwined. Naturally, a description of an entire network and its characteristics is dependent on a definition of the linkages between the organizations involved and their environment. The characteristics, such as interconnectedness, of a given network depend on the attributes of the interlocking directorates involved. The most salient characteristics of interlocking directorates include directness, intensity, and directionality. The earlier example of B.F. Goodrich showed that in our framework directionality is an important attribute of interlocking but directness is not. Within the context of strategically interdependent organizations, the direct interlocks are considered important; indirect interlocks are not expected to be relevant for the management of the organization and environment. Nevertheless, directness is a prevalent concept in the literature of interlocking, while directionality is rarely mentioned. After reviewing these characteristics, we shall return to the issue of networks and organizations embedded in networks.

A *direct* interlock exists when one individual is a director of two organizations; a direct interlock is a single path between two organizations. In contrast, an *indirect* interlock exists when two organizations are linked by a path through one or more third organizations. Channels for potentially surreptitious communication exist, although the communication has to follow a longer route before reaching a terminal point. The previously mentioned Congressional study (U.S. Senate, 1978) shows that the length of a route is often substantial, depending on the number of intermediate companies that one considers. For example, American Telephone and Telegraph Company (AT&T) has 31 direct routes and 624 indirect ones. It has 22 indirect routes to Chase Manhattan, which it can reach through 12 intermediate companies. If one were to consider interlocks at two or three removes, the number of indirect routes would be even larger. For example, AT&T might be linked with Equitable Life Insurance Company, which, in turn, is linked with Citicorp which, in turn, is linked with Chemical Bank, and so on. Several branches originate from each organization; these branches, in turn, divide into many additional branches. The number of indirect linkages multiplies exponentially as we trace the branching.

Many indirect interlocks, however, have little relevance for interorganizational relationships. There are two reasons for this, one theoretical and one methodological. In theory, a firm's benefits from indirect interlocks are marginally decreasing ones, especially if the indirectness includes two or more intermediaries. Information that is transmitted through several consecutive intermediaries is likely to lose validity and richness during the transmission. The indirectly linked director's attention is much more diffused than that of a directly interlocked director; thus the former is a less effective liaison.

The second reason that indirect interlocks may have only minimal effects on interorganizational relationships is that these interlocks are only one form of indirect access between firms. Examining a network of interlinked firms, Levine (1975) removed the best-linked organization, Equitable Life, from his data set; when he reexamined the direct and indirect linkages, he found that the routes between firms remained largely intact. Such explorations led him to conclude that individual linkages (both direct and indirect) are rather irrelevant for evaluating the multiple access routes from one organization to the other.

It is hard to judge whether all indirect linkages are irrelevant. Some might be relevant in reference to the joint consideration of vertical and horizontal interdependence. Representatives of relevant, vertically interdependent organizations may function as common messengers (that is, indirect interlocks) for competitively interdependent organizations. For example, a commercial bank or investment bank could promote the development and monitoring of normative behavior among competing manufacturers that rely on the bank for financing. This hypothesis, however, is highly speculative and has never been tested. It seems likely that many indirect linkages, especially those two or more degrees removed, have little significance.

The *intensity* of an organization's interlocking behavior is the proportion of its directors that the organization shares with other organizations. For example, if a manufacturing organization and a bank create a second interlocking director, their linkage is said to become more intense, particularly if the size of their boards remains the same. Bearden and others (1975) propose the following formula for determining intensity: Intensity is the number of interlocking directorates between two organizations divided by the square root of the product of the two boards' number of directors.

In addition to their intensity, interlocks are described by their *directionality* and *strength*. Directionality was mentioned in our earlier discussion of interlocking directorates among vertically interdependent organizations. As noted, the interdependence between two organizations favors one of them, and presumably the interlocking directorates reflect the asymmetry. If an interlocking director is an officer of organization A and sits on the board of organization B, the benefits from the interlock to organizations A and B are not equal. Interlocking directorates are not reflexive, that is, the link from organization A to B is not equivalent to the link from B to A. Indeed, it will become clear that distinguishing the direction of an interlock is very useful for exploring coordination and communication between vertically interdependent organizations. Directional interlocking directorates may be the single most interesting class of directors for researchers. Other interlocking directors, such as neutral outsiders (business school deans, representatives from ethnic or other interest groups) have probably little relevance for interorganizational coordination, although they can be significant in the diffusion of innovation.

In order to clarify the preceeding statements, it is useful to introduce the concept of *strength*. A distinction between strong and weak ties was made by Granovetter (1973), who classified interpersonal connections on the basis of their communicative function. According to his argument, strong ties are more likely to cluster individuals into well-bounded, closely knit groups. The strength of connections is indicated by the amount of time the individuals spend with each other, their emotional investments, and their mutual attraction; strong ties act to shield the group from exposure to weakly tied individuals. Weak ties, in contrast, are single bridges between individuals who belong to different groups. For example, five individuals of a group frequently interact (they are strongly tied) and one of its members, John, has a remote acquaintance, Peter, affiliated with a different group, with whom he interacts occasionally (a weak tie). Here, information might flow from John to Peter, and vice versa, even though the members of their respective groups may never interact with each other. Granovetter considers the weak tie between John and Peter "strong" because it acts as a liaison between well-integrated groups. The usefulness of this model for research on interlocking directorates seems obvious. Consider, for example, a set of steel firms, heavily interlocked by directors who are Republican, who belong to the same private clubs, and who have known one another for several decades. One of these directors might occasionally interact with a financial analyst who serves as a trustee for the steel workers' pension fund. Such a weak connection might be a "strong" link between the steel industry and its unions.

The stronger the ties between two interlocking directors, the larger the number of other directors with whom they are strongly tied. Also, if organization A is strongly tied with a set of organizations, S_1, and organization B is strongly tied with another set of organizations, S_2, then the stronger the connection between A and B, the greater is the overlap of organizations in S_1 and S_2. By determining the strength of interlocking directorates (for example, reciprocal interlocking directorates and similarity in club memberships of the directors involved), one may be able to identify cliques of organizations that are founded on strong ties, compared to those founded on weak ties. One may also be able to identify weak interlocking directorates that form the single bridge between well-connected cliques of organizations.

It is possible, however, that weak connections have a distinct significant benefit. Firms that are strongly tied may differ in their numbers of weak ties. Perhaps strongly tied firms that have many weak links enjoy an advantage over strongly tied firms that lack weak links. Firms that have many weak links may be likely to be more successful in their diffusion of innovation, and one would predict that such firms would perform better. Weak links form bridges into areas that are beyond a firm's domain or salient environment, but which could expose it to novel areas and developments. That weak ties confer such benefits seems quite plausible (Granovetter, 1973).

To the extent that background information on interlocking directors were available, one might be able to detect strong interlocks not only by ascertaining directionality but also by examining stock ownership, duration of the interlock, and reciprocity of the interlock. Such factors should enhance the involvement and emotional intensity of the interlocking directors and representatives of the two organizations involved. The strength of the ties might be still greater if the interlocking director shares the same educational background or norms and values as the other members of the board (for example, see

Perrucci and Pilisuk, 1970). One might even speculate that the number of directorships held by a single person is an indication of strength; the greater the number of directorships, the more dispersed the director's attention and involvement, and the weaker is the linkage he or she represents. In Chapter One we suggested that neutral and possibly peripheral members in the boundary subsystem are probably not crucial in the management of the organization and environment. The multiple board member whose attention is diluted cannot muster the commitment and energy that is central among directional (and undiluted) interlocking directors. *Professional directors* who hold five or more directorships would fit into this category. Such directors are typically unaffiliated (hence the adjective *professional*) and, unlike directors who link only two organizations, they devote their time to a wide variety of activities. They could be comparatively detached from the interorganizational dynamics, especially if the director with many directorships is compared with officer-directors who are directors in their own organization and in only one other.

A hint about the correctness of our speculation—that the number of directorships an individual holds indicates strength—is provided by Koenig, Gogel, and Sonquist (1973). These authors compared two samples of directors: a group of directors who held only one board membership and a group who held four or more. Of the latter, 72 percent were found to be members of private clubs, compared to only 17 percent of the former. Thus private club membership and interlocking appear highly correlated. One can speculate that the connectedness among interlocking directors is reinforced by their membership in private clubs. These personal connections are the sinews of a network of social links that cut across the connections between organizations. Patterns of membership in such hidden cliques suggest that weak links have possible strength even if the linkers seem weak. Strong links are the bridges that connect strongly tied clusters of firms, but weak linkages enable firms to stay abreast of developments that, while only remotely relevant, may influence important long-term decisions. Naturally, these speculations are highly tenuous, but they do illustrate the value of examining weak ties and their "strength." It is easy to interpret directional interlocking directors as strong since such individuals are not likely to have dispersed their attention span. They are expected to be more committed to and knowledgeable about the organization they originate from. It is also reasonable to view nondirectional interlocks as weak. This adds theoretical justification for expecting stronger correlates for directional interlocking directorates.

This delineation of strong and weak ties emphasizes those attributes of interlocking directors that are derived from their membership in actual groups (for example, private clubs) or inferred groups (for example, network cliques). Numerous studies have examined the organizational linkages between individuals rather than the individuals as links between organizations. In a general sense, individuals are linked by virtue of their overlapping memberships in two or more organizations, while groups are linked by virtue of their sharing one or more individuals. Specifically, directors are linked by their multiple memberships, while organizations are simultaneously linked when they share directors. This duality of interlocks was well conceptualized by Breiger (1974) as the *intersection* of individuals within groups and of groups within individuals. The overlap between boards of directors due to their sharing a common individual coincides with the overlap of multiple affiliations in the connecting individual; hence, the intersection.

As the study by Koenig, Gogel, and Sonquist (1973) illustrates, membership in a clique is an attribute of some interlocking directorates. Knowles (1974) also illustrates that membership in a network clique is a significant aspect of interlocking, but his study is unusual because he constructs a network on the basis of the membership patterns of the directors involved. Knowles' method of determining memberships in actual groups may be contrasted with research in which an analysis of the patterns of overlapping membership is used to detect inferred groups. Members of such inferred cliques may not be aware of belonging to them, do not see themselves as being affected by them, and do not derive any cost or benefit from them. The detection of cliques or clusters of individuals seems pertinent, however, only when the theorist's construction of social reality matches the social construction of reality by the individuals under study. Unless these two constructions correspond, research on social networks of interlocking directors remains sterile and of little relevance. However, when there is closure between the two, research on interlocking directorates can advance considerably, particularly in the area of weak and strong ties.

While the identification of weak interlocks, their role, functions, and consequences remains difficult, strong ties can be identified rather easily—for example, by ascertaining the primary affiliation of the interlocking director. Bearden and others (1975) are the only investigators who have explicitly examined strong ties by identifying the employment status of the interlocking director. In their attempts to construct an interorganizational network, they do not treat linkages between organizations as reflexive (that is, they consider the link from organization A to B to be different than the link from B to A). They assign a weight of 90 percent to the donor organization of the directional interlock and a weight of 10 percent to the recipient organization. They then proceed to determine a firm's centrality in an interorganizational network. This important study illustrates an attempt to define the organizational relevancy of various types of interlocking directorates.

Although this present work does not treat networks in themselves, the idea of distinguishing strategically relevant interlocks from irrelevant ones prominently enters into our analytic method.

Interlocking Directorates and Networks

Moving from a consideration of interlocking directorates between a focal organization and other organizations to a discussion of a network of interlocks seems to be a small step. We could simply count the number of times a firm interlocks with other firms, but many authors have criticized this procedure (for example, Bearden and others, 1975; Bonacich and Domhoff, 1977; Levine, 1972; Mariolis, 1975). They argue that the number of interlocks alone does not account for the number of indirect interlocks. Bearden and others (1975) have developed a measure of centrality that gives more weight to interlocking directorates with densely interconnected firms than to interlocking directorates with sparsely interconnected organizations. The greater a firm's density, the more central the location of that firm in an interorganizational network. For example, Mariolis (1975) and Bearden and others (1975) use a proximity measure developed by Bonacich (1972) to compute a firm's centrality. This algorithm, however, requires the researcher to gather data on a universal constellation of organizations, since they define centrality to include all indirect interlocks, including those at distant removes. Because this is not feasible, researchers such as Levine (1972), Mariolis (1975), and Bearden and others (1975) have restricted themselves to a limited set of organizations—for example, the 800 *Fortune* corporations. They have constructed a matrix of 800 x 800 organizations and determined how much each firm overlaps with the other firms. Mariolis found a correlation of .91 between the number of interlocks and a firm's centrality score, suggesting that the two measures are highly interchangeable. This finding reinforces our earlier comments on the near irrelevance of indirect interlocks for our understanding of interorganizational behavior. Bearden and others (1975), who followed Mariolis' method using data from 1,131 organizations' 1962 records, were less convinced about the interchangeability. Limiting themselves to directional interlocking directorates, they found that a ranking of the twenty most *interlocked* organizations was rather different from the ranking of the twenty most *central* organizations, although thirteen firms were among the top twenty on both lists. Instead of finding a national network with varying degrees of centrality, they detected the existence of five regional networks in which banks are highly central. We have suggested that this centrality may reflect the vertical dependence of peripheral firms on the central organization. Since Bearden and his associates do not provide interdependence data, this is a matter of speculation.

   A different strategy has been used to show that a network's characteristics have minor significance for the individual organizations. This strategy consists of dissecting the network within which a firm is embedded. Studying the *Fortune* list of corporations Mariolis (1975) found that of the 736 firms with at least one interlock, 722 formed a discrete cluster; that is, if one takes any of these firms as a point of departure, one can follow a route through interlocking directorates from that firm to the other 721 firms. In this cluster, each firm is, in more than 90 percent of the cases, only four steps away from the others. The implication seems clear: U.S. corporations interlock tightly. Accordingly, even if one tries to disrupt such networks by reducing the number of interlocks, there remain other routes through which a firm can reach another firm. Even if the number of connections were greatly reduced, the network would still preserve its structure.

Mariolis' work is complemented by Levine's (1975) analysis of the *Fortune* 800. Among 797 of these corporations, Levine discovered 1,572 interlocking directorates, a ratio of 1:2. This ratio is similar to the baseline norm for so-called random graphs (Erdos, 1973). In networks with edges (spokes) and vertices (knobs), the ratio between edges and vertices can range from very small (approximating zero) to unity. In the first phase, with only a few vertices, the random graph consists only of a few small trees. In the second phase, the number of edges increases—but not beyond a ratio of 1:2. The network still consists of many unconnected trees—or the appearance of single cycles or loops with branches—and the number of unconnected vertices increases asymptotically; that is, beyond a certain threshold, there is hardly any appreciable increase in unconnected hubs. In the third phase, the number of edges is close to one half the number of vertices, resulting in a drastic change in the network. The random graph is now instead a single, well-interconnected structure. Beyond this phase as the ratio of vertices to edges approximates unity, the random graph becomes even more complex, and uniform.

Levine (1975) notes that the magical number one half in the theory of random graphs is surprisingly similar to the number of firms relative to the number of interlocking directorates. Although he admits that there is no simple explanation for the correspondence between random graphs and real graphs (of interlock networks), he hypothesizes that a social engineer could manipulate the "real" network without doing much damage. By the same token, an antitrust agency that unknots some social connections will not have any impact on the integrity of a corporate network. We should note that Levine, like Mariolis, considered only those interlocks with firms belonging to *Fortune*'s 800 corporations. Had he counted interlocks with smaller firms, the ratio 1:2 would have been larger. The comparison with random graphs induces Levine to state that "the facts of corporate data, which some sociologists are at pain to endow with meaning and to adduce in the explanation of current events, are, in fact, the work of some whimsical spirit who shoots 'craps' into the universe" (1975, p. 36). Although only suggestive, his assertion illustrates, in yet another way, that interlock-based networks and their properties have little relevance for explaining the behavior between strategically interdependent organizations. The direct and indirect connections between organizations are so frequent, abundant, and pervasive that they cannot be used to differentiate among organizations. Moreover, limiting the number of connections studied, as Bearden and others (1975) did by restricting their study to directional interlocking directorates, does not resolve this problem. Rather, this method only shifts the various threshold levels, as can be inferred from the theory of random graphs. When the number of linkages are fewer, it might appear that the randomness vanishes and that a "real" structure emerges; but, in actuality, such methodology imposes an order on the data that, as the theory of random graphs suggests, is the result of chance. The theory of random graphs seems equally applicable to a wide variety of interlock-based networks and thus renders invalid studies of networks based on graphing. In this study, therefore, we will discard such approaches to networks.

To get a true picture of organizational networks derived from interlocks, one has to visualize the proverbial forest, obscured by a dense intertwining complexity of trees. The situation is even more complex because the forest, unlike a natural one, is not geographically well-defined, but spreads its dense complexity beyond our picture. One cannot clarify the picture merely by excluding the smaller trees as Levine (1972) did; nevertheless, it is not feasible to include the smaller firms—even the largest data-processing facilities are unable to accommodate a matrix whose rank would exceed one hundred thousand. Thus, this forest cannot be completely mapped.

One might conceivably produce a more complete picture, however, if the forest were more bounded, if one examined smaller economies. Countries such as the Netherlands, Canada, and Sweden have comparatively small sets of firms, and the researcher might be able to identify a comprehensive national network (see Berkowitz, Carrington, and Corman, 1978; Berkowitz and others, 1978; Porter, 1965; Wallace, 1976). However, intercorporate affairs reach across geographical boundaries, as a study on interlocking directorates in the Netherlands (Helmers and others, 1975) dramatically illustrates. The Netherlands is the origin of four giant multinational corporations whose combined budget dwarfs the budget of the Dutch government. The relevant environment of these four multinationals (Royal Dutch, Unilever, Philips, and Akzo) reaches far beyond the geographical boundaries of the Low Countries; any useful analysis of their interlocking behaviors must not be restricted only to organizations having Dutch incorporation.

Thus, it is difficult to construct patterns of interfirm networks for even supposedly well-defined national economies. These difficulties provide additional support for the proposition that the study of interlocks is better approached by focusing on interorganizational connections than by attempting to construct elaborate networks based on national aggregate interfirm connections. The research presented in this book, therefore, consists of an examination of direct interlocking directorates between focal organizations and firms in their relevant environment rather than an attempt to locate a focal firm in a network of interorganizational relationships. Furthermore, since vertical interdependence between organizations usually has directional character, we shall deal extensively with the directionality of interlocking directorates. This position naturally determines the design of study, the direction of the analysis, and the presentation and interpretation of results.

Boards of Directors

Boards of directors are, by their very nature, boundary-spanning units; their members perform important duties in the management of the organization's interactions with its environment. Research on boards of directors is related to research on interlocking directorates, although their relatedness is somewhat equivocal, as is particularly noticeable in research on the proportion of *inside* and *outside* directors (Helmich, 1977; Juran and Louden, 1966; Pfeffer, 1972). Inside directors are those board members whose primary affiliation is with the organization. Outside directors are individuals who have been recruited from outside the organization and they form a highly diverse group. The distinction between these two groups is not always clear-cut, however. Some directors could be classified as outside or inside; for example, many organizations have board members who are partners in the law firm that represents the organization. Such individuals could be considered outside directors, although they obviously have a strong allegiance to the organization and therefore could be labelled inside directors. Many boards of directors include private investors who, although not employed by the firm, have such strong vested interest in the firm that they could be classified as inside directors.

Anecdotal evidence suggests that many outside directors are selected by one or two members of the senior management team—for example, by the chief executive officer. Allegations about the existence of a "buddy system" are not infrequent. If such hearsay is correct, the distinction between inside and outside directors is even more blurred, because many outside directors in fact belong to the chief executive officer's "inner circle." Informally speaking, such outside directors are therefore almost insiders.

The category of outside directors can be differentiated into subsets of directors originating from various types of organizations— assuming that all outside directors have a primary affiliation with some other organization. There are outsiders who are employed by competing organizations, those who work for vertically interdependent organizations, and those who come from organizations that are strategically irrelevant.

In order to determine which outside directors were recruited from competing organizations, we must first address the difficulty of defining sets of competitively interdependent organizations. A common guideline is to use the Standard Industrial Classification (SIC) that is maintained by the U.S. Bureau of the Census. This system is based on the technical and commercial traits of products or services. Each industrial classification is given a number of two to seven digits that represents different degrees of specificity within a general category of products. For example, the two-digit class coded 36 represents the electronics industry, while the four-digit class 3662 refers to radio and television communications equipment. It is convenient to consider firms that belong to the same two-digit class as competitors, but sometimes their products are so different that they are not competing in the same market. It is therefore desirable to compare the firms' products in order to determine if they are competitors. The more similar their products, the more reasonable to assume they are in competition.

The reasonableness of this assumption and, by implication, the correctness of classifying a director as originating from a competing organization can be challenged by referring to the notion of product differentiation. As noted in Chapter One, firms with seemingly identical outputs can decrease their competitive interdependence by forming different market segments. Product differentiation among oligopolists exists when they succeed in creating superficial distinctions in their offerings through advertising and packaging, resulting in different use functions or different customer-generated functions. A difference in use function is illustrated by artificial Christmas trees and fluebrushes—uncompetitive although they are similar in composition. A difference in customer-generated functions is exemplified by Volkswagen and Rolls Royce automobiles—two products with the same use function but different generated functions such as economy, status, or conspicuous consumption. These examples demonstrate that product differentiation sometimes leads to uncompetitive firms in the same industry.

We can isolate those outside directors who come from vertically interdependent organizations only if we know the firms' suppliers and customers. Suppliers include providers of raw materials, capital, equipment, and industrial products. Customers include manufacturers, wholesalers, and retailers. If information on specific interfirm transactions is not available—and usually it is not, as such data are considered proprietary—one may rely upon circumstantial evidence, such as the capital structure of the firm or the magnitude of types of supplies needed. At the aggregate level, there are economic input-output tables that describe the demand and supply between different industries and reveal the relative importance of a particular industry for each of the others (Leontief, 1966). Thus, one can determine the aggregate transactions between the petroleum industry, the rubber industry, and the automobile industry. Since petroleum and chemicals are important resources for a rubber manufacturer, we would classify a director on B. F. Goodrich's board who is employed by Standard Oil of Ohio as a vertical, outside director because of the presumed correspondence between transactional relations and corresponding vertical interlocks.

Finally, many outside directors have backgrounds and affiliations that escape classification; for example, the so-called professional directors who sit on many boards have no distinct organizational allegiances or identity. Other individuals in this category include university professors, retired businessmen, government officials, military officers, and representatives from social pressure groups such as the National Association for the Advancement of Colored People and women's organizations. These directors are recruited for their expertise, reputation, or goodwill; but they usually might have little bearing on interorganizational communication and coordination.

Outside directors from horizontal or vertical organizations are the most important within the framework of this study. It must be stressed, however, that outside directors convey only limited information. While interlocking directorates do connect two or more organizations, simple measures of a board's composition, such as the proportion of outside directors, are not adequate to reflect the complexity of these connections. As noted earlier, these interlocks are not reflexive relationships. Some outside directors might be important but unless their employment or institutional affiliation is known, they remain a poorly understood heterogeneous class of boundary spanners. Background information is needed, particularly for vertical interlocks and their presumed role in managing vertical interdependence. Thus, if we know that the outside director has an additional directorship and is a senior executive in a critical organization, we have a firmer basis for imputing important boundary-spanning behavior compared with individuals who are merely outside directors, even if they represent a directional tie. Interlocking directorates have an explicit relational meaning and permit the identification of both to- *and* from-interlocks. Outside directors do not connote such a relational meaning.

It is also incorrect to assume that "It is through the use of outside directors that corporations interlock with one another" (Bearden and others, 1975, p. 25). Since many inside directors can form interlocks with other organizations, a firm can have many interlocks even though there are no outside directors on its own board. Measures of board composition such as proportion of outsiders or proportion of investment bankers represent only those interlocks present on a firm's own board. Even this assumption is sometimes questionable, because such measures do not necessarily include directors' past associations. We will return to this point later. Lastly, a measure of the aggregate number or proportion of outside directors ignores the specific boundary-spanning activities that are unique to the focal organization and other organizations that are strategically salient.

Empirical Determinants of Interlocking Directorates

We have thus far reviewed interlocking directorates between organizations, interlocking directorates as elements of interorganizational networks, and boards of directors. We have briefly surveyed the motivations for interlocks, the consequences of interlocks, and the major attributes of interlocks: directness, intensity, directionality, and strength. Relevant characteristics of networks include connectedness and centrality. Finally, discussing boards of directors, we distinguished inside and outside directors and subcategories of outside directors.

At this point, we need to briefly survey pertinent empirical studies on the propensity of organizations to form horizontal and vertical interlocking directorates. This review includes studies that treat the composition of boards of directors, studies that explore the social linkages between focal organizations and organizations in their environment, and studies that examine the location of an organization in a network. Thus, these studies reflect different approaches to social linkage.

Horizontal Studies. Among the studies on horizontally interdependent organizations, there is only limited evidence that competition is an incentive for the creation of interlocking directorates. Dooley (1969) and Warner and Unwalla (1967) report that interlocks occur among competing organizations. Approximately one eighth of all interlocking directorates occur between firms that belong to the same broadly defined industry. Neither study shows whether specific characteristics of market structure, such as concentration or entry barriers, are related to interlocks. Fennema's (1974) study is exemplary in its detailed examination of the different types of linkages. Studying the European automobile industry, Fennema did not discover any support for the assumption that relatively many linkages exist among competing firms. Since he focused primarily on a single industry, he was unable to relate the differing structures of industries to their pattern of social linkages. In contrast, Pfeffer and Nowak (1977) examined the relevance of different industries' structures but, unlike Fennema, used measures of board composition rather than focusing on interorganizational linkages. Assuming that outside directors constitute linkages with other organizations, they found the proportion of such directors to be highest in industries having an intermediate level of concentration. This study, however, presents a methodological problem in its units of analysis. While board composition is an organizational attribute, the independent variable of industrial concentration is a characteristic of a higher level of aggregation, that is, the market of industry.

Knowles' (1974) investigation uses yet another unit of analysis. He examined those interorganizational linkages in the petrochemical industry that were based on closeness in belonging to the so-called Rockefeller financial group. This author delineated a set of individuals whom he considered to belong to this group and the interorganizational ties among members of this group. He found that firms in the petrochemical industry that were connected by having directors who were members of this group showed a greater amount of product duplication than the set of firms that were not tied in this way. Product duplication exists when two firms manufacture the same product and they jointly possess a large share of the market. Their combined market share, in turn, may enhance their market power— that is, their ability to affect parameters of the market such as price and quantity. The study of Knowles, like the research by Fennema, is of restricted generalizability in that it examines only a single industry. As mentioned before, research on horizontal interdependence must compare various industries in order to determine the significance of concentration for the creation of social linkages.

Vertical Studies. Researchers studying vertical interdependence tend to focus on the relationship between financial institutions, dependence, and interlocking directorates. This preferred or imposed focus on financial interdependence may be due to corporate accounting practices that usually limit themselves to reporting financial information. The researcher does not have access to data on interdependence in other types of buyer-seller relationships—for example, between a steel company and an automobile manufacturer or between a brewery and a metal container firm. The Aston group (Pugh and others, 1969) used the firm's volume of business with its largest supplier and customer, but such data are incomplete and often unavailable (Mindlin and Aldrich, 1975). At the aggregate level, there are input-output tables that indicate the aggregate flow of resources to and from firms belonging to two-digit industries (Leontief, 1966).

Whether these measures reflect the vertical interdependence between two organizations belonging to vertically adjacent industries is questionable, although authors such as Pfeffer and Salancik (1978) have treated aggregate interindustry transactions as reflecting the flow of resources between industrial firms. In view of this problem and the lack of available data on nonfinancial interorganizational transactions, it is not surprising that the studies under consideration have dealt primarily with relationships between firms and their banks.

Most of the relevant studies have relied on indices of capital structure. These indices reflect the reliance of a firm on outside financial sources. The greater the volume of long-term or short-term debt relative to shareholders' (or owners') equity, the higher the dependence; conversely, firms that rely on internal financing enjoy a great deal of independence. Some of the studies use an index such as the debt-equity ratio, a crude index because it combines all forms of external debt obligations, both short-term and long-term (for example, Allen, 1974; Helmich, 1977; Pfeffer, 1972). The debt-equity ratio is an inadequate measure because it amalgamates all outside sources of financing. In addition to this defect, moreover, the debt-equity ratio does not weigh the critical aspect of the firm's size, which often affects the substitutability of available capital. It is very critical to consider the firm's size since small firms are more likely to rely on long-term bank loans while large firms can issue bonds for long-term financing, thereby bypassing external suppliers of long-term capital. Likewise, capital intensity should be considered in examining vertical interdependence (for example, see Allen 1974). It seems plausible to state that dependence on banks and other financial institutions will be larger for capital intensive firms that have a high debt-equity ratio. Finally, it is important to adjust for types of industries since some industries show a much faster turnover of inventory than others; the retail industry, for example, has a far faster turnover than steel. As a result, the retail industry is more dependent on commercial banks because industries with a fast turnover rely heavily on short-term financing.

This difference between short-term and long-term capital requirements has instigated some researchers to develop measures of short-term vertical interdependence (for example, Dooley, 1969; Gogel, Koenig, and Sonquist, 1976). These authors have created measures such as the acid test ratio (the sum of a firm's cash, marketable securities, and receivables, divided by current liabilities) to evaluate solvency. Solvency is likely to be a very sensitive measure of a firm's dependence on short-term resources. Unlike labor and raw materials, credit is a highly substitutable resource; solvency measures, however, reflect the criticality of capital; *criticality*, as noted previously, refers to the vital importance of the main resource in the exchange relationship. In some industries, capital is such a critical resource that organizations with inadequate solvency may be extremely dependent on providers of short-term financing. However, Dooley (1969) and Gogel, Koenig and Sonquist (1976) found very weak associations between dependence on short-term debt and financial interlocking directorates. Dooley's results are primarily significant for this subsample of utility firms.

The research by Daems (1977) and Fennema (1974) treats European organizations. Daems found a very high incidence of interlocking directorates between manufacturing organizations and banks but did not examine the degree of interdependence. Fennema found a high incidence of interlocks between automobile firms and firms in the ferrous metal industry. Presumably steel and other metals are a very critical resource for automotive firms.

Other studies have related measures of interlocking directorates to indices of capital structure. Allen (1974) and Pfeffer (1972) correlated debt-equity ratio with the number of interlocks and number of outside directors, respectively. Pfeffer's results are rather insignificant. Allen showed a weak negative association, but his use of the crude debt-equity ratio, a measure too insensitive to specify the interdependence between banks and industrial, utility, and other types of firms, renders speculation difficult. Furthermore, Allen did not provide information on performance, which may be an important moderator variable for the relationships between debt-equity ratio and interlocking directorates. The findings of Helmich (1977) are rather puzzling since he correlated temporal variations in a firm's proportion of financial directors to variations in its debt-equity ratio; the relationship was negative and moderate in size. Ignoring the methodological problems of this study, we can say only that his results might be consistent with several other studies that also uncovered a negative relationship.

The negative relationship between solvency ratios and financial interlocking directorates revealed by Dooley (1969) and Gogel, Koenig, and Sonquist (1976) seems to suggest that financial institutions are active in establishing interorganizational linkages with firms that are not financially solvent. It is of interest to note that Dooley did not find a significant effect when he analyzed the total sample. However, when he restricted his analysis to utility firms, he found the number of financial interlocks negatively affected by the acid test raio and positively affected by total assets. In other words, the frequency of financial interlocks increases as capital intensive firms, such as utilities, become less solvent and as their assets become larger. The magnitude of the effects of these variables, however, is too small to signal major support for a hypothesis about vertical interdependence. As Chapter Five will show, the results of my study require taking issue with Dooley's conclusions.

Finally, it is of interest to again refer to the extensive study by Bearden and his colleagues (1975). While their investigation had a macroscopic focus, they obtained a configuration of interorganizational linkages that revealed considerable geographical clustering. In these regional clusters, banks and insurance firms occupied central positions. One could speculate that the peripheral firms are more interdependent on the banks than they are on each other; furthermore, differential interdependence should be reflected in the different densities of interorganizational linkages. This is sheer speculation, however, as the investigators did not provide information on vertical interdependence.

While all these studies have made useful contributions to our understanding of the motives for the establishment of interlocking directorates, they are inconclusive. Some studies yield inconclusive results either because they fail to distinguish between cooptation and persuasion or because they do not consider the directionality of interlocking directorates among vertically interdependent organizations. Other studies are too aggregative, and their inferences about social linkages are tenuous. Research on interlocking directorates must move from description to explanation so that hypotheses about the rationale for interlocks can be subjected to empirical testing.

Interlocking Directorates and Organizational Effectiveness

Horizontal interlocks might be construed as the development of a collective structure to facilitate interfirm transfer of information and thereby solidify the so-called shared monopoly that exists in oligopolistic industries. Vertical interlocks might alleviate transactional inefficiencies and conflict and generate superior intelligence about the relevant markets. As suggested earlier, Katz and Kahn (1978) would classify interlocking directorates as strategic devices for achieving *political effectiveness*, as distinct from *efficiency*, which reflects a firm's internal effectiveness—for example, the economy of its method of production. Interlocking directorates enhance political effectiveness by facilitating an organization's attempt to gain information and control conditions in its environment. For example, if a horizontal interlock does provide information that enables competing firms to predict one another's behavior, it is highly likely that the firms' combined profits will be higher. A well-interconnected firm is better informed and may enjoy higher returns than an unconnected, but internally efficient firm.

The fundamental question is whether interlocking directorates do indeed promote a firm's effectiveness. Stigler (1968), for example, argues that interlocking directorates among competitors are a clumsy technique for sharing information and that, therefore, they do not significantly affect performance. In an earlier article on oligopoly (1964), he contends that firms can use statistical inference techniques to detect a competitor's price cutting or other infractions of norms. As Williamson (1975) has suggested, this hypothesis assumes that competitors belong to a market with perfect information, that there are no mutations in the market and its members, assumptions that he considers inappropriate. Oligopolies are markets with a small number of participants, and it is primarily in such markets that the withholding and distortion of information take place. The small size of the market encourages a common awareness but also creates the preconditions for opportunism, cheating, and other symptoms of market failure. We have suggested, however, that interlocking directors might circumvent the lack or distortion of information in inefficient markets, particularly if the concentration is intermediate. Even if interlocking directorates improve the dissemination of information and the sharing of decision making, they will always be a comparatively deficient moderator since they do not strongly diminish a firm's autonomy and capacity to withhold information. For example, Williamson (1975) notes that collusive behavior among oligopolists is doubtful, as the parties do not have the means to implement and enforce agreements— a problem that interlocking directorates may not alleviate. An advocate of vertical integration when transactional difficulties are severe, he regards the noncontractual commitments that may prevail among interlocking directors as insufficient to enforce market norms. Although such commitments entail some minimum level of mutual courtesy and consideration, Williamson argues that the limited authority of such commitments and the firms' inability to impose sanctions on offenders render these agreements ineffective deterrents against opportunism and cheating.

While economists tend to be sceptical about the efficacy of interlocks in promoting internal efficiency, there remains the question of whether interlocks do indeed enhance external control and effectiveness. Some scientists ascribe an information- or decision-sharing function to interlocks, but they do not present sufficient data to justify this assumption. Several historical case studies have explored the archival data and uncovered records that reveal parts of an interorganizational communication process. Stern (1976), for example, was able to reconstruct the social linkages among banks in Bismarck's Germany. These linkages were highly efficient— disseminating not only information about the German or European capital markets but also intelligence about political events and trends. Such historical-ideographic research seems more empirically sound than comparative organizational research that attributes benefits to the interlocked organizations without examining data on interorganizational effectiveness, communication processes, their richness or timeliness, and their presumed implications for the well-being of the organizations involved.

Several studies impute control over strategic decision making to interlocks without providing evidence. Among these are the macroscopic studies referred to earlier (for example, Levine, 1972) that make unwarranted inferences about the "sphere of influence." Of the interorganizational studies, there is the research of Gogel, Koenig, and Sonquist (1976) that, in examining the relationship between a firm's solvency and interlocking directorates, reasoned that basic strategic decisions bearing on effectiveness (for example, dividend payout, acquisitions, and stock issuance) "will tend to be *decided, or at least supervised* by dominating outside financial institutions" (p. 22; italics added). While such inferences have been made rather frequently, the empirical evidence does not offer much support for the hypothesis that interlocked firms have better information, exert more control over their environment, and perform more effectively than noninterlocked firms.

Several researchers have examined the relationship between interlocking directorates and organizational effectiveness. Their sampling techniques and choice of variables are so diverse, however, that one cannot extrapolate shared conclusions. Pfeffer (1972), in his study of eighty nonfinancial corporations, devised a procedure for estimating the "optimal" proportion of inside directors on a board and subtracted this from a firm's actual proportion of inside directors. The absolute size of this deviation correlated negatively with performance measures for the industry; that is, the greater a firm's deviation from the optimal board structure, the lower its performance. This research provides modest support for the contention that organizations that develop an optimal balance between inside and outside directors have superior political effectiveness.

Two other studies, however, fail to corroborate this result. Bunting and Liu (1977) found a very strong relationship between total assets and number of interlocking directorates in some industries (for example, basic processing, machines, and equipment), yet they did not detect a relationship between frequency of interlocks and return on assets. Blankenship and Elling (1962) investigated nonprofit organizations and attempted to relate the amount of financial support that hospitals received to the number of environmental linkages that they had developed. They could not find any support for the hypothesis that strongly tied hospitals enjoyed more community support (as measured by dollars per bed).

Pfeffer (1973), in his study of hospitals and their boards, reached a conflicting conclusion. He found that hospitals whose boards included more representatives from such organizations as financial institutions had greater increases in budgets, new facilities, and number of beds. Pfeffer concluded that a hospital's choice of board members was based on its need to establish linkages with important sources of support; this was especially true for private hospitals, which are more dependent than public ones on their external environment.

The evidence is also inconclusive about the role of cooptation, as enforced through interlocking directorates, in determining organizational support and effectiveness. It seems desirable to compare firms' strategic motivations for interlocking and the results of interlocking so that we can trace effectiveness and other consequences not only to interlocking behavior but also to horizontal and vertical interorganizational interdependencies.

Ideally, researchers should also consider the different implications of horizontal and vertical interdependence. Vertical interdependence results from dyads of organizations that exchange resources. In contrast, horizontally interdependence is a relationship between organizations that are members of a set, such as an oligopoly. The antecedents and consequences of vertical interlocks are primarily attributable to characteristics of the dyad, while horizontal interlocks reflect aspects of the individual organizations as well as the entire horizontal set of competitors.

This book focuses on patterns of interlocking directorates between strategically interdependent organizations with a secondary emphasis on boards of directors and their composition. Treating interlocking directorates as social linkages between organizations obviates the need for constructing interorganizational networks. Such networks, as we have seen, are assumed to be irrelevant to the interorganizational framework thus far presented, in which material dependencies among organizations are viewed as the central issue in understanding interlocking directorates.

Having completed this review of the methodology of interlock research, its most representative findings, and areas in which further research is needed, we must next consider the nature of contemporary activities in interlocking among large strategically interdependent organizations.

~~~~~~~ *THREE* ~~~~~~~

Extent of Board Ties Among 800 Large Firms

~~~~~~

This chapter presents the results of a nationwide survey designed to measure the pervasiveness of interorganizational ties in the contemporary American economy. These data will enable us to explore several basic questions about the presence and significance of interlocking: How common are interlocking directorates among American corporations? What types of interlocking directorates are most prominent? Are there differences among industries in the nature and extent of interlocking behavior? Such inquiries will provide evidence from which to draw conclusions about the importance, and relative danger, of interlocking behavior.

This survey sampled 797 large American corporations that had a total of 8,623 directors on their boards. The subset of 1,572 individuals who sit on more than one board forms the nucleus of social connections between the firms. Information about these individuals and boards enables us to determine the extent of interlocking behavior between various types of organizatons in this country. Such knowledge not only is important for its own sake but also documents the role that interlocks have among strategically interdependent organizations.

Consider, for example, a set of industrial firms that requires substantial capital. Within this distinct set of homogeneous organizations, some firms have more financial interlocks than others. If we can detect that these well-interlocked firms outperform their competitors—because they benefit from easier access to financing or superior industrial intelligence—we can fairly conclude that interlocking directorates interfere with the equitable distribution of scarce resources by giving an undue superiority to well-tied corporations.

As this hypothetical example illustrates, interlocking may have consequences for an individual firm's effectiveness and for the maintenance of a free enterprise economy. If interlocking is a widespread phenomenon in which some firms are more involved than others, it is only natural to ask whether interlocks give undue advantage to strongly tied firms. We also need to know whether the 1,572 individuals who sit on two or more boards are evenly distributed or whether, in the aggregate, they tend to be associated with certain types of organizations. For example, are they more likely to belong to larger firms, or to financial institutions? By investigating their linkage behavior and by identifying the kinds of firms they belong to, we obtain additional insights into the phenomenon of interlocking.

It seems that banks, in particular, are bound to be important suppliers to the pool of interlocking directors; a disproportionately large number of the 1,572 interlocking directors have banks as their principal affiliation. A directional interlock in which an employee or officer of a bank sits on the board of a client-organization is likely to be biased in favor of the bank. If an empirical survey were to show that banks are exceptionally well-bestowed with directional interlocks, it would provide additional impetus for the examination of banks' roles in interorganizational transactions. It seems that banks and other financial institutions might be even more important in the management of interorganizational interdependence than previous investigations have implied (for example, Allen, 1974). Further research might clarify the need, if any, for public policy measures to curtail interlocking between financial and nonfinancial organizations. This

chapter, therefore, examines the preponderance of financial interlocking as well as other types of interorganizational connections.

Method: The Sample and Measures

The sample of 797 organizations, selected from *Fortune*'s May
1970 listing, comprises the 500 largest industrial firms (ranked by
sales); the top 50 firms in each of the following categories: banks
(ranked by assets), insurance companies (ranked by assets), merchandising firms (ranked by sales), utility firms (ranked by assets), and
transportation firms (ranked by assets); and 47 firms in such fields as
film, entertainment, and broadcasting. As always, the *Fortune* rank-
ings are based on data from the preceding year.

A list of corporations, their directors, and these directors'
memberships on the boards of other corporations was provided by a
research team led by Michael Schwartz at the State University of New
York at Stony Brook. Additional data were obtained from the *Dun
and Bradstreet Million Dollar Directory* (1970) and *Poor's Register of
Corporations, Directors, and Executives* (Standard and Poor, 1970,
1971).

There were discrepancies between the 1970 *Poor's Register* and
the 1970 *Fortune* listing for thirty-three organizations. Twenty of
these discrepancies involved closely related organizations. For example, *Fortune* lists the holding company while the *Poor's Register* lists
the operating company. (The Stony Brook team always used the data
on the board of directors of the operating company.) The thirteen
other discrepancies were companies not listed in the 1970 *Poor's
Register*. Many of these organizations were involved in mergers or
acquisitions or underwent name changes. In these cases, information
was obtained from the 1971 *Poor's Register* and the *Dun and Bradstreet Million Dollar Directory*.

The *Poor's Register*'s list of directors was checked against a
number of sources, including *Directory of Directors in the City of
New York* (Directory of Directors Company, 1971), *Dun and Bradstreet Million Dollar Directory, 1971* (Dun and Bradstreet, 1970),
Reference Book of Corporate Managements (Dun and Bradstreet,
1971), and the following volumes published by Marquis Who's Who:
*Who's Who in America 1970-1971, Who's Who in America 1972-
1973, Who's Who in Finance and Industry 1972-1973, Who's Who in*

the East 1972-1973, Who's Who in the West 1971-1972, Who's Who in the Midwest 1970-1971, Who's Who in the South and Southwest 1971-1972.

These reference works were consulted to ensure the identity of directors—particularly whether two or more directorships belonged to the same individual. The majority of directors held only one directorship. Only 4,595 of 11,290 directorships were involved in interlocking. There were 133 individuals whose identity could not be determined unequivocally. Naturally, in a few cases this might have resulted in erroneous coding. However, the number of errors is probably smaller than 133.

We consulted the *Million Dollar Directory* to determine the composition of the organizations' boards of directors. For each board, we ascertained the number of inside directors, outside directors, directors from insurance companies, directors from banks, directors from investment companies, and directors who are private investors. We classified as inside directors those directors who are employed by the organization, those who are officers or directors of subsidiaries or parent organizations, and those who are retired officers of the corporation. In cases of mergers and acquisitions, officers of the acquired company who had joined the board during 1969 were classified as inside directors. Private investors could be classified as inside directors because, as stockholders, they "own" the corporation. But they exercise control indirectly—primarily through their trading behavior on the stock exchange and their proxy voting at the annual meeting. Board members who own a big block of shares or who act on behalf of individuals and families with substantial stockholdings sometimes exercise direct control. Under some circumstances, those directors could be classified as inside, as the separation between "ownership" and "control" is more diffuse. Nevertheless, we have not identified them as inside directors; rather we have listed them as private investors.

Additional problems exist in classifying outside directors into subsets. Since we had no information on the transactional relationship between suppliers and customers—such information is often considered proprietary—we refrained from second-guessing whether a director belonged to a vertically interdependent firm. In the absence of data documenting specific exchanges between buyers and suppliers, one could follow a less stringent procedure and assume that the aggregate flow of goods and services between different industries, as revealed by input-output tables (Leontief, 1966), reflects the actual vertical interdependence between firms belonging to the respective industries. But the aggregate flow of goods and services between industries does not permit us to draw inferences about the actual flow between individual firms. Since we could not, therefore, verify vertical interdependence, we could not isolate vertical interlocks.

The information from the sources noted earlier provides this study with a complete and fairly accurate listing of individuals who are directors of the 797 organizations in our sample. Although our primary concern is with interlocking directors, the information on individual directors' affiliations nicely supplements the data on interlocks as some of these individuals are directors of firms not belonging to the sample. For example, a director of a manufacturing firm might be an officer of a small local bank that is not listed by *Fortune*.

By analyzing this information, we can give an empirical overview of the directors, the boards, and the overlapping membership of 797 American corporations.

Board Size. The size distribution of the boards of directors of the 797 organizations fits a rather nice bell-shaped curve. Figure 3 shows how smooth this range is, although a slight bimodality is noticeable. This distribution is considerable, from boards of fewer than six individuals to those of forty-seven. Only one company has three directors, the minimum number required by law (Daniel Construction Company). The largest board belongs to First Wisconsin Bankshares, followed by Equitable Life Insurance Company and a number of other life insurance companies and banks. Banks and life insurance companies have by far the largest number of individuals on their boards. The smallest board among these institutions has eleven members, a size that approximates the median for the entire sample of organizations. By way of comparison, the largest boards among industrial organizations have twenty-six members (Du Pont and Nemours). The median is thirteen members for nonfinancial organizations; the median for banks is twenty-four members, for insurance firms sixteen. Financial organizations clearly constitute a distinct category by nature of their large boards; they are clustered at the high end of the distribution in Figure 3.

Figure 3. Size of Firms' Boards of Directors (N = 797)

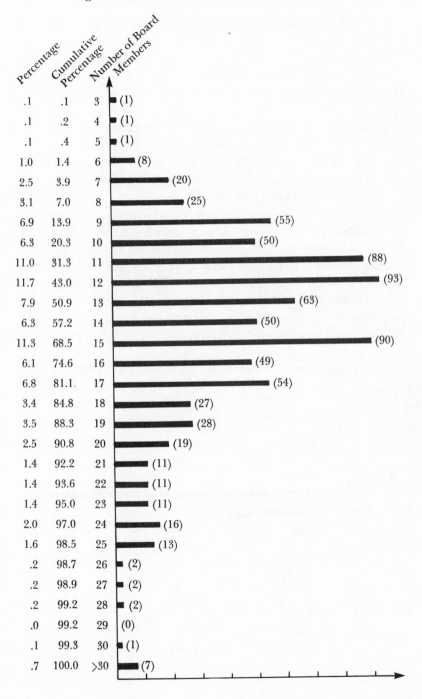

Percentage	Cumulative Percentage	Number of Board Members	
.1	.1	3	(1)
.1	.2	4	(1)
.1	.4	5	(1)
1.0	1.4	6	(8)
2.5	3.9	7	(20)
3.1	7.0	8	(25)
6.9	13.9	9	(55)
6.3	20.3	10	(50)
11.0	31.3	11	(88)
11.7	43.0	12	(93)
7.9	50.9	13	(63)
6.3	57.2	14	(50)
11.3	68.5	15	(90)
6.1	74.6	16	(49)
6.8	81.1	17	(54)
3.4	84.8	18	(27)
3.5	88.3	19	(28)
2.5	90.8	20	(19)
1.4	92.2	21	(11)
1.4	93.6	22	(11)
1.4	95.0	23	(11)
2.0	97.0	24	(16)
1.6	98.5	25	(13)
.2	98.7	26	(2)
.2	98.9	27	(2)
.2	99.2	28	(2)
.0	99.2	29	(0)
.1	99.3	30	(1)
.7	100.0	>30	(7)

The median size of thirteen directors for the subset of nonfinancial firms is quite similar to the median of the individual industries. Publishing and printing organizations have somewhat larger
boards, a median of fifteen members, and the boards of aerospace
firms are somewhat smaller, with a median of twelve. The firms that
have smaller boards tend to be smaller firms, that is, firms that rank
rather low on the *Fortune* list; they are not associated with any
particular industry. The normal bell-shaped distribution shown in
Figure 3 suggests that the 797 organizations are drawn from a single
population and differ only gradually from one another.

Number of Directorships Held by Individuals. In stark contrast, Figure 4, which shows the number of board memberships each
director holds, has a heavily skewed distribution. More than three
fourths of all directors have only one directorship. Quite surprisingly
interlocking directors are in fact a minority when we count their
number from the total set of directors of the *Fortune*-listed corporations. Of the 8,623 directors in our sample, only 1,572 have more than
one directorship; the remaining 7,051 directors sit on only one board.
By definition, this latter group has no role in interlocking behavior.

Figure 4. Board Memberships per Director (*N* = 8,623)

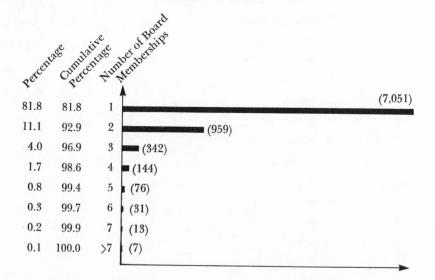

The former group of 1,572 directors hold a total of 4,239 directorships; of this group, 613 individuals—or 40 percent—hold three or more directorships. But the total of all directorships held by the 8,623 directors is 11,290. Therefore, the interlocking directors comprise only 38 percent of the total directorships. Again the interlocking directors constitute a minority of the entire group of directors in this study.

The 1,572 individuals who hold two or more directorships are central in this study because they are among the agents of interorganizational coordination and communication. It is striking that they represent such a small proportion of all directors. It is also striking to note that the twenty individuals who are the strongest linkers, holding seven or more directorships, are .3 percent of all directors—but they reach 16 percent of the 797 organizations. This finding reinforces the conclusion that only a very small proportion of all directors have multiple board memberships. The prominence of banks and insurance firms in that 16 percent further accentuates the pronounced role that banking directors play in forming social linkages between organizations.

The contrast between Figure 3 and Figure 4 nicely illustrates the earlier discussion on the duality of directors and organizations (Breiger, 1974). In view of the ubiquity of financial directors in nonfinancial organizations, it is only natural to find such a preponderance of interlocking between financial and nonfinancial organizations. The financial directors belong to a distinct class: they are disproportionately active in the formation of interlocking directorates and, at the same time, put financial organizations at the center of interlocking among organizations. Their large share of multiple board membership naturally tempts one to attribute a huge amount of influence to them. However, while interdirector relationships might be interesting—for example, for investigating "who rules America"—the present study is primarily concerned with relationships between organizations. In other words, in the present study, organizations are identified as hubs and directors as nodes—that is, organizations as interconnected by individuals, not individuals as interconnected by organizations.

Interlocking Directorates

Having reiterated our emphasis on social linkages between organizations, we now need to examine the distribution of interlocking directorates among the organizations. This distribution (see Figure 5) shows that only sixty-two organizations, less than 10 percent of our sample, have no director interlocks with other organizations in this study's sample. Therefore, almost all organizations can reach at least one other organization through a shared director. In contrast with these sixty-two unconnected organizations, moreover, twenty-four organizations have forty or more interlocking directors. Figure 5 shows that the distribution of interlocking directorates is smooth; there are few discontinuities between the unlinked organizations and the heavily linked organizations. Among the firms that interlock most heavily are those firms that have a large number of individuals on their board. Banks and insurance firms have more interorganizational links than any other types of organization. The average number of interlocks for banks and insurance firms is eighteen, considerably higher than that for other industries, including manufacturing, transportation, merchandising, and utilities. The pattern for the number of interlocks is fairly similar to that for the number of board members: bigger firms not only have more individuals on their boards but also more interlocks. Banks are a distinct category: they have more directors on their boards and comparatively more interlocking directors with other boards. With a few exceptions, banks and insurance companies prevail on the high end of the distribution of Figure 5. Equitable Life Company, the organization having the second largest board, leads the sample in the number of interlocking directorates; immediately following are New York's Chemical Bank, First National City Bank, Metropolitan Life, Chase Manhattan, and Morgan Guaranty Trust. These organizations resemble a hypertrophied octopus, having thirty or forty tentacles. A second cluster of predominantly financial organizations have fewer than thirty interfirm ties, but still have considerably more than the bulk of firms of this study. Such results help explain why, in several recent investigations (for example, Bearden and others, 1975; Mariolis, 1975), banks and other financial institutions appear highly central in interorganizational networks. Large organizations with large boards tend to be

Figure 5. Frequency of Interlocking Directorates (N = 797)

Cumulative Percentage	Percentage	Frequency	
7.8	7.8	0	(62)
14.9	7.2	1	(57)
20.8	5.9	2	(47)
27.5	6.6	3	(53)
32.6	5.1	4	(41)
38.8	6.1	5	(49)
42.3	3.5	6	(28)
45.9	3.6	7	(29)
50.2	4.3	8	(34)
55.0	4.8	9	(38)
57.7	2.8	10	(22)
61.0	3.3	11	(26)
63.6	2.6	12	(21)
66.6	3.0	13	(24)
69.0	2.4	14	(19)
71.5	2.5	15	(20)
73.3	1.8	16	(14)
75.4	2.1	17	(17)
77.4	2.0	18	(16)
79.7	2.3	19	(18)
81.6	1.9	20	(15)
82.8	1.3	21	(10)
84.1	1.3	22	(10)
85.3	1.3	23	(10)
86.4	1.1	24	(9)
87.5	1.0	25	(8)
88.8	1.4	26	(11)
90.1	1.3	27	(10)
90.8	0.8	28	(6)
91.5	0.6	29	(5)
92.5	1.0	30	(8)
92.8	0.4	31	(3)
93.7	0.9	32	(7)
94.5	0.8	33	(6)
95.2	0.8	34	(6)
95.7	0.5	35	(4)
96.1	0.4	36	(3)
96.4	0.3	37	(2)
97.0	0.6	38	(5)
97.1	0.1	40	(1)
97.2	0.1	42	(1)
97.5	0.3	44	(2)
97.7	0.3	45	(2)
100.0	2.1	>45	(18)

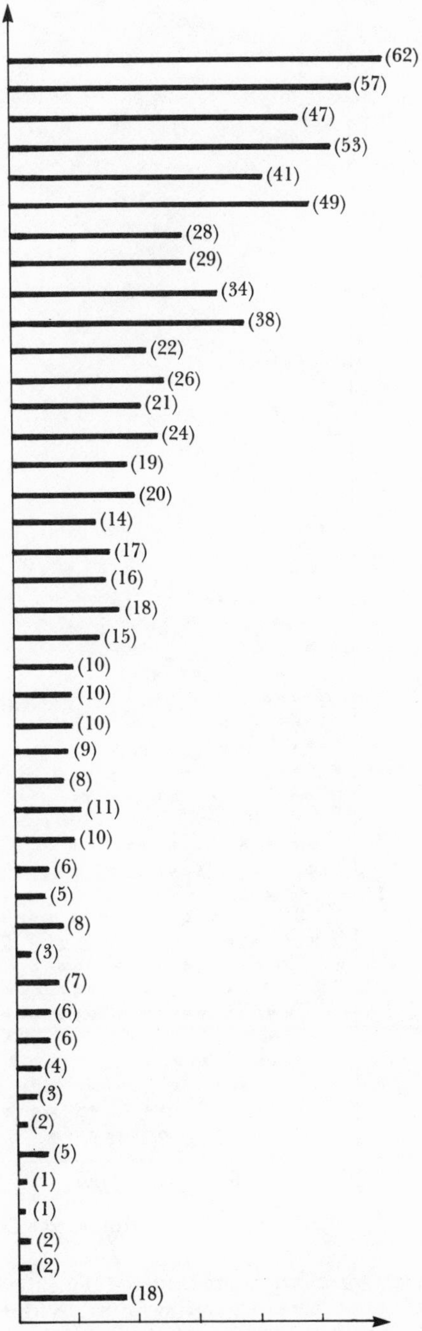

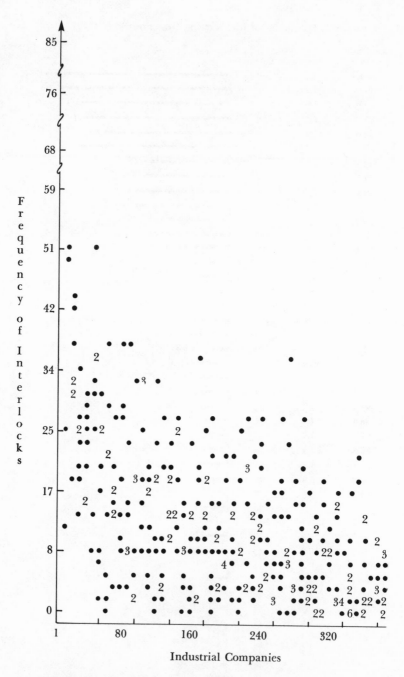

Note: Organizations are clustered along the horizontal axis by type (industrial, banking, and so forth). Within each type, organizations are presented in order of their rank on the *Fortune* (1970) list.

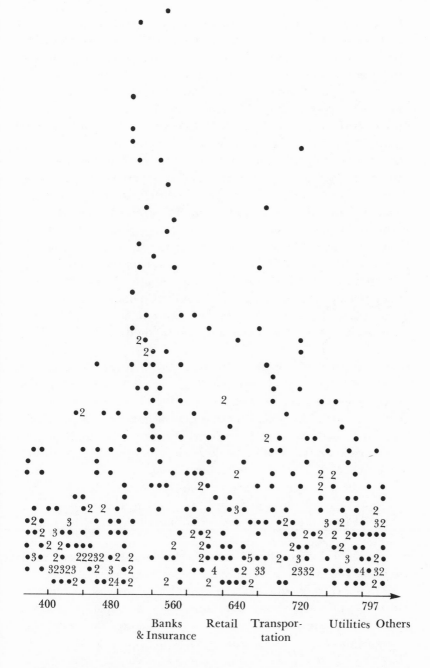

Figure 6. Scatterplot of Number of Interlocking Directorates (*N* = 797)

comparatively well interlocked with other organizations. A scatter diagram of the number of interlocks per firm reveals that an organization's rank on the *Fortune* list is strongly associated with its number of interlocks (see Figure 6). The largest industrials, banks, insurance companies, retail, transportation, utility, and miscellaneous organizations have a greater number of interlocks than smaller firms in their respective fields; a firm's rank in its category and that firm's number of interlocks are strongly correlated. Most of the sixty-two firms that have no ties at all are among the smaller firms in their category. These firms, however, are not necessarily isolated; they may be interlocked with firms not listed by *Fortune*. While the size of their boards is smaller than that of larger firms, their proportion of outside directors is not as different from that of the larger firms. These smaller firms are not completely isolated, but they are isolated from the larger organizations, those on the *Fortune* list. The nature of the matrix used in Figure 6 gives the appearance of isolation, but a larger matrix or a matrix based on a regional sample might alter our impression of the relative peripherality of the smaller organizations. We will bear this limitation in mind during our evaluation of the data about interlocking directorates.

The correlation between rank and frequency of interlocks holds for banks and insurance companies but, as Figure 6 shows, these organizations are distinct because their level of interlocking is considerably higher than that of other categories of organizations. Again, the boundaries of the interlock matrix, the *Fortune* list, gives the impression that smaller banks are less prominent in their interlocking. But, within the subset of banks, we notice that some of the smaller banks are more active in their interlocking than one could have predicted on the basis of their rank. Again, a matrix of smaller, regional firms would yield even more interlocks for these smaller banks.

Figure 7 shows the regression line of rank of assets compared to frequency of interlocks. The standardized regression coefficient is -.68 ($p \leqslant .01$), suggesting that assets are a strong predictor of interlocking. The plot also shows some interesting discrepancies between observed and predicted frequencies of interlocking directorates. The now defunct New York Franklin Bank, which then ranked twentieth, has far fewer interlocks than would be expected; yet, some regional

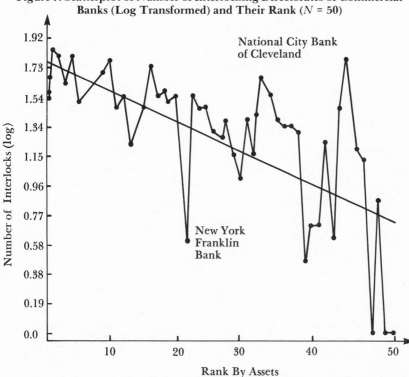

Figure 7. Scatterplot of Number of Interlocking Directorates of Commercial Banks (Log Transformed) and Their Rank (N = 50)

banks, such as National City Bank of Cleveland, have many more interlocks than expected. Several of these more active regional banks are among those cited by Bearden and others (1975) in their study of cliques. Some of these regional banks have fewer interlocks than such giants as Citibank, Chase Manhattan Bank, Bank of America, and Western Bank Corporation but, in relative terms, they are strongly linked. Their number of links would be even greater, were we to examine local, instead of national, interlock data. These banks play a regional role that is likely to be analogous to the national role of the large banks.

Directional Interlocks

A distinctive contribution of this study is the analysis of directional interlocking directorates. Directional interlocks are comparatively infrequent: 332 firms (41.7 percent of the sample) have no directional links coming from other organizations. The distribution of directional interlocks is heavily skewed with a long straddle. One organization has fourteen interlocking directorates originating from other organizations, but most firms rarely exceed two directional ties. The total number of directional interlocks is 1,236—considerably smaller than the total number of all interlocks (4,239). Although the average number of interlocking directorates—both directional and nondirectional—for our sample is almost twelve, the average number of directional interlocks is approximately one-and-a-half. Naturally the limitations imposed by the nature of the sample, as reviewed in the previous section, apply equally to our data on directional interlocks. The number of directional interlocks would quite likely be higher if the matrix of organizations included smaller, regional firms. Nevertheless, it is remarkable that only a small portion of the interlocks have a directional identity.

Consistent with our earlier observations, banks and insurance companies play a very prominent role in directional linkages. Many officers of banks and insurance companies sit on boards of other organizations, and many organizations enjoy directional linkages to banks and insurance companies. Of the 1,236 directional interlocks, 556 (43 percent) involve financial institutions. Therefore, those institutions are even more overrepresented in directional interlocks than they are in interlocks whose directionality was not specified. Although directional interlocks are a relatively rare phenomenon, they are comparatively frequent for financial organizations. They are also more frequent than horizontal interlocks between competing organizations. The mean numbers of directional interlocks for banks and insurance companies are .716 for to-interlocks and .681 for from-interlocks. As explained in Chapter One's B. F. Goodrich example, we refer to *to-financial interlocks* and *from-financial interlocks* when considering the directional ties between financial and nonfinancial organizations. A to-financial interlock exists when a financial organization has an interlocking director who is employed by a nonfinancial organization. A from-financial interlock exists when an officer-director from a bank or insurance firm sits on the board of a nonfinancial organization. That so large a portion of all directional ties involve financial firms as donors or recipients suggests that financial organizations have comparatively many strong ties with nonfinancial companies. This distinction becomes even more significant when we recall that there are only 100 financial firms in our sample.

By way of comparison, the average number of horizontal interlocks for all firms in our sample is .304, and the majority of the 697 nonfinancial firms have no ties at all with organizations that belong to their same industry. In addition, very few firms have more than two interlocks with competitors. These horizontal interlocks include both directional and nondirectional ones, but are presumed to be reflexive because they act as common messengers, transmitting information to both parties. Even if a horizontal director was employed by one of the two competitors, the situation is considered a reflexive tie. Ignoring possible interindustry differences, we find horizontal interlocks not nearly as common as the directional ties between financial and nonfinancial firms. These latter ties, therefore, are most worthy of our attention.

Since banks and insurance firms are deeply involved in directional interlocking, they have a central place in the research reported here. The overwhelming presence of bank officers on nonfinancial organizations' boards suggests that the transactions between financial and nonfinancial organizations are among the most important for American corporations. The high propensity of corporations to place their own officers and directors onto the boards of banks and insurance firms also signals the importance to nonfinancial firms of maintaining close connections in the financial community. It also warns us that financial interlocks should not be interpreted exclusively as forms of persuasion and cooptation. Although we shall examine financial interlocks in reference to a firm's dependence on external financing, financial interlocks might also serve as common messengers. This possibility seems to fit the directional interlocking director particularly well. That a disproportionately large number of directional interlocks involve financial institutions seems to indicate that banks and insurance companies can also act as conduits between competing organizations, transmitting market information among them.

We refrain from identifying other types of vertical interlocks and from determining their empirical distribution because it is virtually impossible to ascertain a firm's dependence on suppliers or customers or even to determine the volume of its transactions with firms vertically adjacent in its industrial chain. Also, it is obvious that the number of vertical interlocks other than the financial ones are rather few; moreover, since most firms have many suppliers and customers, the number of directional interlocks involving any one category of these vertically dependent firms is exceedingly small. We have observed that directional interlocks are rather infrequent and that financial institutions are involved in almost half of those directional interlocks. On all counts, therefore, it seems necessary to focus on this particular type of interlocking behavior.

This review has shown that banks and insurance companies play a prominent role in the establishment of interorganizational linkages. Compared to other firms, they have rather large boards, more interlocking directorates, and substantially more directional interlocks. Such findings underline the importance of the role of financial organizations within the context of strategically interdependent organizations.

Boards of Directors

To avoid confusion about the full extent of interlocking, note that the interlocking directorates reviewed thus far are those among organizations included in the *Fortune* listing. For example, the earlier mentioned 62 organizations with no interlocks are only isolated with respect to the remaining 735 organizations. Naturally those 62 organizations might have interlocks with organizations outside our universe of organizations. In fact, as we shall see, they do. Barring some exceptions, their outside directors must be "from" directors, associated with some employer regardless of whether the organization is mentioned by *Fortune*.

Excluded firms include smaller firms but also various types of larger organizations not mentioned by *Fortune*—for example, law firms, universities, the military, and foundations. Ties with such excluded organizations may be important. By studying publicly available information about the background of board members we can deduce some of these ties. Examining the membership of the boards permits us to draw conclusions about firms' connections with organizations not included in our sample. Furthermore, although interlocking directors comprise the focal connections between firms, there are additional connections among organizations in that some board members do not sit on the board of another organization but are strongly affiliated with that second organization. An individual employed by organization A—a bank, perhaps—may be a director of organization B but not of A. By definition, this individual is not an interlocking director; nevertheless, the behavior of recruiting firm B can be interpreted as coopting the bank to improve credit availability. In order to detect connections between our sample firms and others and in order to detect connections that are not interlocks, we must, therefore, examine the composition of the boards of directors. In this section, we look at nonfinancial firms.

Figure 8 shows the proportion of outside directors on the boards of nonfinancial firms. Outside directors are individuals who are neither employed by nor previously associated with the organization. Figure 8 provides a global impression of the openness of boards by showing the extent to which officer-directors share their board deliberation with these outsiders. The distribution of outsiders is

Figure 8. Proportion of Outside Directors (N = 645)

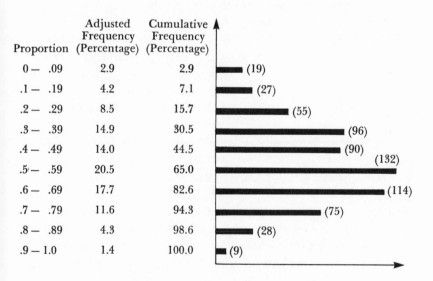

Proportion	Adjusted Frequency (Percentage)	Cumulative Frequency (Percentage)	
0 — .09	2.9	2.9	(19)
.1 — .19	4.2	7.1	(27)
.2 — .29	8.5	15.7	(55)
.3 — .39	14.9	30.5	(96)
.4 — .49	14.0	44.5	(90)
.5 — .59	20.5	65.0	(132)
.6 — .69	17.7	82.6	(114)
.7 — .79	11.6	94.3	(75)
.8 — .89	4.3	98.6	(28)
.9 — 1.0	1.4	100.0	(9)

surprisingly normal, with most organizations striking a balance between insiders and outsiders. In fact, the average proportion of outside directors is .5003. The distribution is slightly skewed to the left, but a large part of these organizations has an equal number of insiders and outsiders. During crises in which management faces the possibility of dismissal, it may be to management's advantage to have more insiders than outsiders, assuming that insiders are more loyal to senior managers and the president. The political role that outside directors can perform is often limited, not only because they are often inadequately informed about the internal operations of the organization but also because they often rely on the senior management for their information.

The presence of so many outside directors is attributable, in part, to the regulations of the Security and Exchange Commission (SEC). The SEC regulations stipulate that all members of a firm's audit committee (a committee composed of board members) must be outside directors. Some companies have had to recruit additional outside directors to meet this regulation. Privately owned firms, however, are not required to meet SEC regulations. While the activities of the SEC have resulted in greater apparent openness of boards, as organizations have been forced to acquire outsiders, it is not clear what effect they have had on the governance of the firms involved. The presumed independence of outside directors might often be compromised because, lacking inside information, they are dependent on insiders for essential knowledge of the firm. Indeed, they seem often to be selected by senior management to serve management's needs, especially the need to obtain superior intelligence. Outside directors might thus aid, rather than check, the concentration of power.

Some researchers have argued (for example, Faris, 1979) that the number of outside directors indicates the cohesiveness of a firm's management team. Cohesiveness describes the degree of control that a group's members exert over one another, or the degree to which they are insulated from external influence. Firms with many inside directors have a cohesive management team because the scarcity of outsiders restricts outside influence. But extreme cohesiveness poses dangers for a firm's officers; it induces them to derive their judgments, perceptions, and decisions from their colleagues alone; it therefore makes them subject to groupthink (Janis and Mann, 1977). According to this line of reasoning, firms that open up their management structure to include many outside directors thus permit the entry of new information and might be in a better position to make sound decisions. The actual effects of outside directors on corporate practices have not been adequately investigated and remain largely a matter of sheer speculation.

In the popular financial press (for example, "End of the Directors' Rubber Stamp," 1979), the trend toward a greater number of outside directors has often been interpreted as a departure from traditional practice in which the board of directors rubber-stamps important strategic decisions. According to this argument, increasing the number of outside directors on the firm's board, or on any of its committees, will provoke an independent and fresh review of long-term decisions, will effectuate impartial, uncontaminated audits of managerial performance, and will counterbalance the influence of top management. Except for a limited number of anecdotes and case histories, however, we still do not know whether the number or proportion of outside directors has had a substantive effect on the governance of corporations or on their definition of their strategic mission.

Outside directors can be categorized by their primary affiliation. Figure 9 shows the number of outside directors that financial firms donated to the nonfinancial firms in our sample. Figures 10, 11, and 12 show the number of directors originating from banks, insurance companies, and investment banks, respectively. Relationships with financial organizations are among the most significant of interorganizational relationships. These interlocks can be construed as directional interlocks emanating from financial organizations to the focal organization.

Figures 10, 11, and 12 show a remarkable difference between banks, on the one hand, and insurance companies and investment banks, on the other hand: While banks are very well represented on the boards, insurance companies are not. Fewer than 10 percent of the firms have a board member from an insurance company. Investment banks are intermediate in their representation on the boards of nonfinancial organizations. These data accentuate the unusual role of banks in the director-based connections between organizations.

Figure 9. Outside Directors Originating from Financial Organizations

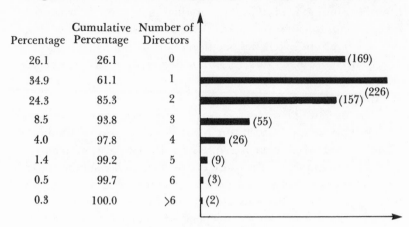

Percentage	Cumulative Percentage	Number of Directors
26.1	26.1	0
34.9	61.1	1
24.3	85.3	2
8.5	93.8	3
4.0	97.8	4
1.4	99.2	5
0.5	99.7	6
0.3	100.0	>6

Figure 10. Outside Directors Originating from Commercial Banks

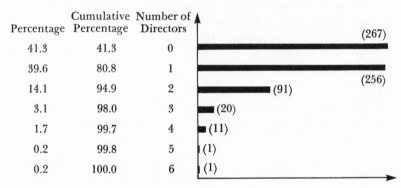

Percentage	Cumulative Percentage	Number of Directors
41.3	41.3	0
39.6	80.8	1
14.1	94.9	2
3.1	98.0	3
1.7	99.7	4
0.2	99.8	5
0.2	100.0	6

Figure 11. Outside Directors Originating from Insurance Companies

Percentage	Cumulative Percentage	Number of Directors
91.8	91.8	0
7.0	98.8	1
0.9	99.7	2
0.3	100.0	3

Figure 12. Outside Directors Originating from Investment Banks

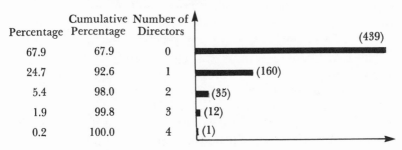

Percentage	Cumulative Percentage	Number of Directors
67.9	67.9	0
24.7	92.6	1
5.4	98.0	2
1.9	99.8	3
0.2	100.0	4

Banks, rather than insurance companies, form the bulk of linkages between financial and nonfinancial organizations. This finding might reflect the fact that insurance companies operate in the long-term capital market, while banks operate in both the short-term and long-term markets; banks therefore play a more important role in a firm's external financing. Furthermore, insurance companies have primarily a regional or national basis, while banks are much more localized, catering to both local and cosmopolitan firms. The data presented in Figures 10, 11, and 12 can be contrasted with those presented in Figure 6, which shows only a slight superiority of banks compared to insurance companies in the frequency of interlocks. But the data in Figures 10, 11, and 12 suggest that the superiority of the banks would have been greater had the sample matrix included more banks. As a specific example, let us isolate the data in Figure 8 that apply to industrial firms: the average number of outside directors originating from banks is .754. In contrast, the average number of directional interlocks originating from the fifty banks on the *Fortune* list is .252. These averages suggest that banks not in our sample are important and visible providers of directors for the 500 largest industrial firms; they are important for industrial organizations, despite the smaller size of their assets. The average number of banking directors is even higher for retail, transportation, and utility firms (1.45, 1.65, and .81, respectively) whereas the number of directional financial interlocks with banks in our sample is approximately .3. Some minor difficulties in comparing the two sets of numbers arise because we were unable to obtain information on the composition of approximately 7 percent of the boards. Most of these companies are among the smallest, however, so that our results are likely to be slightly biased to the conservative side; smaller firms have an even greater propensity to interlock with local banks, as distinct from the larger banks in our sample. The overall preponderance of banks, therefore, seems far more pervasive than suggested by examining the *Fortune* list.

An analysis of interlocking based exclusively on the behavior of firms on the *Fortune* list is, therefore, a limited one. The extent of interlocking with banks is even more pronounced than the earlier analysis implied. It is difficult, however, to draw any inferences about the significance of this phenomenon for interorganizational relationships. Certainly, representatives from the larger banks are better connected than are their counterparts from local banks and could, therefore, perform as more effective agents of interorganizational communications. However, in view of the regional nature of many banking transactions, the smaller local bankers might be more instrumental in the management of interorganizational relationships. Recurrent personal interactions between local banks and organizations in their territory create personal contacts, continued business, and trust. Although not likely to be detected by empirical analysis, such contacts may generate strong ties between firms.

Differences Among Industries

Much of the preceding overview has concerned the distinct position of financial institutions and the prevalence of financial interlocking directorates. Now let us explore the distribution of interlocking directorates and the composition of boards as they differ among the various industries. Table 1 presents data regarding the frequency of interlocking directorates and the composition of boards for twenty-seven industries, as defined by the SIC codes (see p. 48). Comparisons among industries show considerable variation on all variables. When we examine the frequency of interlocking, we notice that mining, petroleum refining, rubber, steel, transportation equipment, and railroads are industries with well-connected organizations. Railroads exceed all other industries in interlocking (mean number of interlocks, 17.4), followed closely by the automotive industry (16.2), and mining (15.5). At the other end of the distribution, we find oil producers (3.3), general contractors (3.7), textiles (6.8), and trucking (2.8) among the industries with relatively few interlocking directorates. (Recall that the average number of interlocking directorates for all firms in our sample is approximately 13.) The railroad companies dominate all other industries in their frequency of interlocking; like banks, they tend to have bigger boards, averaging eighteen members. Their high frequency of interlocking is further accentuated by the fact that three fourths of their board members are outside directors (see Table 1). Despite their regional characteristics, railroads interlock with many firms that have a national base, as can be inferred from their interlocks with firms on the *Fortune* list. The mining industry and SIC industry group 37 are also heavily involved in interlocking. SIC group 37 includes manufacturers of motor vehicles, trucks, and auto parts (SIC 371), aerospace and defense (372), ship building (373), railroad equipment (374), and trailers and campers (379). These manufacturers of transportation equipment approximate the transportation industry in their amount of interlocking.

In addition to showing overall interlocking activity, Table 1 presents some specific types, including ties with financial institutions and horizontal interlocks between competitors. Industries that have high levels of overall interlocking also maintain frequent connections—both reflexive and directional—with banks. For example, railroads, transportation equipment, and mining firms have the largest number of interlocks with banks. The pattern of directional interlocks with banks, however, differs from that of reflexive interlocks. The mining, rubber and plastic, and railroad industries donate surprisingly few of their own directors to the boards of banks. The most important sources of industrial directors for bank boards are the chemical, petroleum refining, and transportation equipment industries. It is striking that the railroad industry, which provides few directional linkages to financial firms, nevertheless receives the largest number of directional interlocks from financial institutions. It is one of the few industries that receives more linkages from financial institutions than it gives to them. That most industries donate more directors to banks than they receive from banks, however, does not mean that nonfinancial organizations infiltrate financial firms more than the latter infiltrate the former. Because there are many more

Table 1. Interlocking Directorates and Board Membership by Industry.

Industry (SIC Group)	Number of Firms	Number of Interlocks	Financial Interlocks	To-Financial Interlocks	From-Financial Interlocks	Horizontal Interlocks	Proportion of Outside Directors	Financial Directors
Mining (10)	7	15.5	3.9	.57	.43	.00	.62	2.14
Oil production (13)	3	3.3	1.0	.33	.33	.00	.40	1.33
Contracting (15–17)	10	3.7	0.9	.20	.10	.06	.38	0.55
Food (20)	58	9.9	2.7	.60	.30	.24	.46	1.40
Tobacco (21)	5	7.0	2.0	.60	.00	.00	.25	1.00
Textile (22–23)	24	6.8	1.7	.63	.21	.08	.39	1.40
Paper, wood (24–26)	26	10.0	3.0	.65	.23	.00	.53	1.68
Publishing (27)	9	11.6	2.7	.33	.22	.00	.44	1.25
Chemicals (28)	55	11.8	3.1	.75	.40	.73	.43	1.48
Petroleum refining (29)	28	13.2	3.3	.89	.28	.36	.44	1.14
Rubber, plastic (30)	9	15.2	2.8	.11	.22	.00	.45	1.56
Leather (31)	3	8.3	1.7	.33	.00	.00	.83	1.50

Industry							
Building materials (32)	15	12.5	2.9	.40	.47	.27	.55	1.57
Primary metals (33)	30	14.2	3.6	.60	.37	.53	.45	1.35
Metal products (34)	17	7.2	1.6	.24	.06	.00	.54	1.20
Equipment (35)	44	11.3	2.7	.52	.27	.68	.52	1.21
Electronics (36)	33	11.3	2.4	.76	.21	.24	.49	1.15
Transportation equipment (37)	47	15.1	3.9	.81	.38	.94	.50	1.26
Automobile (371)	27	16.2	4.3	.74	.41	.67	.51	1.17
Aerospace (372)	15	13.2	3.5	1.07	.33	1.07	.53	1.00
Precision instruments (38)	10.	9.2	2.4	.80	.30	.00	.51	.78
Jewelry, toys (39)	5	8.3	.5	.00	.25	.00	.51	1.50
Railroads (40)	17	17.4	5.2	.35	.59	.59	.75	2.93
Trucking (42)	8	2.8	1.3	.13	.00	.00	.54	.71
Shipping (44)	2	3.5	.5	.00	.00	.00	.75	2.00
Airlines (45)	13	13.5	3.5	.39	.31	.00	.69	2.15
Utilities (49)	50	12.0	3.8	.86	.34	.20	.69	1.62
Retail food (53)	20	13.6	3.7	1.15	.25	.10	.40	1.67
Retail merchandising (54)	22	6.3	1.6	.36	.28	.00	.44	1.25

nonfinancial firms than banks and insurance companies among this country's largest organizations, the insurance companies and banks have a large number of organizations to which they donate directors. In contrast, the nonfinancial companies have a huge pool of directors to donate to banks and insurance companies. The average number of from-financial interlocks each industry has is thus bound to be smaller than the to-interlocks. The last column of Table 1 shows that most industries have at least one representative from the financial community on their boards. Railroads and mining companies average two or more members from the financial sector on their boards.

In spite of some variation in financial interlocking, all industries appear to enjoy a certain amount of their connections with banks and other financial institutions. In stark contrast, industries differ greatly in their frequency of horizontal interlocks. Approximately half of the industries do not show any interlocking between similar firms. In view of the broad definition of industry (the two-digit SIC groups), not all interlocks between members of the same industry are true horizontal interlocks between competitors. For example, General Motors might have an interlock with a manufacturer of auto parts; although both firms belong to SIC 37, the relationship between the two firms might be a vertical one between buyer and seller, rather than a horizontal one. Since such information is often not available, these assertions are a matter of conjecture. However, firms belonging to the same SIC group are comparatively similar in technology and rely on nearly identical occupational groups and other expertise. The Bureau of the Census continuously redefines these groups to reduce heterogeneity among them. Firms themselves may have contributed to unity in diversity by establishing domain consensus, for example (Thompson, 1967). Such consensus indicates that firms collectively recognize that each has a different and separate portion of the domain, thus allowing them peaceful coexistence. In spite of the heterogeneity of SIC groups, it is possible to point to domain characteristics in the defense of employing these groups for identifying horizontal interdependence.

While these classification problems are acknowledged, interlocks between firms belonging to the same two-digit SIC group are assumed to be horizontal interlocks. On that assumption, the chemical, steel, transportation equipment, and transportation industries have the best interconnected firms (see Table 1). Firms in these industries have the highest frequency of interlocks between competitors. These organizations would appear to be the most blatant violators of Section 8 of the Clayton Act.

Finally, as Table 1 shows, the boards of mining, railroad, and utility firms have the highest proportion of outside directors. The general contracting, tobacco, and retail industries are visibly inbred, having a much larger proportion of inside directors. The group of outsiders, however, includes a wide variety of directors, and it would be simplistic to consider the proportion of outsiders as a measure of cooptation. In this connection, it is useful to note that some industries that have relatively many outside directors have comparatively few directors from financial institutions, while others that have extensive bank connections have very few or no interlocks with competitors.

Industries that were not included in the preceding interindustry comparisons were those represented by only one firm in our sample and those that comprise a small number of competitively heterogeneous industries. For example, SIC 48 includes a small number of telephone companies and one radio-television broadcasting company. The average number of interlocks for this group is approximately twenty-two, considerably higher than any other category, including banks and insurance companies. However, this high rate can be primarily attributed to American Telephone and Telegraph Company (AT&T)—a monopolist which, by any definition, does not have any competition except for some manufacturers of minor and peripheral products and services, such as telephone equipment. AT&T is not only an economic giant, its frequency of interlocking also dwarfs that of many firms: it enjoys sixty interlocking directorates, of which twenty-two are with banks. Its officers sit on the boards of four banks, while only one bank officer sits on the board of AT&T. Approximately 80 percent of its board members are outside directors. We, therefore, excluded industries such as SIC 48 from our interindustry data. They have not only too few and very heterogeneous firms, but also a large standard deviation on measures of interlocking directorates. This heterogeneity presents specific problems in defining an industry, as will be further specified in the next chapter.

Despite differences of size and heterogeneity, our data—as presented in Table 1—illustrate substantial differences in interlocking behavior among industries. Most importantly, they show that interlocking in the United States is a ubiquitous phenomenon that has survived a succession of antitrust legislation.

Horizontal interlocks between competing organizations obviously violate various antitrust regulations, in particular, the stipulations of the Clayton Act. The deeper ramifications of such interlocks are, however, rather difficult to evaluate for several reasons. The first, previously alluded to, is the difficulty one encounters in defining strategically meaningful categories of firms. The SIC numerical code is somewhat inadequate for this purpose, as we have seen. Second, one has to consider the size of the industries: if a given industry is broadly defined and therefore includes a large number of firms, it is likely that this industry will appear to have a high number of competitive interlocks. For example, if one were to combine several of the smaller SIC industries into one larger category, the average number of horizontal interlocks between firms in that category might well exceed the separate averages for the smaller groupings.

Warner and Unwalla's (1967) study is a case in point. In order to ascertain the frequency of horizontal interlocks, they combined heterogeneous manufacturing industries into three large categories: Manufacturing I included tobacco, food, textiles, and the like; Manufacturing II, lumber, furniture, and paper; Manufacturing III, metal and machinery. They found that 18.6 percent, 22.0 percent, and 32.5 percent of the directorships originated from firms belonging to the three respective categories. They concluded that "managers of big business of all types who are outside directors are most likely to choose to be on the board of their own kind of enterprise and less likely to choose the boards of other types" (p. 150). By way of comparison, the average numbers of competitive interlocks for firms in the present study for categories similar to those defined by Warner and Unwalla are .18, .15, and .50, respectively. Because Warner and Unwalla's figures are based strictly on directional interlocks, they do not lend themselves to comparisons with the data of the present study. While both sets of data would seem to favor those who demand stronger enforcement of the Clayton Act, such data distort the actual prevalence of horizontal interlocks. Such broadly defined categories do not accurately reflect the boundaries of sets of strategically interdependent organizations. Only when one defines the categories more narrowly, so that they represent actual groups of competitors, can one determine more precisely the frequency of horizontal interlocks.

Such groups of competitors are usually defined in terms of the similarity of their product or service; the more similar their products, the greater the firms' awareness of interdependence. There is obviously little such similarity between a manufacturer of garments and a manufacturer of tobacco products, although they were grouped in Manufacturing I by Warner and Unwalla (1967). Our recognition of the limitations imposed by such a method enhances our ability to properly assess horizontal interdependence and horizontal interlocking directorates. A review of the data presented in Table 1 shows that we cannot share their conclusion about intraindustry linkages. These linkages are relatively few when contrasted with the interlocking directorates between financial and nonfinancial organizations. The individual industry's frequencies of horizontal interlocks do not, in themselves, suggest that strong enforcement of antitrust legislation is in order.

Relationships Between Interlock Variables

Table 2 shows the correlation coefficients for the variables presented in Table 1. The size of the board of directors is rather strongly associated with the number of interlocking directorates, except for the from-financial interlocks and the number of horizontal interlocks. Although the correlations between size and these two variables, .11 and .07 respectively, are significant ($p \leqslant .01$), clearly board size has rather minor relevance. Both the total number of interlocks and of financial interlocks correlate strongly with the size of the board; the larger the board of directors, the higher the number of interlocks and the greater the number of financial directors. Organizations that have large boards, however, are not necessarily more likely to open themselves to outside directors; the proportion of outside directors is not related to the number of directors on the board.

Since many of these measures are related to board size, Table 2 also reports the correlations after that variable was statistically controlled. These first-order correlations, therefore, show the intensity of

Table 2. Correlations Between Selected Measures of
Interlocking Directorates (N = 641).

	1	2	3	4	5	6	7	8
1. Size of Board		.40	.33	.27	.11	.07	.03	.37
2. Number of Interlocks			.82	.56	.64	.19	.34	.29
			.84	.47	.42	.31	.35	.16
3. Number of Financial				.63	.88	.02	.27	.26
Interlocks				.62	.48	.19	.27	.15
4. Number of To-					.52	.03	.03	.08
Financial Interlocks					.25	.11	.02	.00
5. Number of From-						.03	.17	.32
Financial Interlocks						.11	.17	.30
6. Number of Horizontal							.11	.07
Interlocks							.11	.05
7. Proportion of Outside								.32
Directors								.33
8. Number of Financial								
Directors								

Note: The first line in each cell shows the zero-order correlations; the second line, the first-order correlations with the size of the board of directors having been statistically controlled.

interlocking, as defined earlier. The number of interlocks is strongly related to measures of financial interlocks and board composition, but only weakly related to horizontal interlocks. The frequency of horizontal interlocks is unrelated or only weakly related to the other measures; such interlocks constitute a separate cluster of linkages and therefore will be considered separately.

The three measures of financial interlocking correlated so strongly that they can be treated as forming a distinct cluster. The correlation between the numbers of to- and from-financial interlocks is .52 (.25 when we control for board size). Thus firms that donate directors to banks and insurance companies are also likely to receive directors from those organizations. However, although the to-financial interlocks do not correlate with the porportion of outside directors or the number of financial directors, there is a strong relationship between from-financial interlocks and the number of financial directors. This pattern indicates a pronounced difference between organizations that reach out to financial organizations and those that are the "target" of financial organizations—a pattern which will be further analyzed in succeeding chapters. The correlation between from-financial interlocks and the number of financial directors also clarifies an earlier observation. The firms receive financial directors from a large array of banks, insurance companies, and investment bankers; our data on the nonfinancial firms' boards include all of these financial directors. But our data on financial organizations to which nonfinancial firms donate directors are restricted to those 100 financial organizations in our sample. The number of directors received from the financial community thus must appear larger than that of those donated to it. It is reasonable to speculate that many of the small firms are isolated relative to the fifty large banks in our sample, but are connected to local banks in their region.

In order to further explore this possibility, correlations between the relevant variables were computed for the fifty largest and the fifty smallest industrial firms. The zero-order coefficient between to-financial interlocks and the number of financial directors is .58 ($p \leqslant .01$) for the set of large firms and .20 (nonsignificant) for the set of small firms. Similar differences in coefficients were found for the relationship between from-financial interlocks and the proportion of outside directors and between from-financial interlocks and the number of financial directors. These correlations imply that the number of financial directors is very good proxy for the number of directional interlocks going from financial institutions to those non-financial organizations that rank high on the *Fortune* list. Such organizations have a national or even international mission and are more significant for banks and insurance companies that are similarly oriented.

In contrast, many of the smaller nonfinancial organizations on the *Fortune* list have a local, regional basis and appear to be relatively detached from the national financial community. If they form financial interlocks, they are inclined to do so with local banks and insurance firms. The regional nature of many banks is due not only to congressional or state legislation that prohibits banking in multiple states (or even multiple counties) but also to the banks' having developed a base of regional customers with whom long-term

relationships of trust and competence provide an impetus for linkages. The large banks, operating in major metropolitan areas and
primarily catering to firms with a cosmopolitan orientation, are
highly unlikely to donate directors to small, local firms. These considerations appear reasonable, although the present study provides
no information about the differential propensity of large banks to
conduct business with firms of different sizes.

Some of the largest banks are now strategically modifying the
diversity of their clientele by moving into the so-called middle market
(firms with sales of $100 to $500 million). This middle market is
showing a comparatively high rate of growth and represents an
attractive new strategic option for banks that, in the past, focused on
large firms. If this trend continues, national banks will figure more
prominently in regional business, and they might donate more directors to the local, smaller firms. At this time, these smaller firms
establish linkages with local financial organizations that are not in
our sample.

As Table 2 indicates, the first-order correlation coefficients
(controlling for board size) are fairly similar to the zero-order correlations, except for those involving financial interlocks. The frequencies
of the other types of interlocks, therefore, are not contingent upon the
size of the board of directors. The correlation coefficients also remain
substantially unchanged when we control for the size of the organization, as measured by number of employees and size of assets.

Summary

In conclusion, this national survey has shown that a rather
limited set of persons and organizations play a disproportionately
large role in the formation of interorganizational linkages. The relatively small size of this set is even smaller when we consider only the
directional linkages. About half of the directional interlocks involve
banks and insurance companies. They are ubiquitous in all types of
interlocks, and their presence is more pervasive than previous research on interlocking behavior has indicated. Banks and their officers, in particular, are among the most important component of linkages in the American corporate community, visible in industries of all
types and sizes.

We have also seen that horizontal interlocks between competing organizations are relatively infrequent, although there are considerable variations among the various industries. For some of these
industries, horizontal ties might be important. The proportion of
outside directors also differs among industries. Some industries are
more inbred than others, differences that we shall attempt to relate to
differences in the degrees of horizontal interdependence.

These observations summarize the results of the national survey. In the next three chapters, we will focus on interorganizational
relationships, examining the relationships between interlocking directorates, board composition, and horizontal and vertical interdependence. Because there are considerable differences between
individual organizations and the industries they belong to, it is crucial to investigate the organizations' differential propensity to form
interlocks, both financial and horizontal. Similarly, we must examine the composition of the organizations' boards of directors, a factor
that has implications for interlocks and other measures of
organizational behavior.

~~~~~~~~ FOUR ~~~~~~~~~

Links Between
Competing Organizations

~~~~~~

In the previous chapter we detected considerable degrees of interlocking between financial and nonfinancial organizations, and a lesser extent of interlocking between competing organizations. The analysis of these findings suggested that interlocking is not a random phenomenon, but our survey did not enable us to determine whether interlocking is motivated by a firm's desire to improve strategic interorganizational relationships. In this chapter, we address that issue by relating characteristics of markets to the frequency of interlocking among horizontally interdependent organizations. As discussed in Chapter Two, in industries in which the number of competitors is not overly large, competing firms are aware of their interdependence, and they have an incentive to form communication linkages to better deal with their mutual dependence. Therefore, we expect to find a relationship between the structure of given markets and interlocking directorates in those markets. The unit of study is

94

the industry or market—a set of strategically interdependent organizations—and not individual organizations. We are interested in explaining how interlocking satisfies the needs of a set of competing organizations, although any specific horizontal interlock pertains to only a pair of organizations.

Salient difficulties arise when we attempt to infer horizontal interdependence from data on market structure. One useful measure is the *concentration ratio* of the market or industry, defined as the combined market share of the four largest competitors in an industry. In Chapter One, we hypothesized that horizontal interdependence is highest when concentration is intermediate, that is, when the market is neither dominated by a single or a few large firms nor shared by many small firms. At intermediate levels of concentration, there is too much variability in behavior (pricing, advertising, research, and development) for firms to decode or anticipate their competitors' activities. Unlike firms in markets that are monopolistic (high concentration) or open (low concentration), firms in oligopolies (intermediate concentration) must develop strategies for coping with their competitors' withholding or distortion of information; failure to do so will severely reduce the firms' effectiveness. Interdependence on competitors requires firms to improve their information about market conditions so that they can neutralize the adverse effects of competitive interdependence.

Although horizontal interdependence can be defined in theory, we encounter difficulties in applying this term to actual situations. For example, in our analysis of the differences in interlocking among various industries, we discussed the problem of delineating an industry (see Chapter Three). One common solution is to use the Standard Industrial Classification (SIC) codes. As we have noted, however, the two-digit classes are so broad that they include firms that are not competitors. Firms belonging to the same three- or four-digit class have a greater similarity of products of services. Horizontal interdependence is directly related to the similarity of products; the greater the similarity, greater is the firms' awareness that the behavior of one has repercussions for the others. Some four-digit classes, however, represent a miscellaneous category of firms that do not belong to any one of the narrower classes. These firms produce such a variety of products that they are not competitively interdependent on any specific class of firms.

The difficulty of drawing correspondences between formal classifications of organizations and actual economic markets or industries cannot easily be resolved. Some firms are grouped into categories that have little homogeneity; other firms that are classified in different categories are in severe competition with each other. For example, Texas Instruments could be grouped with electronics firms that produce electronics components or with firms that manufacture watches. The firm makes digital watches and thus competes with firms that produce mechanical watches. It also manufactures electronics components and thus competes with electronics firms. As in this case, special problems arise in the classification of firms that produce a variety of related products. Texas Instruments products all derive from varied applications of microelectronics technology, but each product competes in a different market—watches, calculators, minicomputers. A second example of the difficulties of using the SIC codes is the case of container manufacturers. Manufacturers of paper containers belong to a different class than do the manufacturers of aluminum containers; the former are grouped with competitively irrelevant firms, such as those producing periodicals, books, pulp, and other paper products.

Product differentiation is an additional factor in evaluating the argument that SIC groups are sometimes defined too broadly to denote horizontal interdependence. Firms that have differentiated their product from others have acquired some independence and display monoplistic competition. However, an interesting counterargument to product differentiation and its implied diminution of competition has been suggested by the concept of "domain consensus" (Thompson, 1967). Interlocking might contribute to the rise and perseverance of domain consensus, which exists when oligopolists express a shared position about the boundaries of their product and market domains. For example, two department stores may offer merchandising differing in price and quality and thus avoiding competitive confrontation. Interlocking could contribute to the integrity of product differentiation and preserve the status quo in the market. These considerations might soften the difficulty of heterogeneity in SIC groups and the definition of competition.

These considerations point to several other pitfalls. One's definition of what constitutes a set of competing organizations strongly affects one's conclusions about the degree of concentration of the industry. If we define an industry very broadly, the concentration ratio of that industry will appear smaller than if we define an industry in narrower terms. If our definition is too narrow, however, all industries will appear highly concentrated. For example, if we were to compute the concentration ratios for the four-digit classes, we would arrive at concentration ratios which are considerably higher than those for the two-digit classes. The choice of an appropriate unit of aggregation is crucial.

Problems in selecting the appropriate unit also arise when we consider firms in an industry that shows widespread vertical integration, that is, when one division of a firm is a supplier of materials to another division, and the firm thus need not depend on outside suppliers. This problem was briefly mentioned in the preceding chapter, in the example of automobile manufacturers and the producers of automotive parts. If the firms in an industry are highly vertically integrated, the output of that industry will appear smaller than it is, because only interorganizational transactions are included in the measurement of an industry's output. When vertically integrated organizations compete with suppliers of industrial products (because both are manufacturing the industrial products), it is difficult to determine the actual market structure. In the case of the automobile industry, the measure of concentration will depend on the amount of vertical integration in the four largest companies.

Bias can also enter concentration measures if one inappropriately chooses a national, rather than a regional, basis. Nationwide industries, such as food distribution, appear to be unconcentrated if one studies the entire nation, but at regional levels, a different conclusion emerges. For example, the Safeway supermarket chain has many stores in some parts of this country and none in other regions. It has a big market share in the West and a minuscule share in the Northeast. Regional measures of Safeway's market share will obviously differ from national measures. If a national concentration measure is used to describe a basically regional industry, such as retail food merchandising, the concentration measure will be biased, reflecting a lower level of concentration than actually exists. Again, the unit of aggregation selected influences the results.

To control such biases, Weiss (1962) recommends a series of statistical adjustments. Bias caused by the adoption of broad industrial categories can be neutralized by using a weighted average of concentration ratios for five-digit subgroups. Bias caused by the presence of narrow categories can be avoided by interpolating the upper and lower limits of the combined concentration ratios. In other words, by combining two four-digit industries into a single group, we can determine the concentration ratio by taking a single value within the range of the two industries. Finally, regional differences in concentrations that cause bias in a national measure are alleviated by computing weighted averages of the regional concentration ratios. Since this information is generally unavailable, as a substitute, concentration measures for each industry can be adjusted by using constant factors obtained from weighted averages for all local, regional, and national markets. For regionalized, self-contained industries, this adjustment might be too small; the small size of these industries makes them probably more concentrated than a larger national market that involves the same distribution of firms. The adjustment is probably too large for regionalized industries that are dominated by nationwide chains.

Combining the three adjustments, Weiss found them to result in increases in his calculated levels of concentration, although the relative levels for different industries remained the same. (For a complete explanation of the derivation and reliability of Weiss' adjustments, the reader is referred to Weiss, 1962.) In the results to be reported here, we employ both the uncorrected concentration ratios and the adjusted ratios defined by Weiss.

Having statistically tested his adjustments on a sample of fifty industries, Weiss concluded that there exists a uniformity of structure within most two-digit classes. This latter conclusion is critical for the present analysis as the sets of strategically interdependent organizations have been defined at the two-digit level. Having only 500 industrial firms in our sample, it would be difficult to conduct our analysis using a smaller unit of aggregation. The unadjusted and adjusted concentration ratios are used to determine the strategical interdependence of firms belonging to the two-digit industries. The adjusted ratios should alleviate the previously mentioned difficulties of improper aggregation. Strategic interdependence within an industry was evaluated by measuring that industry's deviation from the mean concentration ratios for all industries in our sample. The results reported here are based on the subsample of industrial firms for which concentration ratios were available. Some industrial firms were eliminated because their product portfolio is so heterogeneous that they do not fit any industrial category. The zero-order correlation coefficients between deviation from the mean concentration and amount of interlocking follow. These are correlations between an industry's deviation from the mean concentration ratios and the measures of interlocking:

Deviation from Average Concentration

	Unadjusted	Adjusted
Interlocks (General)	-.016	-.059
Financial Interlocks	-.099 ($p = .01$)	-.061
To-Financial Interlocks	-.025	-.038
From-Financial Interlocks	-.060	-.089 ($p = .04$)
Horizontal Interlocks	-.002	-.049
Proportion of Outside Directors	-.022	-.038
Financial Directors	-.004	-.026

These results are very unambiguous in their negative support for the hypothesis that industries with intermediate levels of concentration have higher levels of interlocking than other industries. The negative sign of the correlation coefficients was expected, but the magnitude is so small that there is little room for assuming that industrial firms that belong to intermediately concentrated industries frequently interlock to enhance their intelligence about the market. Although the coefficients are higher for the adjusted concentration ratios, their size does not warrant any positive conclusion about concentration ratios and interlocking directorates.

This conclusion is strongly reinforced by an examination of various scatterplots (not shown). These plots reveal that many firms in various industries have no interlocks with banks, and that an even greater number of firms have no interlocks with competitors; these firms are equally distributed across the deviation scale. The firms with one or more financial or competitive interlocks are also fairly equally distributed over the two-dimensional area.

Clearly these findings do not square with the current body of knowledge. The reasons for our not having obtained stronger results are difficult to ascertain however. It is possible that the concentration measure, although adjusted, applies to industries that have been defined too broadly. The results might be different if it were possible to circumvent the problems of selecting an adequate unit of aggregation. The adjustments for bias caused by the unit of aggregation have had little effect on the results of this analysis. Perhaps the adjustment for aggregation bias is ineffective. It is also possible that concentration measures alone fail to adequately describe the phenomenon of competitive interdependence. Apart from studying concentration levels, it is important to examine the size of firms in an industry, (Pennings, 1980a). Strategic interdependence can be a function of clusters of small firms that are competing in an industry dominated by a single firm or by several subdominant firms. The set of small competing firms might experience a high level of strategic interdependence, even though their industry has an extraordinarily high degree of concentration. Similarity in size, as well as similarity in products, affects interdependence. The competitive environment, as defined by the two-digit industrial classifications, has a different meaning for organizations that differ in size (see also Grabowski and Baxter, 1973).

Finally, the analysis of the absolute deviation from mean concentration ratios may have incorrectly assumed that the relationship between interlocking and absolute deviation is symmetrical, as implied by the absolute difference measure. This symmetry was assumed correct, because interlocking—unlike merger and other overt behaviors among competitors—is relatively immune from the visibility of antitrust agencies. Merger activity is low in highly concentrated industries because it is monitored by federal antitrust agencies, but such agencies have not had a noticeable effect on interlocking behavior. In spite of this difference, perhaps the relationship between concentration and interlocking is different for industries with high compared to low levels of concentration. The following results, however, suggest that this expectation is not correct. The correlations between concentration and interlocking are virtually identical for two sets of industrial firms, differentiated by concentration ratios. The results for the unadjusted concentration ratios are similar, albeit slightly lower, than for the adjusted ratios reported here.

Adjusted Concentration Ratio

	Below Average (N = 216)	Above Average (N = 181)	Total (N = 386)
Interlocks (general)	.119 (p = .04)	.165 (p = .01)	.206 (p < .001)
Financial interlocks	.113 (p = .05)	.188 (p = .01)	.184 (p < .001)
To-Financial interlocks	.005	.067	.112 (p < .05)
From-Financial interlocks	.012	.142 (p = .02)	.143 (p < .01)
Horizontal interlocks	.123 (p = .04)	.153 (p = .02)	.196 (p < .001)
Proportion of outside directors	.041	.069	-.037
Financial directors	.019	-.018	.046

With the exception of from-financial interlocks, the association between measures of interlocking and concentration are almost the same for both groups. The differentiation into low and high concentration levels has, therefore, little meaning. The more general outcome is that the higher the concentration level, the higher the frequency of interlocking directorates. This conclusion is derived from the third column that shows the product-moment correlations for the total sample of firms for which we had concentration data. These correlations are very similar to second-order correlations that control for the size of the organization and the size of the board of directors. The coefficients indicate that market structure is a rather poor predictor of interlock behavior. They might have been higher, however, if their computation had been based on a more normal distribution of the interlock variables.

The relationship between horizontal interlocking and concentration has been explored further through the use of nonparametric, distribution-free statistical analysis. Although horizontal interlocks do not have the strongest association with market structure, they were hypothesized to be most relevant for the management of horizontal interdependence. The range of adjusted concentration ratios was divided into four intervals, resulting in four categories of firms. Table 3, which shows the distribution of horizontal interlocks for each of the four categories, indicates that the frequency of horizontal interlocks is much higher for firms in industries with high concentration ratios. It is comparatively low for industries in which concentration is

Table 3. Cross-Tabulation of Industrial Concentration Ratio and Frequency
of Horizontal Interlocking Directorates (*N* = 386).

Frequency of Interlocks	Horizontal Interdependence (Adjusted Concentration Ratio)				
	0 - 36	36 - 47	47 - 57	57 - 68	Row Total
0	49	97	89	63	298
	16.4	32.6	29.9	21.1	77.2
	96.1	81.5	78.1	61.8	
1	2	14	16	23	55
	3.6	25.5	29.1	41.8	14.2
	3.9	11.8	14.0	22.5	
2	0	5	5	12	22
	0.0	22.7	22.7	54.5	5.7
	0.0	4.2	4.4	11.8	
3	0	1	3	2	6
	0.0	16.7	50.0	33.3	1.6
	0.0	0.8	2.6	2.0	
>3	0	2	1	2	5
	0.0	40.0	20.0	40.0	1.3
	0.0	1.7	0.9	2.0	
Column Total	51	119	114	102	386
	13.2	30.8	29.5	26.4	100.0

Note: In each cell, the first line gives the number of interlocks; the second, that number expressed as a percentage of the total for the row; the third, that number expressed as a percentage of the total for the column.

A nonparametric test of the relationship is highly significant (χ^2 = 28.81, p = .004 with 12 degrees of freedom).

low, and most of the united firms are in industries with the least amount of concentration. This display of the relationship obviates the need for making a median split to demonstrate that most horizontal interlocks are not at intermediate levels of concentration. Rather, we see that the actual degree of concentration is associated with interlock frequency and that the hypothesis on the deviation from average concentration applies only to firms that have below-average concentration ratios.

The data in Table 3 suggest that there is virtually no interlocking between competitors in highly differentiated, fragmented markets with many small firms. In contrast, industries in which a few oligopolists share a quasi monopoly exhibit widespread interlocking. The assumption that such firms refrain from interlocking because their small numbers make intelligence superfluous and unnecessary is not correct. These firms, which experience considerable competitive interdependence, are apparently inclined to establish communication channels, as inferred from their frequency of horizontal interlocks. It should be added that this conclusion applies almost equally to general and financial interlocks. Cross-tabulation of these variables with concentration ratios yielded results which are similar to those reported in Table 3. In all cases, the relationship was highly significant as revealed by nonparametric test statistics. The approximately 25 percent of firms with horizontal interlocks also show disproportionately high levels of other kinds of interlocking. Thus, there is quite a pervasive relationship between concentration and interlocking.

Two important questions must be considered: Why is the relationship between concentration and interlocking identical for firms regardless of the level of concentration? Why is the relationship between from-financial interlocks and concentration significant only for firms in highly concentrated industries?

The answer to the first question might be simply that interdependence is a linear function of concentration. An industry with only two firms shows more interdependence than an industry with five or ten firms. The smaller the number of firms, or the larger the share that belongs to a small set of large firms, the greater the interdependence. This, in turn, provides an incentive for the sharing of information and diminution of competitive behavior as facilitated by interlocking directorates.

Thus, the assumption that strongly concentrated industries have no need for interlocking, because scarcity of firms obviates the need for such communication, appears false. It is particularly interesting to note that horizontal interlocks, which were unrelated to the deviation measure, are correlated with concentration. Although the magnitude of the correlation continues to be low and explains only 4 percent of the variance, we note that it is stronger for the firms in highly concentrated industries. The finding cannot be dismissed by the argument that firms in highly concentrated industries have more interlocks because they are generally larger. As mentioned before, the zero-order correlations are very similar to the first-order correlations in which organizational size is controlled. Perhaps because interlocking directorates are surreptitious or innocuous, they are very attractive for managing horizontal interdependence, particularly in highly concentrated industries.

The relationship between concentration ratio and from-financial interlocks signals a possibly different and not previously considered role for boundary spanning individuals between financial and nonfinancial institutions. The from-financial interlocking directors might serve not only as conduits between financial organizations and their clientele but as disseminators of information about industry trends and other pertinent developments, even if they do not form a direct link between two competing organizations.

The correlation between concentration ratio and from-financial interlocks did not disappear when controlled for horizontal interlocks. Would such a finding suggest that from-financial interlocks would serve as an outlet through which information stored in the financial community is made accessible to industrial organizations? It seems as if commercial banks are also industry data banks. Conceivably, the from-financial interlocks facilitate the disclosure of information stored, accumulated, and updated by the financial organization. This type of boundary-spanning person might therefore be as likely to diffuse information as to act as common messenger among competing organizations. Unlike the to-financial interlocking director, such a person might promote rich and generalized intelligence. For example, a director from a bank who sits on the board of an industrial firm has experience and a comprehensive overall view of markets and their firms, and she can transmit this knowledge and know-how. In contrast, an inside director of an industrial firm who sits on the board of a bank might be in a good position to negotiate the securing of a loan, but he could probably not match her performance in transmitting information. Indeed, a to-financial director is comparatively limited in acquiring, processing, interpreting, and transmitting information from a bank to his own firm.

Perhaps banks and insurance companies perform a role which is analogous to trade association surveys and so-called Profit Impact of Market Strategies (PIMS) surveys (Schoeffler, 1977). Trade associations collect information from member firms and compile it in a report that does not disclose identities but, nevertheless, permits comparison between similar firms on a number of performance attributes. Banks are also repositories of market information, repositories to which industrial firms may achieve access by, for example, establishing a linkage with a bank. Banks and insurance firms are often in the unique position of obtaining inside information from a number of similar organizations, which enables them to derive behavioral patterns and to extract normative competitive standards. For satisfying a firm's need of information about its industry, directional interlocks from financial institutions may be more attractive than horizontal interlocks, because they provide a more panoramic view of the industry. Horizontal interlocks cannot provide the generality of information that financial interlocks can. Perhaps an analogous interpretation can be invoked to account for the irrelevancy of financial directors, the bulk of which do.not originate from the *Fortune* sample. These firms have more regional horizons. If this assumption is correct, it is only natural to expect that competitively interdependent firms will prefer to recruit directors from large financial organizations, which have a more general and encompassing view of their industry, than from local banks. Furthermore, it is conceivable that industries with high concentration levels are national in character, and thus data about these industries are less subject to bias caused by the unit of aggregation. This observation, if correct, describes the predominantly national or international mission of the financial institutions on the *Fortune* list. These organizations are, therefore, attractive providers of directors, who diffuse information commensurate with the national scope of their domain. The data under consideration, however, do not permit us to offer a more precise interpretation.

In conclusion, this analysis has shown that there is a weak, but very significant, relationship between concentration ratio and interlocking. The relationship is strongest for highly concentrated industries—industries that writers on oligopoly have classified as having the most interdependent firms (Williamson, 1975). These results do not corroborate the hypothesis that the deviation from intermediate concentration explains competitive interlocking. The role and function of financial institutions are difficult to demonstrate empirically, but we can intuitively infer that financial directors perform a role analogous to that of horizontal interlocks. Financial interlocks might not be relevant exclusively to vertical relationships; they also seem to transmit information between competitively interdependent organizations. Financial firms have confidential relationships with a wide variety of firms, and these relationships enable them to be more effective transmitters of information than many other types of firms (for example, suppliers of raw materials or major customers). Perhaps some law firms and management consultants that have many interorganization relationships perform a similar role, but such information is not available. Banks and insurance firms probably have a fairly well-balanced set of financial, marketing, and strategic standards of behavior for various industries; their having such information might render them more effective than law firms as providers of common messengers.

These observations also dramatically illustrate the metaphor of the black box, described in the first chapter. We know only who a firm's directors are, what their backgrounds are, how important they appear in view of a firm's competitive interdependence, but we cannot infer their significance in an organization's actual decision making. That is, we cannot surmise whether a firm, on the basis of its financial (or horizontal) interlocking, is prone to adopt certain strategic decisions that will shape its long-term posture toward its competitors. We do not even know whether interlocking directors do indeed enhance the sharing of information between competitively interdependent organizations. The prevalence of bankers among interlocking directorates is suggestive but enigmatic.

We can only assume that if horizontal interdependence is high, those competitors with comparatively many interlocks are better informed about market developments, competitive fronts, product innovations, and other market conditions. It is then plausible to speculate that such firms will be more effective, as indicated by high profits, market share, or consumer satisfaction. Fortunately, we do not have to assume that well-interlocked firms are more effective; it is possible to indirectly relate interlocking frequency to organizational effectiveness. In Chapter Six we shall address this issue in greater detail.

~~~~~~~ *FIVE* ~~~~~~~

Links Between Financial Institutions and Their Corporate Clients

~~~~~~~~~~~~~~~~~~~~~~~~~~~~~~~~

Unlike the study of horizontally interdependent organizations, which emphasizes sets of interdependent competitors and their collective structure, research on vertically interdependent organizations concentrates on individual firms and how a firm uses vertical interlocks to mitigate difficulties in transactions with its suppliers and customers. In this chapter, we analyze vertical interdependence by examining the relationship between a firm's dependence on external financing and its financial interlocking directorates.

 Financial interlocks were chosen as the focus because, as noted earlier, they are quite prevalent and financial records are more accessible to the researcher than information on suppliers and customers.

Even if data on vertical interdependence between suppliers and buyers were accessible, we would still face major obstacles, such as the relative incomparability of organizations and their dependence on external resources. We would need to develop uniform measures of dependence for a number of organizations before we could examine the relationship between interdependence and interlocking. Characteristic differences between firms or their industries, however, might prevent interorganizational comparisons. Although the issues can easily be defined, there are empirical difficulties in devising and applying uniform measures for a wide variety of organizations.

We have also noted that the researcher needs to identify exchange patterns for each focal organization and, subsequently, relate these patterns to the organization's interlocking behavior. Differences in the vertical integration, concentration of the suppliers' and buyers' industries, regional economic conditions, and many other factors determine a focal organization's dependence on external suppliers of resources. Furthermore, the criticality and substitutionality of resources is important in evaluating interdependence. Criticality, in particular, depends on the strategic posture of the firm and can alter as a result of shifts in strategic planning. Changes in a firm's missions or goals (for example, a move into overseas markets, vertical expansion into manufacturing industrial products, diversification, and product differentiation) alter the relative importance of various resources. The criticality of a resource cannot be deduced simply from the volume of transactions. One must often make subjective judgments about the relative importance of a firm's suppliers or customers. Even after making such subjective choices, one may find that interorganizational comparisons of resource dependency are tenuous.

We can escape these difficulties by studying the financial dependence of the firm. From accessible records, we can make rather objective inferences about the dependence of organizations on their providers of capital. Capital is a resource that all firms—industrial, merchandising, transportation, and utility—require. Lastly, financial resources are expressed in uniform units of measurement, such as national currencies, that allow us to readily compare different types of organizations and industries.

The prevalence of financial interlocks among competitively interdependent organizations has led us to conjecture that they act as distinct disseminators of market information. Nevertheless, this role is not their primary one; rather, they seem to function as a device for managing and coordinating vertical interdependence—particularly, the vertical interdependence between various types of corporations and their providers of capital. Financial interlocks are instrumental in a firm's effort to acquire control over its external financing.

Assuming that financial dependence is comparable across many different types of organizations, we can test the hypothesis that interlocking is a boundary-spanning phenomenon in the realm of capital markets. Even at this level of specificity, however, there are difficulties in collecting relevant data. We usually cannot obtain information on the transactions between specific banks, or insurance companies, and their customers. Most firms maintain financial relationships with several banks—partly to diminish their vertical dependence on any one bank. Capital, a very common resource, is very substitutable, but its suppliers often act as gatekeepers, exercising considerable control over its availability. A firm can decrease its reliance on any specific bank by developing relationships with several banks.

A firm's use of multiple sources for external financing creates problems for the researcher who would relate financial dependence to financial interlocks. A firm may have one financial interlock, yet maintain lasting transactional ties with two or more banks. What is the rationale for the firm's selecting a director from one of those banks or for providing a director for one of their boards? Is the selection predicated upon the firm's relative dependence on the respective financial institutions? We cannot answer such questions in this study, because they require data that most firms do not disclose for proprietary reasons.

Instead, this study relates the aggregate financial dependence of a firm to its financial interlocks. In view of the prevalence of financial interlocks, our data should permit an adequate test of the hypothesis that vertical interdependence leads to vertical interlocking. We have seen that a substantial number of interlocks involve banks and insurance firms—particularly if we limit ourselves to directional interlocking directorates. If differences in financial interlocking are traceable to variations in dependence on external financing, we are justified in inferring that interlocks function as boundary-spanning devices between transactionally interdependent organizations. The framework presented in Chapter One specified that a firm's directional interlocks with organizations providing critical and nonsubstitutional resources are central to the firm's management of its interorganizational relationships. The relationship between directional financial interlocks and financial interdependence should be more pronounced (and more informative) than relationships involving interlocking directorates whose directionality cannot be determined. We assume, therefore, that a firm's need for external financing, its financial dependence, is managed by directional interlocking directorates.

Financial Dependence

Financial dependence can be inferred from an organization's capital structure, specifically, from the volume of a firm's external debt, both short-term and long-term, relative to its equity. The greater the volume of debt, the higher the dependence on outside sources; conversely, the higher the degree of internal financing, the higher the independence. Broadly speaking, a firm finances its investments by debt or by available equity; equity is the sum of common and preferred stockholders' equity. The debt-equity ratio and the solvency ratio express a firm's reliance on external financial sources relative to internal sources. The debt-equity ratio is the ratio of total debt to equity. For example, if a firm has borrowed short-term and long-term capital amounting to $100 million, and stockholders' equity is $60 million, the debt-equity ratio is 1.67. Financial analysts often use this ratio to evaluate the riskiness of a firm. If a firm borrows so freely that its debt is considerably larger than its equity, the firm is said to be risky. Conversely, some firms refrain from borrowing, financing their investments from their equity, such as stock and retained earnings. Debt-equity ratios vary among industries: A ratio of .5 is high for some industries (for example, merchandising) and low for others (for example, railroads). Financial analysts generally feel that firms whose ratios deviate substantially from industry norms are risky.

Two solvency measures, the *quick ratio* and the *current ratio*, indicate how well a firm can meet its current obligations. The quick ratio is the quotient of a firm's cash and receivables, divided by its current liabilities. The current ratio is the quotient of current assets divided by current liabilities. These ratios sometimes give a better indication of a firm's financial state than the debt-equity ratio. For example, short-term debt is a critical resource for some firms, such as merchandisers, whose annual cash flow is highly cyclical. This dependence is not disclosed by the debt-equity ratio, but is revealed by the solvency ratios.

Analysts also compare the volume of a firm's long-term and short-term debt. If long-term debt is large, a high debt-equity ratio is considered even more unfavorable. Likewise, a firm is considered more vulnerable if its current liabilities and long-term debt are large, and its debt-equity ratio is high. Financial dependence factors have a mutually reinforcing effect on one another, often expressed as a multiplicative effect. In considering a firm's financial dependence, then, we must evaluate its debt-equity ratio, its long-term debt, and the joint incremental effect of these two factors. In order to then determine whether these factors correlate to a firm's number of financial interlocks, we compare two regression equations, one without and one with a multiplicative term expressing the incremental effect of debt-equity ratio and long-term debt. If the multiplicative term relates significantly to interlock frequency we can conclude that there is an interaction effect between long-term debt and debt-equity ratio (Cohen, 1968). We can similarly analyze the relationships between financial interlocks and short-term debt obligations, current ratios, and their multiplicative effect. All these factors may be related to either cooptative or persuasive linkages in vertical interlocking.

Apart from considerations of debt, organizations are also hypothesized to form interlocks if they are capital intensive and have extensive capital expenditures. They form interlocks if their investment programs induce them to seek access to capital markets. We can express capital requirements in two ways: capital intensity and capital expenditures. *Capital intensity* is the ratio of a firm's total assets or invested capital divided by the number of its employees. *Capital expenditures* are monies spent for the construction or acquisition of new facilities and equipment. Capital expenditures include investments in joint ventures with other organizations and investments in subsidiaries.

As a preliminary hypothesis, we suggest a positive relationship between inferred capital requirements and financial interlocking directorates. The hypothesis is only preliminary, however, because the relationship may vary among industries, depending on their growth, riskiness, and other attributes. Also, as will be explored in Chapter Six, firms' performance may affect the strength and direction of the relationship. In this chapter, we examine whether firms with large capital requirements have many to- and from-financial interlocks. The relationship between capital needs and to-interlocks are likely to be stronger than those for from-interlocks, because firms with expansive strategies allocate more resources in the management of their interorganizational environment. The relationship is likely to be particularly strong among firms that invest aggressively in joint ventures with other firms. Joint ventures resemble interlocks in that they promote control over the organization's environment; both joint ventures and interlocks are indicative or symptomatic of a firm's external control (Pennings, 1980a). Thus the effects of capital investments in joint ventures are considered in this analysis.

Measures and Methodology

We obtained information on financial dependence from COMPUSTAT, a subsidiary of Standard and Poor's that maintains extensive archives of financial, statistical, and marketing information on more than 1,000 corporations. The data have been collected from balance sheets and income statements; they are fairly complete for industrial firms, but relatively incomplete for nonindustrial firms, especially banks, insurance companies, railroads, and some utility companies. Unfortunately, their data are less complete for some measures than others, and this incompleteness may create a sampling bias that is impossible to isolate. We will use their information on financial structure and capital expenditure to test the hypotheses on the relationship between interdependence and interlocking.

Most of the data we analyzed are limited to the year 1969, the year for which we have the information on interlocking. However, we have incorporated some selected variables for the period 1960–1975. In some respects, the financial posture of a corporation reveals a great deal of inertia. Decisions about long-term commitments are made relatively infrequently and, although short-term measures, such as current ratio, vary from year to year or from quarter to quarter, other measures, such as debt-equity ratio, change only gradually. In the following analysis we supplement the cross-sectional comparisons with some long-term measures in order to explore the relationship between long-term financial dependence and interlocking. For example, we ascertain whether increments in debt-equity ratios during the period 1960–1969 or the period 1969–1975 are associated with frequency of interlocking directorates.

Our variables for measuring financial dependence are the following:

- X_1 = Size of Organization, measured by annual gross sales and other operating revenue
- X_2 = Size of Organization, measured by average number of employees during the year or the number of employees at the year's end
- X_3 = Capital Intensity, defined as total assets divided by number of employees
- X_4 = Capital Expenditures, measured by the amount of money spent for the construction and acquisition of facilities and equipment
- X_5 = Investment in Joint Ventures, measured by long-term investments and advances to "associates" and joint ventures
- X_6 = Current Debt, measured by total of notes, contracts, loans, current sinking funds payable, and current maturity of long-term debt
- X_7 = Current Ratio, defined as current assets divided by current liabilities
- X_8 = Debt-Equity Ratio, defined as long term debt divided by common equity, that is, by the common shareholders' interest in the company
- X_9 = Long-Term Debt, the total of all obligations due after a one-year period
- X_{10} = Retained Earnings, expressed in dollars
- X_{11} = Current Assets, expressed in dollars
- X_{12} = Pension and Retirement Expenses, as reported in the income statement, expressed in dollars.

The first two variables, measuring size, must be controlled in order to ascertain the effects of the other variables, because size is an important predictor of interlocking. Variables X_3, X_4, and X_5 measure capital investments and possible dependence. X_6 to X_9 are measures of external dependence; X_{10} and X_{11} measure external independence as high retained earnings allowed a firm to either finance new investments or replace old investments without having to borrow from external sources. Variable X_{12} has been included as a measure of a firm's dependence on labor—a complement of capital expenditure. We used pension and retirement expenses rather than wages and salaries because many firms do not report the latter. These two variables appear interchangeable because, for those firms that reported information on both, pension and retirement expenses showed a .97 correlation with wages and salaries. A labor variable must be used, because labor expenses are complementary to capital intensity and have been reported as an important antecedent of interlocking directorates (compare Allen, 1974; U.S. Senate, 1978).

Compared with data on horizontal interdependence, financial information is more widely available and pertains to individual organizations rather than an aggregate set. We obtained fairly complete information on approximately 580 nonfinancial firms; various reasons, such as merger and gaps in the data archives, precluded our obtaining all the data for all the firms. The available financial information, however, did permit us to partition the set of organizations into homogeneous subsets: industrial, retail, transportation, and utilities. The association between financial dependence and interlocking varies considerably across these subsets. Because our chosen financial measures are relatively few, we have exercised restraint in drawing conclusions from our data. Furthermore, we present only a few measures of interlocking, particularly those which are germane to boundary spanning between nonfinancial and financial firms. First we present our results for a variety of two-variable relationships. Then we test our specific hypothesis about the joint effect of all financial variables and their interaction. Finally, we present some results on changes in capital structure and interlocking.

Bivariate Relationships

Table 4 shows seven dependent variables that measure overall interlocking and directional financial interlocking. The to- and from-financial interlocks are primarily germane to the firms'

Table 4. Correlations Between Financial Interdependence and Interlocking Directorates.

	Capital Intensity	Capital Expenditures	Investment in Joint Ventures	Current Debt	Current Ratio	Debt-Equity Ratio	Long-Term Debt	Retained Earnings	Current Assets	Pension and Retirement Expenses
Interlocks (General)	-.04	.20[a]	.24[a]	.42[a]	.02	-.05	.10[a]	.08[a]	.46[a]	.28[a]
Financial Interlocks	-.02	.49[a]	.33[a]	.60[a]	-.18[a]	-.11[a]	.11[a]	.05	.70[a]	.79[a]
To-Financial Interlocks	-.02	.25[a]	.37[a]	.40	.09[a]	-.02	.07[a]	.03	.43[a]	.38[a]
From-Financial Interlocks	-.01	.21[a]	.22[a]	.52[a]	-.16[a]	-.12[a]	.04	.04	.63[a]	.39[a]
Proportion of Outside Directors	.02	.03	-.01	.01	-.03	.10[a]	.07[a]	.03	.06	.05
Number of Financial Directors	.00	-.01	.06	-.02	-.04	.15[a]	.05	.03	.05	.02
Number of Investment Bank Directors	.00	.00	.06	-.03	.04	-.04	-.06	.03	-.04	-.06

Note: These coefficients represent second-order correlations in which the firm's size, measured by the number of employees and total annual sales, has been controlled.

[a] $p \leq .05$

boundary-spanning interlocks with the 100 financial firms on the *Fortune* list, while the number of financial and investment bank directors who sit on the board have a relevance beyond the *Fortune* set. The frequency of general interlocks and proportion of outside directors are included to permit a contrast with previous studies on interlocking directorates.

The number of financial directors and the number of directors from investment banks were analyzed separately because these two types of directors can perform different roles in enhancing a firm's access to capital markets. When in need of long-term financing, a corporation can either arrange for long-term external debt or it can procure long-term capital through the issuing of new securities. Banks and insurance companies are instrumental in supplying long-term debt, while investment bankers usually serve to advise, underwrite, and market a firm's new securities. They provide advice (about the timing, price, and types of securities) prior to the issuance of new securities. More importantly, the investment bank often underwrites the securities; it buys all the securities (debentures, shares) and disposes of them at its own risk. As a result, it is usually responsible for marketing the securities, often pooling its efforts with those of other investment banks. In contrast, although banks and insurance companies may underwrite securities or buy corporate securities (as in the case of so-called private placement), their primary function is to lend capital. In view of firms' dependence on long-term credit, as expressed by the debt-equity ratio, and the alternative sources of credit in the capital market, it seems worthwhile to explore the relationships between financial dependence and interlocking with different types of financial organizations. The specialized nature of financial organizations makes it likely that corporations will recruit different types of directors depending on their long-range financial planning. Firms with an inclination toward equity financing are likely to interlock more frequently with investment banks, the largest of which include Merrill Lynch, Salomon Brothers, First Boston Corporation, Goldman Sachs, Blyth, Eastman, Dillon, and Lehman Brothers. The volume of each of these firms exceeded $5 billion in 1975.

Table 4 displays the second-order correlations between financial dependence and frequency of interlocking. These correlations are presented with the size of the organization (number of employees and total sales) held constant. Zero-order correlations would be spurious because size is an important predictor of interlocking.

Overall, the results of Table 4 do not confirm the hypothesis on financial dependence and interlocking. Many of the correlation coefficients are low and insignificant—especially those entries involving board composition measures. Among the higher and significant coefficients are several whose signs are opposite our expectations, particularly the relationships involving current ratio, debt-to-equity ratio, and current assets. Within the total context of all relationships, some coefficients suggest conflicting conclusions. For example, while capital expenditures are associated with higher levels of financial interlocking, there are similar associations in the case of labor expenses. We had expected strong links between financial organizations and capital intensive firms with high outlays of capital expenditures and fewer ties with firms having substantial variable, nonfixed costs, such as pension and retirement expenses. Let us review these results by sequentially discussing the measures of capital dependence.

Contrary to earlier assumptions about capital intensity, there is no significant association between this variable and the various measures of interlocking directorates. The zero-order correlations are also low. Although higher, they are negative and therefore contrary to the hypothesis. Strictly speaking, the zero-order correlations are highly insignificant in a one-tailed test. The lower second-order correlation as contrasted with the zero-order correlation might have been due to a filtering effect. By statistically controlling for the two measures of size, some of the effects of capital intensity are removed. Larger firms are generally more capital intensive so that the holding constant of size was considered desirable. At any rate, both the zero-order and second-order correlation are contrary to the hypothesized relationship, a finding that is consistent with Allen (1974).

However, the capital expenditures variable is positively associated with the first four measures of interlocking. Similar results were obtained for investment in joint ventures. The coefficients are higher for the to-financial interlocks than for the from-financial interlocks, which implies that organizations with relatively expansive dispositions are comparatively active in establishing ties with the financial community. This is particularly evident in the case of joint ventures, an alternative and apparently complementary approach for gaining better external control. The greater the investment in joint ventures, the larger the number of financial interlocks. It seems as if investment in joint ventures—whether with suppliers, buyers, or competitors is not known—clusters together with financial interlocking in forming part of a firm's "outreach" syndrome. Both are vehicles through which firms reach out into their strategic environment; both are elements of the firm's institutional level. Outwardly oriented firms are expected to have a relatively high number of outside directors. More specific information on these and other boundary-spanning activities are needed to conclude that multiple manifestations of external control and intelligence occur simultaneously or are complementary to one another.

While the measure of current debt is also positively associated with frequency of interlocking, the correlation with from-financial interlocks is significantly higher than that with to-financial interlocks. These results clearly support the contention that corporations whose financial dependence is high coopt and persuade banks and insurance firms. Compared with long-term debt, current debt is often more critical because it reflects immediate obligations, to be met within a year; short-term debt is important because a sudden decrease in the supply of short-term capital could quickly impede a firm's operations. Long-term debt also correlates with frequency of interlocking, but the coefficients are small; they do not signal major support for the hypothesis on cooptation and persuasion.

The two ratio measures—current ratio and debt-to-equity ratio —also show unexpected coefficients. First, the coefficients are very low, close to zero for the board composition measures and for the first four measures, which are based on the exclusive sample of 800 *Fortune* firms. Second, many of the correlation coefficients have a sign opposite to that which had been expected. As noted before, the significant coefficients are highly insignificant if one-tailed tested.

For the current ratio, a negative relationship was expected with the assumption that solvent firms are comparatively independent of the supply of short-term debt; hence they should show fewer interlocks with financial organizations. This expectation is only borne out for to-financial interlocks and from-financial interlocks. Recall that current ratio is the quotient of current assets divided by current liabilities; the lower this ratio, the higher the dependence on short-term financing. Although rather low, the second order correlation involving financial interlocks ($r = -.18$; $p \leqslant .01$) and from-financial interlocks ($r = -.16$; $p \leqslant .01$) signal mild support for the hypothesis on interdependence and interlocking. However, these results are somewhat puzzling in view of the positive correlation involving to-financial interlocks ($r = .09$; $p \leqslant .01$). Firms with probable cashflow problems were expected to forge ties with the financial world to protect themselves against the problems of short-term financing. Solvency is a rather poor predictor of interlocking.

In contrast, the financial organizations listed by *Fortune* appear to stay away from corporations with high debt-equity ratios. There is one interesting departure from the pattern of correlation coefficients: Firms with a high debt-equity ratio have a larger proportion of outside directors ($r = .10$, $p \leqslant .01$) and a greater number of financial directors ($r = .15$, $p \leqslant .01$). Perhaps this latter coefficient points to the specific character of firms on the *Fortune* list, compared to smaller financial organizations, an issue mentioned in Chapter Four.

Retained earnings, a measure of a firm's independence from outside financial sources, is unrelated to interlocking. The strongest relationships shown in Table 4 are those that involve current assets and labor expenses. Firms with extensive cash and other liquid financial resources are extraordinarily well interlocked with financial organizations. Banks and insurance companies show a strong affinity with these firms; this affinity seems reciprocal, for there is a fairly even balance of to- and from-interlocks. Perhaps banks find financially sound firms to be interesting financial partners; strong interlocking regulates and seals the transactional relationship. The outcomes involving pension and retirement expenses might be explained by reference to a firm's recurring obligations to labor; well-cemented and closely preserved connections with suppliers of capital will enable a firm to surmount problems of cash flow. Firms that rely heavily on labor are also bound to be more dependent on groups such as trade unions and are, therefore, more inclined to seek allies that can help them alleviate disruptions such as labor disputes. The size of the coefficients for correlations of the labor measure and financial interlocks suggests that a highly plausible motive for financial interlocking is a firm's desire to financially buffer itself.

It is also plausible that large pension and investment expenses imply large funds, which are generally invested. Firms endowed with such large funds have the influence to claim and to secure board representation on other firms. For the focal organization's relationship with financial organizations, this might mean better access to their investment practices or cooptation by financial organizations to acquire new business. Even more speculative, a focal organization might receive representation on the board of other firms because its retirement and pension funds have been used for financing their bonds and other securities. This study does not have data on stock ownership, but this might be an important determinant of interlocking, especially when the large shareholders are institutional investors.

In their totality, these results challenge the hypothesis that financially dependent firms are more prone to establish interlocking directorates. Barring two exceptions, these results are only significant for interlock variables derived from the *Fortune* list. As Table 4 shows, the interlock measures derived from board composition are unrelated to indicators of capital structure. As noted previously, board composition measures can be interpreted as reflecting directional interlocks, except that the formal position of outside directors in their organization of origin is unknown. Perhaps their status in their organization is not as high as that for directors of *Fortune*-listed companies. Perhaps their organizations do not carry as much influence in the interorganizational arena. The results are clearly negative. The only exception in Table 4 concerns financial directors on the board and the debt-to-equity ratio, in which the correlation coefficient is positive: $r = .15; p \leqslant .01$, one of the isolated cases of support for our hypothesis.

Earlier we speculated that firms might recruit representatives from various institutions, depending on their specific financial needs. In the case of investment bankers, this reasoning pertains to long-term financing. The results of Table 4 and the unreported results are unequivocally negative, and there is little relationship between external financing and the number of specific types of financial directors on the board.

Analysis of Homogeneous Subsets of Organizations

Table 4 gives results for all nonfinancial firms for which relevant financial information was available; however, the analysis and results might be too aggregative. By decomposing our sample into homogeneous subsets, results more compatible with the hypothesis might be obtained. To explore this possibility, we computed separately the coefficients for distinct categories of firms, such as automotive, aerospace and defense, energy, transportation, and utility, and for conglomerates (results not shown). The usefulness of such an analysis is often hampered by the small number of observations. Nevertheless, a glimpse of this exploration of industry differences may alleviate some of the ambivalence that flavored the results.

The findings for the various industries dictate a wide array of conclusions about the interlock correlates of capital structure. Generally, board composition measures are independent of capital structure indicators; the results of the measures derived from the *Fortune* list of interlocking are stronger. However, many of these results are seemingly contradictory and without any distinct pattern.

For some industry groups there are no relationships between interlocking and capital dependence, for some other categories there are strong negative relationships, for still some other categories there are strong positive relationships, and for the remaining groups there are mixed results. One is tempted to say that these divergent results are cancelled in the aggregate analysis.

There is virtually no relationship for firms in the food (SIC 20), chemical (SIC 28), and equipment (SIC 35) industries. The major exception applies to investment in joint ventures, which is mostly positive and highly significant. In contrast, firms in the energy (SIC 29, (SIC 531 and 541), and aerospace and defense (SIC 372) fields show pronounced, congruent correlations between capital intensity, capital expenditures, investment in joint ventures, current ratio, long-term debt, retained earnings and the *Fortune*-list-derived measures of interlocking directorates; the relationships are somewhat weaker for the board composition measures. In general these industries are most consistent with the predictions from our theoretical framework: the greater the financial dependence, the higher the amount of interlocking. The pattern of directional interlocking is also balanced; we can discern an aggregate symmetry in the correlations between capital dependence and to- and from-financial interlocks. In other words, the firms in these industries frequently form links with interdependent financial organizations, and these latter organizations appear equally eager to obtain representatives on industrial firms.

A similar pattern for to- and from-financial interlocks does not exist in the primary metals industry (SIC 33). In that industry there are strong negative correlations for to- and from-financial interlocks. The interesting exception involves the investments in joint ventures, which is again positively and significantly associated with interlocking. In this generally stagnant and aged industry, some firms have apparently initiated new steps to move into novel and growing areas. The measures of board composition show strong negative correlations with financial dependence. The more financially dependent manufacturers of such metal products as steel, aluminum, and copper have significantly fewer financial directors on their boards. Their industry reveals a pattern of correlation coefficients that is almost a reversal of the one for energy, retail, and aerospace and defense industries.

The electronics industry (SIC 36) shows an uneven pattern. There is no relationship for to-financial interlocks but a strong negative one for from-financial interlocks. Banks and insurance firms are not represented on the boards of capital dependent firms in this industry. Again the exception is investments in joint ventures: electronic firms that invest heavily in joint ventures have greater financial representation on their boards. Unlike primary metals, electronics is a comparatively profitable and fast growing industry as *Forbes* (1970) indicated in its annual "Who's Where in Profitability." While primary metals ranked very low in growth of sales or growth of assets, electronics scored rather highly. Yet the correlations do not give any clue about growth as a factor in interlocking or disinterlocking.

Conglomerates, which are heavily diversified into different and unrelated industries, show no relationship at all, even for the investment in joint ventures. Typically these corporations are limited to acquisition and investment activities to obtain superior return on investment as compared with security portfolio investments (Williamson, 1975). Their management is usually not involved in the strategic or operational aspects of their business units. This might explain why the capital structure of conglomerates is unrelated to financial interlocking or interlocking in general.

Finally, utility firms show no appreciable relationship with interlocking. However, these heavily regulated organizations have a significant correlation with capital expenditures. We can most easily compare utility firms with some of the previously discussed industries by listing several zero-order correlations for each industry. These correlations are similar to the correlations in which the size of the board and the size of organizations are held constant. The coefficients for relationships between directional financial interlocks and capital intensity (CI), capital expenditures (CE), and long-term debt (LT) are:

	To-Interlocks			From-Interlocks		
	CI	CE	LT	CI	CE	LT
Energy (N = 47)	.42*	.43*	.23	.26	.48*	.44*
Automotive (N = 23)	.22	.23	.47*	.29	.58*	.66*
Aerospace and defense (N = 15)	-.02	-.04	.79*	.06	.13	.69*
Department stores (N = 16)	-.29	.28	.05	.03	.39*	.75*
Primary metals (N = 33)	-.21	-.22	-.45*	.26	.33	.16
Conglomerates (N = 16)	-.10	.30	.09	-.10	.05	.22
Utilities (N = 46)	-.02	.26*	.15	-.12	.07	.15

The coefficients do not permit an unequivocal conclusion. (An asterisk indicates a 5 percent significance level.) The results do not support negative relationships reported previously by other researchers, nor are they consistent with our hypothesis. The to- and from-financial interlocks are the interfirm ties most critical to that hypothesis, yet the correlations do not suggest any pattern. The associations involving to-financial interlocks could be construed as reflecting the industrial firms' effort to persuade financial organizations to commit financial resources. The from-financial interlocks as cooptive ties could further enhance the acquisition of debt financing. Such interpretations are not always congruent with the findings, especially for electronic and utility firms, which have major capital expenditures and long-term debt. The relationship between capital intensity and directional interlocks also varies among the different types of corporations. Considered jointly, these results are ambivalent in their support for our hypothesis.

Retroactively, the mixed results could be explained by referring to interindustry variations in growth, innovations, stage of the product life cycle, and product differentiation—for example, the differences between primary metals and electronics. Other industries, such as energy and aerospace and defense, are similar to electronics in their profits and high growth; these industries show results congruent with our hypothesis.

As "Who's Where in Profitability" (1970) indicates, there are vast differences in industry medians of "management performance." At face value there seems to be a tendency for industries with correlation coefficients consistent with our hypothesis to rank higher on measures of profitability and growth (for example, increase in sales during the past five years). Industries with mixed or negative results tended to rank below the industry median. Primary metals (steel) is among the poorest industries, and financial institutions avoid interlocking with its capital dependent firms. However, as we have seen, there are exceptions. Electronic firms are far above the median in both profitability and growth, yet financial firms do not interlock with financially dependent manufacturers of electronic products.

Effectiveness might thus be an important factor in dealing with the ambiguity of the results. In all likelihood, effectiveness considerations are also important at the analysis-of-firm level. Before such questions are discussed in Chapter Six, we review two additional sets of findings on interdependence and interlocking: (1) the combined effects of all capital structure indicators and (2) fluctuating financial ratios and interlocking directorates.

Joint and Interactional Effects

Our analysis thus far has studied the relationships between pairs of variables (with size controlled for). The analysis of bivariate relationships is useful for descriptive purposes, but it is somewhat inadequate for evaluating the combined effect of all aspects of financial dependence. To the degree that the independent variables are correlated, the correlation coefficients between the independent and dependent variables will show an upward bias. We can eliminate this bias by simultaneously considering all the financial dependence measures. This method will also permit us to isolate interaction effects. To a regression equation that incorporates the financial dependence variables, we can add interaction terms (such as the product of two dependence variables, for example, debt-to-equity ratio multiplied by long-term debt). We can then determine whether this additional term results in a significant increase in explained variance. As explained earlier, the detection of such interactional effects is crucial for testing the hypothesis relating vertical interdependence to interlocking directorates.

Table 5 shows the results of multiple regressions involving all financial dependence measures except investments in joint ventures, which was deleted because information about these investments is not available for a great many firms. To have excluded these firms from our sample would have drastically altered the distribution of our sample, limiting the investigation to those organizations that are extending themselves externally—through joint ventures—presumably to gain more influence over their environment. Therefore, we decided to eliminate that one variable from the regression analysis. Although the elimination of this variable caused the regression coefficients to have an upward bias, the bias was small.

Table 5 lists the remaining financial variables and two interaction terms: debt-equity ratio × long-term debt and current ratio × current debt. The significant effect of these two terms was determined by subtracting from the squared multiple correlation coefficient (R^2) of the equation with the interaction term the R^2 of the equation without the interaction term. If the inclusion of the interaction term results in a significant increment in explained variance (that is, in R^2), the interaction effect is said to be nonrandom (Cohen, 1968).

An interaction between the debt-equity ratio and the amount of long-term debt is quite plausible. The debt-equity ratio might be particularly important for disclosing the hypothesized effect on financial interlocks if the amount of long-term debt is large. It probably has little effect if long-term debt is relatively small. The interaction between current ratio and current debt is also consistent with our hypothesis. A corporation is more dependent on banks if it has extensive short-term debt and is not too solvent.

Table 5. Multiple Regression Analysis of Selected Measures of Interlocking

Independent Variables	Number of Financial Interlocks β	Number of Total Financial Interlocks β	Number of From-Financial Interlocks β	Proportion of Outside Directors β	Number of Financial Directors β	Number of Investment Bank Directors β
Size (employees)	.1289	-.0918	-.3352	-.0646	-.0840	.4360
Size (sales)	.2886	.0453	.3991ᵃ	.2843	.4944ᵃ	.3235
Capital intensity	.1413ᵃ	.0517	.0650	.1485ᵃ	.0632	.0689
Capital expenditures	.1990	.2794	-.4885	.0848	-.4785ᵃ	.9156ᵃ
Current debt	-.9143ᵃ	-.1468	-.3480	-.1764	-.7124ᵃ	-.3182
Current ratio	-.1311ᵃ	-.0921	-.0643	-.1242ᵃ	-.0943	.1015
Debt-equity ratio	-.1985ᵃ	-.1178ᵃ	-.1638ᵃ	.1319ᵃ	.0486	.0725
Long-term debt	.0766	-.0201	.3548	-.1269	.2453	-.4171
Retained earnings	-.3116	-.4510ᵃ	.2612	-.0397	.4102	-.5255ᵃ
Current assets	.0708	.6346ᵃ	.3464	-.1845	-.3573	-.4076
Pension and retirement expenses	.1532	.0451	-.2138	.0297	-.1108	-.2140
Debt-equity ratio × Long-term debt (a)	.2627ᵃ	.1145	.3264ᵃ	.1246	.2468	-.1361
Current ratio × Current debt (b)	.8251ᵃ	.1113	.0664	.1086	.5831ᵃ	.3586
R² with (a) and (b)	.391	.218	.131	.130	.105	.063
R² without (a) and (b)	.370	.217	.123	.129	.093	.057
R² difference	.021ᵃ	.001	.008	.001	.012	.006

ᵃ p ≤ .05

Table 5 thus includes two interaction terms: *debt-to-equity ratio* × *long-term debt* and *current ratio* × *current debt*. They were included to more specifically test the hypothesis that interlocking would be higher when resources are critical and nonsubstitutable. It was expected that long-term debt is more critical when the debt-to-equity ratio is high; similarly, short-term debt should be critical if a firm faces an unfavorable current ratio. The regression coefficients of Table 5 are therefore expected to be positive. The significance of the interaction effect is tested by comparing the explained variance of interlock variables with and without the two interaction effects included in the equation. The effects are significant if the increment is explained variance exceeding a statistical confidence interval.

For the firms in our sample, current debt and debt-equity ratio negatively affect the frequency of financial interlocks. Although this finding is similar to that of Allen (1974) and Gogel, Koenig, and Sonquist (1976), it was not expected. It corroborates the results of the correlational analysis and not only contradicts our hypothesis but suggests an entirely different one: Nonfinancial firms that have extensive short-term debt and a high debt-equity ratio do not interlock with banks and insurance companies; this disinclination to interlock is mutual.

Also consistent with previous findings is the negative effect of capital expenditures. The effects of this variable on from-financial interlocks (β = -.4885) and on the number of financial directors (β = -.4785) strongly indicate that financial firms refrain from interlocking with firms saddled with considerable capital outlays. An interesting opposite relationship, however, holds for capital expenditures and investment bank directors (β = .9156, $p \leqslant .0001$). It has been speculated that these directors are more instrumental in the placement of new equity and (convertible) bonds than in the acquisition of short- and long-term debt, and the beta coefficient is certainly congruent with this line of reasoning. Corporations making major new investments to replace old equipment or to add new equipment need substantial capital to finance this growth. The issuance of new securities is one source of financing, and investment bank directors can aid a firm in the issuance.

The results of the remaining three dependence measures are generally not significant. The negative effect of retained earnings was expected because it indicates the extent to which a firm relies on self-financing. The effect of this variable on to-financial interlocks is high (β = -.4510, p = .054) suggesting that self-financing firms refrain from forming persuasive ties. Retained earnings also has a negative effect on the number of investment bank directors (β = -.5255, p = .02), reinforcing the interpretation that self-financing firms refrain from establishing ties with institutions that facilitate the acquisition of external financing. There are, however, positive effects on from-financial interlocks (β = .2612, p = .21) and number of financial directors (β = .4102, p = .07), indicating that financial institutions are not disinclined to interlock with firms with higher amounts of retained earnings. This behavior, which does not fit the notion of cooptation, indicates a desire on the part of financial organizations to be associated with financially healthy organizations.

Finally, the current-assets and the pension-and-retirement-expenses variables are not related to the various measures of interlocking directorates. The only exception is the effect of current assets on to-financial interlocks (β = .6346, $p \leqslant .001$); its effect on from-financial interlocks is not significant (β = .3464, p = .21). Because the regression coefficients for pension and retirement expenses have decreased in importance compared with the earlier mentioned correlation coefficients, they are unimportant when considered with all the other capital structure variables.

Table 5 also shows results for the two interaction terms. The effects of the interaction terms are rather strong for the number of financial interlocks. With two exceptions, the remaining entries show no significant interaction effects. Note, however, that the sign of the coefficients is positive and hence congruent with our hypothesis. The increment of explained variance is only significant for the first variable, the number of financial interlocks. The firms whose need for debt is critical and scarce have significantly more financial interlocks.

Directional interlocks have a different inference. The increment of explained variance is not significant for each of the directional measures of interlocking. Inclusion of interaction terms having a sizeable effect has reduced the main effects. Naturally, there is multicollinearity between the original variables and the interaction terms derived from them. The ensuing redundancy has led to the reduction of individual regression coefficients.

The interaction effects on directional interlocks would have satisfied our theoretical expectation that firms facing critical dependence will coopt financial organizations to shield themselves against the contingencies arising from that dependence. We have stressed the importance of directional financial interlocks. The results of Table 5 induce us to dismiss those considerations. The interaction effects do not suggest that financially dependent firms reach out into the financial community nor do they absorb representation from financial organizations into their decision-making structure to ensure their cooperation and expertise.

Although merely a summary statistic, the multiple correlation coefficients shed a different light on Table 5. The indicators of capital structure explain a greater amount of variance of the to-financial interlocks than they do for the four from-interlocks, both financial and general. They also explain slightly more than 6 percent of the variance for the number of investment bank directors. All four types of from-interlocks are poorly explained compared with to-financial interlocks. Capital dependent firms may be disinclined to interlock with financial firms or they may have executives for whom there is little demand among financial institutions.

Clearly, there are some striking differences between the various industries with respect to the apparent effects of financial dependence. Rather than present the same multiple regression analysis on each industry's data, we will briefly review the main departures of Table 5. There are generally sharper results for to-financial interlocks as revealed by the multiple correlation coefficients; these results tend to reappear at the industry level. The major exception involves the two interaction terms. The interaction effects are negligible for the to-financial interlocks. In contrast, we find frequent strong and significant interaction effects for long-term debt $\times$ debt-to-equity ratio on two critical dependent variables: (1) the number of from-financial interlocks and (2) the number of financial directors. For the transportation equipment industry (SIC 37), equipment (SIC 35), and chemical products (SIC 28) the increment in explained variance is approximately 20 percent. The effects are smaller for the second interaction term, current ratio $\times$ current debt, although in several cases the increment in explained variance is substantial—for example, for the equipment and energy industries. These results are only suggestive. An examination of industry differences beside their structure is beyond the scope of this book. We need more information on industry-idiosyncratic factors to further account for these variations in dependence and interlocking.

Although they are not uniform, these results clearly suggest that interlocking directorates between nonfinancial and financial organizations are rooted in their transactional relationships and cannot be dismissed as mere random phenomena. The findings are sometimes enigmatic; however, several of the relationships yield support for our hypotheses and corroborate our earlier speculations about directional interlocks, their relevance for managing interorganizational transactions, and the consequences of resource dependencies.

There are puzzling discrepancies, however, particularly those which involve strong negative relationships. The data lead us to ask why banks shun firms with high debt-equity ratios and why corporations do not develop the expected cooptative interlocking patterns. Do risk-wary institutions, like banks and insurance companies, avoid such firms because they equate excessive debt-equity ratios with poor past performance? Financial companies seem to distance themselves from corporations that are heavily in debt, rather than seeking new business opportunities with them.

Fluctuating Financial Ratios

The results thus far reported have been derived from a cross-sectional analysis. Such an analysis precludes the detection of causal relationships, although we have implied that they exist. Since we were able to obtain information on the firms' capital needs before and after 1969, the year to which the interlock data refer, we can supplement our analysis by examining changes in debt-equity ratio, long-term debt, and capital expenditures during the periods 1960–1967 and 1969–1975. We correlated these variables with the frequency of financial interlocks, but the results of this investigation were generally negative. Most of the correlations, controlling for organizational size, approximate zero. The absence of relationships holds for the total sample as well as for most subsets of organizations.

Some of the coefficients are very significant, but they explain only a small percentage of the variance of interlock frequencies.

Furthermore, the sizes of the coefficients are not always intelligible. For example, the correlations between change in capital expenditure during the period 1960–1969 and to- and from-financial interlocks are -.08 and -.14 ($p<.001$). The correlations between change in long-term debt during the period 1969–1975 and these interlock measures are .03 (nonsignificant) and .08 ($p\leqslant.001$). Although such findings are extremely weak, they tempt one to ask why corporations that have decreasing capital intensity or long-term debt also have a greater number of financial interlocks. One would expect to observe a positive relationship between financial interlocks and subsequent increments in long-term debt, an expectation predicated on our assumption that such interlocks coopt or persuade financial institutions to make more long-term debt available. Increments in long-term debt prior to 1969 should likewise show a positive relationship with interlocking, but financial institutions have a slight tendency to avoid interlocks with such firms.

These findings also hold for the subsets of industrial firms. Variations arise among the subsets of manufacturing organizations, but it would be too cumbersome to describe all these relationships. For example, we found positive correlations for both periods for the food and electronics industries, negative correlations between change and some measures of financial interlocking for various energy producers, and positive relationships for the period 1960–1969 for the equipment and primary metals industries. It is doubtful that one could give a meaningful and convincing interpretation of such differences.

Financial economists often argue that firms with fluctuating financial ratios are more risky, show inferior performance, and are less desirable enterprises for the investor. Firms showing pronounced variations or instability in their financial ratios are more likely to face bankruptcy (Lev, 1974). The preponderance of negative weak relationships between changes in financial ratios and the frequency of financial interlocks might therefore be explained by reference to effectiveness; for example, increases in debt-equity ratios indicate inferior performance and organizational ineffectiveness. The criterion of effectiveness, however, does not explain the positive relationship between changes in financial ratios and interlocking in some industries. The data collected for this study are not sufficient for us to disentangle the dynamic relationships between financial dependence and interorganizational ties.

Although the relationship between interlocking and organizational effectiveness is the subject of the next chapter, a clarification of the association between interdependence and effectiveness will help us to more correctly interpret the findings in this chapter. The connection between interdependence, as inferred from indicators of capital structure, and aspects of organizational effectiveness is rather complex, and a comprehensive discussion of this topic is beyond the scope of this book. We can, however, consider some major issues in this area.

Capital structure, in general, and the debt-equity ratio, in particular, are pertinent to an evaluation of an organization's effectiveness in that many performance indicators are expressed in terms of the shareholders' investments or equity. Given that a firm earns a certain net income, the income per share will depend on whether the debt-equity ratio is large or small. Other things being equal, the earnings per share are dependent on the size of equity, while profits derive from total invested capital. Those earnings are greater if, at a given profit level, the proportion of debt is larger. The interest rate is fixed; therefore, higher profits reflect a greater exploitation of debt for the benefit of the shareholders. The management and owners of the firm have, therefore, an incentive to become financially dependent in order to gain the benefits of leverage.

This statement, however, is incorrect according to the well-known study by Modigliani and Miller (1958) in which they showed that the debt-equity ratio, in general, has no appreciable effect on the shareholders' returns. Borrowing capital might yield high returns, but it also entails some risk. Investors' funds will always flow to stocks that yield the greatest benefits and the lowest risks. Thus, if a firm enjoys considerable leverage, the price of its stock will increase to reflect this advantage. In the long run, the returns to debt and to equity are similar. Modigliani and Miller's position is well-established in economics, although their argument loses some of its strength if one considers the tax advantages. The firm's interest payments to its creditors are tax deductible, thus the firm enjoys a tax advantage.

Modigliani and Miller's paradigm focuses exclusively on the criteria for investment decisions by financial institutions. It is less applicable to a firm's strategic decisions to borrow capital in order to finance investments. The banks' decision to invest and the firms' decision to borrow are not unrelated, but Modigliani and Miller discuss only the first decision.

A firm's decision regarding how to finance its investments is related to its long-term strategies. If a firm acquires long-term debt in order to promote future growth that is focused, stable, and well directed, its high debt-equity ratio implies less risk than if its growth were predicted to be erratic and its income unstable. Stable growth is achieved by innovation, long-term contracts, and product differentiation (Mansfield, 1962; Pennings, 1980a). For example, long-term contracts ensure a firm that its income will be steady. The execution of such contracts is often interrupted by unforeseen events but, in conjunction with such coordination measures as joint ventures and interlocking directorates, a firm might be able to remedy some of the unexpected transactional contingencies. Stable future income is also enhanced if a firm is more innovative and acquires an immediate advantage over its competitors; innovative firms grow faster than others (Mansfield, 1962). A firm that is an innovator or leader in its industry will be able to borrow, because its steady growth seems assured, and it can thus enjoy considerable leverage.

Debt-equity ratio in itself cannot always be equated with leverage and risk. Firms that have high levels of performance and steady growth can allow themselves to have higher debt-equity ratios. Norms for debt-equity ratios also vary among industries. Firms in younger, less institutionalized, and more volatile industries cannot afford to borrow extensively because they have not established a stable flow of income and are, therefore, vulnerable to the embarrassment of not being able to meet their loan payments. Furthermore, such young firms ideally should apply a relatively large portion of their income to finance their growth rather than applying their earnings to interest payments.

Another important measure that relates a firm's financial dependence and its organizational effectiveness is coverage—the firm's ability to meet its interest expenses. If a firm's debt-equity ratio is 1.0, it has relatively little coverage and it is extremely vulnerable if its profitability drops below the minimum required level for meeting its interest obligations. In contrast, a firm whose debt-equity ratio is .2 has exceptionally good coverage in that it can easily meet its relatively small interest expenses. If its profits drop or become irregular, the firm is in little danger of not being able to repay its loans.

Firms have to balance the respective advantages of leverage and coverage. As the debt-equity ratio increases, the return on equity increases due to increased leverage but, simultaneously, the higher ratio results in a lower coverage. The risks of low coverage can be minimized only if the firm ensures itself of steady growth and stable earnings. In other words, a firm is relatively immune from the pressures of banks and insurance companies if it has low debt-equity ratio or if it has a high level of organizational effectiveness. The implications of this proposition for the findings reported in this chapter are clear: Financial ratios alone do not determine financial dependence. Dependence is a factor of a firm's capital structure and its performance.

The findings of this chapter could therefore be refined by incorporating measures of effectiveness into the relationships between vertical interdependence and interlocking directorates. A joint investigation of interdependence, interlocking, and organizational effectiveness might then explain the equivocality of some of the above results, which were not always consistent with our hypotheses. In Chapter Six, we will analyze organization effectiveness and relate measures of performance to interlocking behavior.

SIX

Impact of Interlocking on Organizational Effectiveness

~~~~~~~~~~~~~~~~~~~~~~~~~~~~

In the preceding chapter, we traced variations in interlocking to patterns of interorganizational interdependencies. Implicit in that analysis and reasoning were the assumptions that an organization acquires superior control over environmental contingencies by coordination with other organizations. In this chapter, we investigate whether differences in interlocking are associated with aspects of organizational effectiveness. We are particularly concerned with discovering whether well-interlocked firms enjoy high levels of political effectiveness (Katz and Kahn, 1978), which we earlier contrasted with efficiency (see Chapter One).

In theory, interlocking directorates enable firms to acquire better intelligence about their deficiencies in their transactions with other firms. Horizontal interlocks aid firms in coping with the competitive uncertainties that prevail in oligopolistic industries. By anticipating these contingencies, a firm might realize higher profits or perform better in other respects. Vertical interlocks contribute to superior effectiveness by circumventing the "information impactedness" (Williamson, 1975) that exists when one firm in a market is comparatively better informed than its competitors about the market's parameters. A lack of parity invites opportunistic behavior that damages the less well-informed firms. Interlocks between transactionally interdependent firms reduce the information impactedness either by equalizing the information among the firms involved or by instilling commitments that neutralize any incentive towards opportunistic behavior. Vertical interlocks are therefore also expected to contribute to political effectiveness. Both forms of interlocking directorates are thus assumed to give the organization better knowledge and control of environmental contingencies that, in turn, effect better performance.

The fundamental question is whether this assumption is correct. Evaluating this assumption is difficult because there are many approaches to the definition and measurement of organizational effectiveness. Organizational effectiveness is defined differently by various interest groups (management, shareholders, unions, employees, financial institutions, regulatory agencies, environmental pressure groups, and others). Researchers may choose to develop their own criteria, select criteria from the various interest groups, or adopt criteria that are conveniently available. Because the number of interest groups and their criteria is large, an unequivocal judgment about organization effectiveness seems impossible (Pennings and Goodman, 1977).

We have chosen to focus on the relationship of interlocking as a *determinant* and several other factors as *indicators* of a firm's effectiveness. Rather than attempt to consider all possible determinants and indicators, we find it useful and practical to focus on a limited set of effectiveness indicators, while recognizing that other indicators exist and that the outcomes have limited generalizability. Before proceeding to this analysis, however, it is necessary to further delineate the concept of organizational effectiveness.

Organizational Effectiveness

There is little agreement among researchers about the elements that should be comprised in a definition of organizational effectiveness. Researchers also disagree about the multidimensionality of effectiveness and about the appropriate criteria for assessing effectiveness. Finally, researchers disagree about the relevant antecedents of effectiveness, that is, which organizational aspects (structure, process, long-range planning, political behavior, and the like) should be investigated in explaining observed variations in organizational effectiveness.

Apart from the question of what determines organizational effectiveness, there are problems in identifying the structure of the effectiveness criteria. Organizations are open systems that have exchange relationships with individuals and organizations in their environment. They comprise various interest groups, or constituencies, that make claims on the organization (Pennings and Goodman, 1977). An organizational constituency is any group within or outside the organization whose members have indentifiable common interests in the organization's functioning. Internal constituencies include stockholders, management, and employees; external constituencies include consumer groups, regulatory agencies, suppliers of raw materials, and financial institutions. There is often a correspondence between the importance or influence of constituencies and the effect they have on determining which goals and policies the organization will adopt (Pennings and Goodman, 1977). Internal constituencies often derive their influence from the importance and centrality of their function (Hickson and others, 1971), whereas external constituencies can exercise influence because they provide critical and nonsubstitutable resources (Pennings and Goodman, 1977). For this book, with its emphasis on organizations' interdependence on their environment, the role of the external constituencies is central.

The firm's goals, against which it measures its effectiveness, are determined by a coalition of individuals who represent, directly or indirectly, the various constituencies. The firm's definition of its effectiveness is then a function of the consensus among the members of the dominant coalition and the relative power that they wield in affecting the organization's decision making. External constituencies are particularly influential when they have a potentially great effect on the organization's well-being—that is, when they have some control over the focal organization's acquisition of resources or marketing of products. In the present study, we have assumed that banks and insurance companies play an important part in the firms' decision making because they exert great control over a firm's access to the capital market; such financial institutions are an important constituency whose preferences are incorporated in the strategies of the dominant coalitions. For example, when a bank has extended large loans to a firm, it can be expected to monitor the firm closely, especially if the firm shows signs of insolvency or financial unsoundness that puts the bank's interest in jeopardy. It seems likely that the bank will attempt to influence the firm's decision makers to adopt strategies that bank representatives deem necessary to ensure the firm's survival. Likewise, a particular supplier of raw materials or a regulatory agency, such as the Environmental Protection Agency, might be an important constituency in a firm's decisions about its definition of effectiveness. Thus, the character of a firm's interdependence determines the importance of groups and organizations that are relevant to the firm's decision making. By identifying the critical resources that are needed by the focal organization and by assessing which groups or organizations control them, we can identify and weigh the influence of the external constituencies.

Identifying the internal and external constituencies and their relevance for the well-being of the organization, however, is not sufficient. We must also determine the criteria by which the constituencies evaluate the organization's effectiveness. These criteria for effectiveness can be differentiated into goals, constraints, and referents (Pennings and Goodman, 1977). *Goals* are ideal states that organizations try to attain; *constraints* are minimum conditions to be satisfied; *referents* are the standards against which the firm's actual achievements are evaluated. Referents can be either internal or external to the organization. *Internal referents* are standards unique to the focal organization, whereas *external referents* are based on information from other organizations. Referents can also be described as static or dynamic. *Static referents* are standards for achievements at a particular point in time; *dynamic referents* are standards for rates of change over time. A measure of net income as a percentage of total assets is an example of an internal static referent; a comparison of the market share of the focal organization and that of a rival firm is an example of an external static referent. The variability in income over a number of quarters is an example of an internal dynamic referent; changes in market share between rival firms over a number of quarters is an external dynamic referent.

Implicit in this discussion is the assumption that organizational effectiveness is a multidimensional concept that cannot be evaluated by use of a single referent. The task in evaluating effectiveness is one of comparing actual results in the context of a firm's constraints and goals.

The various internal and external constituencies propose sets of goals, constraints, and referents to the members of the dominant coalition who must reach a consensus. The process through which this occurs is complicated and, for the most part, poorly understood; it is also beyond the scope of this book. The result of this process is disclosed by management in the annual report and other formal publications. The information on effectiveness in these reports is not necessarily a summary of the state of the organization. Not all aspects of a firm's behavior and achievements can be represented by accounting reports. Furthermore, annual reports do not include the goals, constraints, and referents that are emphasized by constituencies not represented in the dominant coalition. The annual report presents the owners' or managers' evaluation, and criteria from other constituencies can be ignored or concealed by the accounting data. Finally, senior management is predisposed to present information that favorably reflects the organization; it may try to conceal data that might cast the organization in an unfavorable light. The standardization of accounting information, however, allows the researcher to make comparisons between organizations' performances on specific criteria, although there are problems in comparing the significance of a criterion for different firms (Hannan and Freeman, 1977b). For example, market share might have different significance as an indicator of effectiveness for different organizations. Since it is impossible to determine which referents are significant for each firm, one must rely on data that are conveniently available and assume that they have comparable significance for all firms involved.

In this study, we supplement information that is disclosed by the firm with some information that is disclosed by outsiders. The limitations imposed by this information restrict us to providing only a partial answer to the questions raised before. Still, an examination of these data will help us settle some of the controversy about interlocking directorates and their consequences. In the following sections, we examine the relationship between interlocking and effectiveness, recognizing that if different measures of effectiveness were available, the findings about the effectiveness correlates of interlocking might differ from the findings reported here. At the same time we must stress that the use of these "hard" effectiveness measures enables us to conduct an unprecedented and rigorous investigation of the effectiveness correlates of interlocking. The general hypothesis to be tested is that well-interlocked firms show higher levels of organizational effectiveness. We consider a selected set of independent variables. By limiting the number of variables, we are able to present specific insights into the effectiveness determinants unique to this study.

Measurement of Organizational Effectiveness

We derived our effectiveness measures from the financial statements that firms publish annually or quarterly. As noted above, our assessment of effectiveness is based solely on financial measures; we recognize that nonfinancial indices of effectiveness might yield a different set of findings. The firms' financial statements often exclude information that bears on effectiveness but that has little or no relevancy to standard accounting procedures—for example, safety of working conditions, labor strikes, customer satisfaction, and pollution. Furthermore, a firm's financial report may not always include financial information that is of interest to constituencies other than the stockholders or senior management. For example, the development of new products or changes in efficiency, as a result of economy of scale modifications, affect a firm's competitive market position and financial strength. Such information, however, is not published in any reports because it is considered proprietary. Regulatory agencies, antitrust officials, and congressional investigators sometimes use their subpoena powers to obtain financial information that is of concern to the public sector. Such investigators can acquire sensitive and confidential data about a firm's performance that satisfies the needs of governmental agencies and other external constituencies. Their examination of such proprietary data permits them to make an assessment of the organization that may differ from assessments based on published financial statements.

A commonly held assumption is that the financial statements contained in annual reports are addressed to the investment community, in general, and to the stockholders, in particular. Investors are a generalized external constituency that exercises control over the firm through their investment decisions. They use the information in annual reports in making their investment decisions, analyzing the relevant information so that they can maximize their profits and minimize their losses. For example, if the financial statement contains negative indicators, the stockholders will sell their holdings. The resulting drop in price for the securities reflects the investors' scepticism about the future of the company. Conversely, firms that perform well attract investors, and their increased interest is reflected in the rising price of the securities. In general, the price of securities conveys all the necessary information about the investment community's assessment of corporate performance; the price serves as a condensation of all relevant information about the market value of the firm. The market value depends on both financial performance as well as nonfinancial considerations. The nonfinancial considerations are relevant when they affect performance or when they are expected to affect future performance. After an airplane crash, the public's faith in the effectiveness of the airplane's manufacturer decreases, and this pessimism results in lower stock prices and a decline in the firm's market value. Similarly, the stock prices of a manufacturer of nuclear reactors dropped dramatically after one of its products was involved in a serious accident. When a firm develops a new process or product that is expected to increase its profits, the price of its stock rises accordingly. These examples illustrate that the market value of the firm, as reflected by stock prices, contains information that is of interest to noninvestors. Although the financial statements give only a partial picture of a firm's effectiveness, these examples suggest that pressures from nonfinancial constituencies often affect the public valuation of the firm.

Another limitation in using financial statements to measure a firm's effectiveness lies in the reliability and validity of the accounting information itself. This issue has been closely scrutinized by writers in accounting research (for example, Beaver, 1968; Brown and Kennelly, 1972). Critics argue that financial reports have to be read and analyzed with great caution, that they are unreliable sources for assessing an organization's effectiveness because they are equivocal and subject to distortions within the wide latitude of accounting standards. Treynor (1972) proposes that if "accountants want to continue to enjoy a role in the investment management process, they should prepare to focus their energies on supplying whatever data a workable theory of security valuation requires, rather than defending the present ritual" (p. 43).

The financial research to date suggests, however, that financial statements do contain a great deal of information that is not available prior to their publication. Financial economists explain the statements' function within the framework of efficient capital markets. Such markets are defined as those in which stock prices always convey all publicly available information about the stocks traded. Financial reports contribute to efficient markets because they disseminate information that enables investors to optimally allocate financial resources. Stock prices alter rapidly whenever new relevant information is disclosed to the public.

The most important information the financial statement discloses is the discrepancy between expected and actual results. This discrepancy is useful not only in determining the usefulness of an annual report, but also in measuring effectiveness itself. A positive discrepancy, when actual earnings exceed expectations, indicates good performance; a negative discrepancy signals poor performance. Financial research has shown that such discrepancies result in increases or decreases in the firm's stock price and the volume of trade in its securities (Beaver, 1968). Beaver found, for example, that the volume of transactions shortly after the publication of the financial statement was substantially larger than the average volume during the rest of the year.

Brown and Kennelly (1972) found a relationship between unexpected earnings and stock price changes by using the residual analysis technique. This technique consists of attributing variability in stock prices to two classes of factors. The first class includes national and international economic factors, such as political shocks and recession, that equally affect all firms. The second class includes specific factors, such as the frequency of interlocking directorates, that affect only the focal organization. It is misleading to examine changes in stock prices in conjunction with the publication of a financial statement without considering other contemporaneous events (for example, an OPEC meeting) that might have caused changes in the stock prices of the focal organization and those of all other organizations. By performing a regression analysis of the returns of a specific firm compared to an indicator of aggregate stock returns, such as the Standard and Poor's Index, one can examine the residuals. Residuals from this regression equation indicate the part of the firm's performance that cannot be explained by the conditions of the overall economy. In other words, the residuals indicate what portion of the firm's performance is unique to the firm in question. If the residuals are greater than zero, the firm is performing better than the overall economy; if they are less than zero, it is performing below the general level. As mentioned earlier, investors in the stock market will quickly react to the firm's performance, and the stock's price will rise or fall accordingly.

The residual analysis technique assumes an efficient capital market—weak forms of which have been repeatedly shown to be correct. The accounting research mentioned above also shows unequivocally that information disclosed in financial statements can have effects not anticipated by the investment community. Research within this same tradition has shown that changes in a firm's accounting techniques do not have a statistically significant effect on stock prices (Kaplan and Roll, 1972). Changes in accounting measures such as depreciation and inventory methods are ignored by the capital market. Such findings provide additional support for treating financial statements as fairly reliable sources of data on effectiveness. There are some celebrated exceptions to this, most notable among them the last financial statement that was issued by W. T. Grant prior to its demise. In that instance, the senior management successfully concealed the seriousness of the firm's morbidity. It is also instructive to note that not only the management team, but also Ernst and Ernst, Grant's auditing firm, was the target of criticism, presumably because the auditors had failed to adhere to established accounting standards ("Investigating the Collapse of W. T. Grant," 1978). But the general reliability of the expected or unexpected information in financial statements seems strong.

A major advantage of the discrepancy between expected and actual performance is its dynamic character. Earlier, we made a distinction between static and dynamic referents. The discrepancy measure has also a general, external referent in that it contrasts a firm's distinct profitability with all other types of firms—regardless of type, local economic conditions, and general economic trends.

These advantages have led us to adopt this discrepancy as a generalized indicator of an organization's effectiveness. We call our measure of this discrepancy the *performance forecasting error,* and define it as the difference between predicted earnings per share and actual earnings per share, as reported in the annual report. We ascertained expected earnings per share from *Standard and Poor's Earnings Forecaster* (1968, 1969), which contains the predictions of some of the most important financial analysts, for example, Goldman Sachs, Merrill Lynch, and Standard and Poor. We used the forecasts of predicted earnings per share that were published nine months prior to the publication of the annual report. If more than one prediction was listed, our measure was the average of all predictions. These predictions are assumed to reflect all the pertinent information available to the capital market about the value of firms whose securities are traded on the most important stock exchanges. Since analysts do not always agree in their forecasts, clearly their expectations are not faultless. Analysts use different models and assumptions in determining the expected performance. Our use of the mean expectation provides a composite measure of these differing models.

We ascertained the actual earnings per share from the COMPUSTAT archives, and we adjusted this variable for stock splits and stock dividends if these took place in the period between the publication of the relevant issue of the *Earnings Forecaster* and the release date of the annual report. Stock splits are conversions of old shares into a multiple of new shares; for example, one old share becomes three new shares, with each one having one third the nominal value of the old share. Stock dividends are dividends paid in the form of stock rather than cash. Information on stock splits and stock dividends is available from Standard and Poor's *Security Owners' Stock Guide* (1973) and the Commerce Clearing House's *Capital Changes Reporter* (1977).

The forecasting error is an attractive indicator of an organization's effectiveness. It is relatively free of confounding factors such as inflation and general economic developments, and it may reflect conditions or factors that have a nonfinancial character, such as political and international disruptions. We will treat it as a generalized performance indicator to be supplemented by other indicators that might have a more salient relevance for two visible constituencies: the stockholders and the providers of external financing.

The measures of effectiveness used in this book are the following:

- Y_1 = Performance Forecasting Error, defined as the percentage of increase or decline of the difference between the firm's actual earnings per share, as reported, and the expected earnings per share
- Y_2 = Return on Assets, defined as net income (the difference between operating income and taxes) divided by fixed and current assets—such as buildings, equipment, and inventory—but excluding accumulated reserves for depreciation
- Y_3 = Return on Net Plant, defined as net income divided by the value of tangible fixed property
- Y_4 = Return on Sales, defined as net income divided by the volume of sales; this indicator can be interpreted as the after-tax profit margin
- Y_5 = Price-Earnings Ratio, defined as the quotient of the year-end price per share stock price divided by earnings per share
- Y_6 = Net per $100 of Market Value, defined as the quotient of net income divided by year-end price per share, multiplied by adjusted number of common shares outstanding
- Y_7 = Net and Interest on Assets, defined as the sum of net income and interest expenses, divided by total assets
- Y_8 = Net, Deferred Taxes, and Depreciation on Assets, as defined by the sum of net income, funds that represent deferred tax payments, and funds allocated for the replacement of buildings and equipment—that sum divided by total assets
- Y_9 = Sales per $100 of Market Value, defined as total sales, divided by year-end price per share multiplied by adjusted number of common shares outstanding
- Y_{10} = Sales on Assets, defined as the quotient of total sales divided by total assets

Indicators that are relevant for stockholders include: return on assets, return on net plant, return on sales, price-earnings ratio, and net per $100 of market value. Two indicators relevant to financiers are Net and interest on assets and net, deferred taxes, and depreciation on assets. The latter indicators differ from those of the shareholders since financiers must, in evaluating a firm's ability to meet long-term debt obligations, consider the payment of interest expenses and the allocation of funds for deferred taxes and depreciation. Financiers are interested not only in net income but also in the depreciation and amortization of equipment and other fixed assets that enable the organization to finance replacement of obsolete equipment without incurring new capital expenditures. The indicators relevant to stockholders' interests are straightforward and are commonly listed in the financial publications. As we shall see, there are considerable differences among industries, but, by controlling for such differences, we can make sound interindustry comparisons.

In addition to these indicators, we also include two marketing variables: sales per $100 of market value and sales on assets. These indicators reflect a firm's ability to generate sales and are known to be strong predictors of bankruptcy (Beaver, 1972). Management and other interest groups are often more concerned about these indicators than about profitability. The marketing indicators represent the firm's potential for growth, and it is not uncommon for a firm to sacrifice some profitability for the sake of growth and long-term survival. Analysts often evaluate firms on both profitability and growth, using such criteria as long-term corporate strategies, anticipated life cycles of products, and competitive trends. Above all, it must be repeated that effectiveness is a multidimensional concept incorporating multiple goals and referents. Any assessment of organizational effectiveness must conform to this assumption.

In the remainder of this chapter, we will investigate relationships involving the effectiveness variables. First, we will treat the measures of interlocking as variables to explain variations in organizational effectiveness by conducting bivariate analyses and multiple regression analyses to determine the individual and combined effects of interlock variables on effectiveness. We will supplement this latter regression analysis while statistically controlling for differences between industries to reveal the extent to which interlock-effectiveness relationships are not confounded by variations in aggregate industry effectiveness. To test Chapter One's hypothesis that interlock effects are stronger under high levels of horizontal interdependence, we will examine the effects of interlocking in industries with high concentration ratios.

We will analyze vertical interlocks and vertical interdependence to answer the question of whether the effects of interlocking on effectiveness are stronger when organizations are confronted with high levels of vertical interdependence.

Finally, we will reverse the status of the effectiveness variables and examine whether the association between interlocking and interdependence is contingent upon the degree of organizational effectiveness. This analysis was prompted by the counter-intuitive and unconfirming results of Chapter Five and the ensuing desire to view effectiveness as a variable that might mediate the relationship between financial and nonfinancial organizations. The results of that analysis are rather provocative. In the context of this research, we also examine the cost of debt in relation to financial interlocks. These results, too, are thought provoking.

Interlocking, Board Composition, and Organizational Effectiveness

The bivariate associations between interlocking, board composition, and organizational effectiveness are listed in Table 6. The results show that, in general, interlocking is positively associated with performance, while the board composition measures—with one exception—are weakly and negatively related to performance.

Among the interlock variables, the financial interlock frequencies, in particular, are related to performance. The relationship is strongest for Y_7 (net and interest on assets) and to some lesser extent for Y_3 (return on net plant) and Y_4 (return on sales). Y_1, the performance forecasting error, is only very weakly and mostly insignificantly related, and so is Y_5 (price-earnings ratio). Striking is the negative finding involving the most common profitability measure, return on assets (Y_2). The two turnover variables (Y_9 and Y_{10}) also are negatively related to interlock frequencies. The significance of the financial interlock measures compared to the insignificance of the measures of

Table 6. Product-Moment Correlations Between Interlocking and Board Composition Measures and Indicators of Organizational Effectiveness (N is 634 for interlock variables and 561 for board composition variables).

Organizational Effectiveness Variables[a]	Frequency of Interlocks (general)	Frequency of Financial Interlocks	Frequency of To-Financial Interlocks	Frequency of From-Financial Interlocks	Frequency of Horizontal Interlocks	Proportion of Outside Directors	Number of Financial Directors
Y_1	.07	.08*	.04	.07	.01	-.09	-.10
Y_2	-.15*	-.27*	-.14*	-.26*	-.08*	-.06	-.07
Y_3	.24*	.46*	.37*	.45*	-.05	-.02	-.09
Y_4	.28*	.39*	.29*	.39*	-.02	.10*	.11*
Y_5	-.05	-.06	-.02	-.07*	.01	-.01	.02
Y_6	.01	.06	.00	.08*	.02	.01	-.01
Y_7	.40*	.71*	.52*	.67*	-.09*	-.04	-.16
Y_8	.03	.05	.11*	.07*	.02	-.04	-.07
Y_9	-.21*	-.18*	-.15*	.17*	-.04	-.05	-.09*
Y_{10}	-.12*	-.04	-.03	-.03	-.05	-.08*	-.14*

[a]Y_1 = Performance Forecasting Error
Y_2 = Return on Assets
Y_3 = Return on Net Plant
Y_4 = Return on Sales
Y_5 = Price-Earnings Ratio

Y_6 = Net per $100 of Market Value
Y_7 = Net and Interest on Assets
Y_8 = Net, Deferred Taxes, and Depreciation on Assets
Y_9 = Sales per $100 of Market Value
Y_{10} = Sales on Assets

*$p \leq .05$

horizontal interlocks and board composition is also interesting. Interlocks with the *Fortune* financial institutions have important correlations with effectiveness, while horizontal interlocking and board composition have rather little relevance for predicting performance.

The performance forecasting error, Y_1, is considered to be one of the more interesting performance variables, but its variance is not explained by interlocking to the degree that might have been anticipated. Since this variable has been identified as rather important, it is desirable to further examine our expectations in light of this finding. One would surmise that interlocks between organizations are rather permanent ties and change only gradually. Likewise, a firm's board composition might show considerable inertia. If analysts assume that well-interlocked firms are likely to be high performers, their predictions for a well-interlocked firm's earnings will reflect the advantageous position that is associated with superior interfirm ties. Thus even when the well-interlocked firm has high actual earnings, since such high earnings were predicted in the analyst's forecast, the firm may not substantially outperform the predictions. Furthermore, we could also consider the magnitude of the deviation that emerges from the comparison between expected and actual earnings per share. Perhaps well-interlocked firms perform better but only within "reasonable limits." Firms that are doing exceptionally well or extraordinarily poorly—for example, an increase or decline of 75 percent—might have been affected by factors other than those associated with interfirm ties.

Most firms in our sample show a discrepancy in the vicinity of zero. The average difference is -12.6 percent (with a standard deviation of 46.3 percent). The median forecasting error is zero.

If we eliminate the extremely deviant firms—for example, those performing 75 percent worse or better than anticipated—and recompute the product-moment correlations, the coefficients increase in size. For example, the correlations between the forecasting error and to- and from-financial interlocks become .10 ($p \leqslant .05$) and .11 ($p \leqslant .01$), respectively, while the negative correlations involving board composition vanish.

It might seem somewhat arbitrary to eliminate the deviant firms from the computations. The justification for this decision is founded on the assumption that firms that deviate substantially from expected predictions follow a different pattern than do firms whose deviation from predicted performance is slight. Presumably, firms that have experienced major shocks behave differently than do other firms. Major performance deviations require explanations other than those associated with interlocking patterns. With the present information, we cannot account for the behavior of the deviant firms, that is, we do not know what factors caused their unpredicted performance. In the previous chapters, we noted that it is important to consider not only actual performance but also the variability of performance. Any inferences about variability based on only two factors, actual and predicted earnings, are somewhat tenuous, but excessive departures from expected performance clearly are unhealthy symptoms. Because the elimination of deviant firms produces only a minor increment in the size of the correlation coefficients, however, the elimination of such firms is not necessary in analyzing this variable.

The distribution of the forecasting error is normal, but its variance is strongly correlated with the level of interlocking. If we plot the forecasting error against the interlock frequencies, the plot shows a considerable amount of heteroskedasticity; it resembles a slanted triangular cloud with the base against the Y-axis and its peak in the upper middle of the right hand side. The plot indicates that there is a large variance in forecasting errors if the frequency of interlocking is low, and relatively little variance if the frequency is high.

In order to eliminate this heteroskedasticity, we modified both the performance forecasting error (Y_1) and each of the interlock variables (X_1) by dividing both Y_1 and X_1 by the square root of X_1. This adjustment has the effect of normalizing the variance. The regression model for investigating the relationship between variables is based on the method of generalized least squares (Johnston, 1972):

$$Y_1^* = \beta X_1^* + \beta (1/N) + \epsilon$$

where Y_1^* and X_1^* are the adjusted dependent and independent variables, respectively, and $1/N$ is a weight factor derived from the sample size while the intercept is suppressed. If we follow this estimation procedure, we notice that the predictive power of the interlocking measures is stronger than that obtained from the zero-order correlation coefficients mentioned earlier. The standardized regression coefficients and their t-values are as follows:

	β	t-value
Number of Interlocks (general)	.33	7.66
Number of Financial Interlocks	.26	6.01
Number of To-Financial Interlocks	.16	3.64
Number of From-Financial Interlocks	.15	3.45
Number of Horizontal Interlocks	.07	1.56
Proportion of Outside Directors	.05	1.14
Number of Financial Directors	-.14	-2.92

From these results, we can conclude that well-interlocked firms perform better than do poorly interlocked firms. The effect of the from-financial interlocks appears to be strong, as does the effect of to-financial interlocks. Quasi-competitive collusion, in the form of horizontal interlocks, does not enhance effectiveness. The proportion of outsiders also has little predictive power: the presence of many outside directors contributes little to performance.

In contrast, the number of directors that have a financial background has a negative effect on this measure of performance, $\beta = -.14$, and the t-value exceeds the 5 percent level of confidence. This negative effect was not expected and paradoxically differs from the effect of from-financial interlocks. As previously defined, the from-financial interlocking directors are officers of large financial organizations, those which are ranked by *Fortune* as the largest ones in the United States, who are directors of nonfinancial firms. The measure of financial directors, however, includes all directors from banks or insurance firms, regardless of size or national significance, whether or not they sit on the board of the organization with which they are primarily affiliated.

In summary, the forecasting error points to the differential advantages of interlocking, although the advantages are not as strong as might have been expected. There is a striking difference between the effects of interlocking (which, although weak, tend to be positive) and the effects of board composition, which tend to be negative. We shall frequently return to this paradoxical finding. Before we elaborate on the asymmetrical effects of interlocking compared to board composition, it is desirable to review the relationships involving the other effectiveness variables.

Among the five profitability variables, Y_2 (return on assets) stands out because it is *negatively* associated with the interlock variables. Unlike the other effectiveness variables, whose positive relationship with interfirm ties was expected, we encounter here a puzzling outcome. Perhaps this finding can be attributed to systematic differences between industries that have considerable assets relative to their net income and industries that have relatively few assets. For example, the return on assets is 7.7 percent for retail firms, 7.1 percent for electronics, and 8.4 percent for the chemical industry, but only 2.7 percent for transportation and 4.6 percent for utilities firms. Thus it would be desirable to control for such differences, especially because we have also observed considerable interindustry variations in interlocking. Perhaps the age of the industry, or the stage of its product's life cycle, should be considered when relating return on assets to interlocking.

It is also useful to compare the coefficients for Y_2 (return on assets) and Y_7 (net and interest on assets), because the only difference between the two measures is that the latter is adjusted for interest expenses. Although Y_2 shows negative associations with the interlock variables, Y_7 shows very pronounced and positive relationships. Net income accrues to the interest of the stockholders, and interest expenses are payable to bondholders and other providers of debt. When the returns to these two constituencies are combined, the earlier mentioned negative relationship (involving return on assets) becomes a positive one.

It is similarly consistent with the hypothesis to see a positive, albeit weak, relationship between interlocking and Y_8 (net, deferred taxes, and depreciation on assets). For the providers of debt, this is an even more pertinent performance indicator than the profitability measures. The result corroborates the contention that well-interlocked firms do better. This indicator, as well as the previous one (Y_7), is more commensurate with the evaluative predisposition of banks and insurance firms. Both Y_7 and Y_8 amalgamate the returns that are due the two most important and most visible interest groups: stockholders and financiers. These two groups monitor and control the behavior of management, and they are among the first to make claims on the firm's return. If we compare the financial interlock correlations for the performance indicator most relevant to financiers (Y_7) with those for the pure profitability measures (such as Y_2 and Y_3), we find that the coefficients are much higher for relationships involving Y_7. In other words, firms that perform better on an evaluative measure like Y_8 tend to have a greater frequency of interlocks with financial firms, a constituency that is attuned to the organization's ability to accumulate returns above those that belong to the shareholders.

Based on these results, as well as on the findings on previous profitability indicators, we have to conclude that better performing firms tend to be those which maintain the most frequent ties with firms in their environment, in particular, ties with financial firms. The horizontal interlocks, in contrast, have little relationship to performance. Because the weak significant correlations are mostly negative, it is obvious that such interfirm connections are inconsequential.

Finally, Table 6 includes two turnover measures, Y_9 and Y_{10}, that indicate how fast a firm generates sales to sustain a given level of assets. Firms that have higher rates of turnover have fewer interlocks, as is especially evident on the measure of sales per \$100 of market value. Firms with higher growth levels appear thus to have fewer interlocks. It is desirable, however, to postpone speculations on this point until we have explored variations among different markets and industries, since turnover ratios are somewhat idiosyncratic to the various markets.

Most importantly, we note that among all the interlock variables, the from-financial interlock measure is particularly conducive to organizational effectiveness. This variable consistently has the highest correlations with the dependent variables. This finding becomes even more pronounced if we compute first- or second-order correlations in which the frequency of interlocks (general) or the frequency of financial interlocks is controlled. This control does not have an appreciable effect on the correlations involving the from-financial interlocks. However, if we control for from-financial interlocks and examine the first- and second-order correlation for the frequencies of general interlocks and financial, nondirectional interlocks, we notice a dramatic decline in the correlation coefficients. For example, the second-order correlations between the first two interlock measures and Y_4 (return on sales) drop to .01 and .06 (compared to the zero-order correlations of .28 and .39, respectively). Similarly, the second-order correlations for these two interlock measures and Y_7 (net and interest on assets) are .14 and .28, which differ significantly from the original zero-order correlations of .40 and .71. Such dramatic reductions in the correlation coefficients indicate that the high correlations in the first two columns of Table 6 are partly due to the frequency of directional financial interlocks that are included in these general measures. We see, therefore, that to the extent that effectiveness is contingent upon the management of interfirm boundaries, such effectiveness is primarily due to directional interlocks. One might conjecture that the transmission of information from the capital market to the focal organization, through interfirm liaisons, is highly conducive to economic performance. Moreover, the linkages from financial organizations to nonfinancial organizations appear to be somewhat more relevant than the linkages from nonfinancial to financial organizations.

By way of contrast, the measures of board composition are weakly and mostly negatively associated with the ten effectiveness variables. With the exception of Y_4 (return on sales), all the significant coefficients are negative—contrary to expectations. Firms that have permitted a greater influx of outside directors have a slight tendency to lower performance levels, but the relationships are insignificant for most of the effectiveness indicators. We had anticipated that firms having executive cohesiveness, as measured by a low proportion of outsiders, would be less effective. Perhaps the lack of any substantive relationship can be attributed to the interaction of two opposing underlying factors. We would expect a cohesive board, dominated by insiders, to be better informed about critical environmental conditions and to be more active in specifying the firm's long-term strategic options. A board dominated by outsiders might be less cognizant of the firm's particular problems or have less business acumen to contribute to the strategic decision-making process. However, we might also expect that a board dominated by insiders might be a parochial board whose directors suffer from groupthink and discourage the search for information or for different and unconventional ways of processing it (Janis and Mann, 1977). From the results of Table 6, it appears that boards dominated by insiders benefit from their cohesiveness rather than suffer from groupthink. However, since the coefficients are extraordinarily small, it seems preferable to conclude that the proportion of outside directors is invariant with respect to organizational effectiveness. Perhaps the measure of the proportion of outside directors is too aggregative to reveal any specific pattern.

It is also difficult to account for the negative results involving the number of financial directors because the frequency of from-financial interlocks correlates so strongly with effectiveness. The differences between national and local banks—particularly the contribution that cosmopolitan financial organizations make compared with their local counterparts—bear on an explanation of the results. Perhaps local firms are more prone than larger financial firms to bail out firms with inferior performance levels. Or perhaps local financial firms possess comparatively little information. One could also speculate that local bank representatives often sit on the boards of firms that perform poorly in order to help such firms restore their financial soundness. Another possible explanation is that local banks are comparatively less well endowed with representation on boards. The current data do not permit us to test these speculations. The results of Table 6 are certainly not spurious. Indeed, when we subtract the from-financial interlocks from the total number of financial directors, the negative coefficients increase in magnitude.

The differential role of national and regional financial institutions were further explored by a second analytic method. As noted earlier, Bearden and others (1975) identified five regional clusters in which a nationally prominent bank had entrenched itself into a regional network. These authors labelled these networks "empires": the Morgan Empire, Mellon Empire, United California Bank Empire, Bankers Trust Empire, and Continental Illinois National Bank and Trust Empire. The five clusters include thirty-eight organizations.

For the present analysis, an interesting aspect of these empires is the regional or metropolitan nature of the clusters, although the financial connection is a nationally prominent bank. We therefore compared the firms in our sample that belonged to the five regional clusters and the remaining unconnected firms. The results were somewhat inconclusive. In general, the connected firms performed better, except on the mean return on assets (4.1 percent, compared to 5.5 percent; F = 2.18, $p \leq .001$) and the price earnings ratio (13.6 percent, compared to 17.3 percent; F = 25.4, $p \leq .001$). On most effectiveness variables, the connected firms outperformed the unconnected firms. The performance differences are even more pronounced if we compare the connected firms with those firms that have financial members on the board, but no ties with banks and insurance firms on the *Fortune* list. Further speculations that seek to explain such negative results are extremely tenuous, however.

We should complement the current analysis by examining the simultaneous effects of all interlock and board composition measures. Table 7 shows the standardized regression coefficients.

The effects are most prominent for frequency of from-financial interlocks and the number of financial directors, and the effects of these two measures are manifest for almost all the effectiveness variables. The joint effects—considering all seven independent variables—are highest for return on sales (Y_4), net and interest on assets (Y_7), net, deferred taxes, and depreciation on assets (Y_8), and sales on assets (Y_{10}). The respective multiple correlation coefficients are .16, .16, .23, and .22. The price-earnings ratio (Y_5) remains totally unexplained by the measures of interlocking and board composition.

The measure of to-financial interlocks relates surprisingly weakly to effectiveness. Its predictive power is certainly weaker than that of the aggregate financial interlocks. These financial interlocks include any tie between financial and nonfinancial organizations, and apparently they are fairly important in predicting organizational effectiveness. Many of these ties are made by "third parties," that is, by individuals who are presumably neutral or equally loyal to the two organizations that they connect. Horizontal interlocks are totally irrelevant to these measures of effectiveness.

From these results we conclude that the frequency of interlocking directorates and board composition predict effectiveness, although the individual and joint predictive powers of these variables are fairly small. We also conclude that the study of such vaguely defined interorganizational linkages as general interlocks and horizontal interlocks, in which institutional affiliations are not specified, do not strongly contribute to our understanding of an organization's political effectiveness.

Table 7. Multiple Regression Analysis of Indicators of Organizational Effectiveness.

Dependent Variable[a]	N	Frequency of Interlocks (general) β	Frequency of Financial Interlocks β	Frequency of To-Financial Interlocks β	Frequency of From-Financial Interlocks β	Frequency of Horizontal Interlocks β	Proportion of Outside Directors β	Number of Financial Directors β	R^2
Y_1	(465)	.05	.06	-.06	-.02	.02	-.10*	-.10*	.022
Y_2	(552)	-.07	-.02	.05	.15*	.04	-.05	-.11*	.028
Y_3	(552)	-.04	-.10	.05	.11*	.04	-.01	-.10*	.020
Y_1	(552)	-.10	.19*	.07	.05	-.01	.08*	.06*	.041
Y_5	(552)	.01	-.05	.04	-.03	-.01	.00	.00	.003
Y_6	(553)	-.09	.12	.11*	.07*	.05	.01	-.04	.015
Y_7	(529)	.00	-.16*	.05	.08*	.04	-.02	-.15*	.041
Y_8	(429)	-.07	.15*	.04	.05	-.04	.11*	.07*	.048
Y_9	(552)	-.12*	.03	-.06	-.01	.00	-.04	.06	.030
Y_{10}	(552)	-.11*	-.07	.01	.03	.01	-.06*	-.11*	.046

[a] Y_1 = Performance Forecasting Error
Y_2 = Return on Assets
Y_3 = Return on Net Plant
Y_1 = Return on Sales
Y_5 = Price-Earnings Ratio

Y_6 = Net per $100 of Market Value
Y_7 = Net and Interest on Assets
Y_8 = Net, Deferred Taxes, and Depreciation on Assets
Y_9 = Sales per $100 of Market Value
Y_{10} = Sales on Assets

*$p \leq .05$

Having thus completed the correlational and regression analyses of the effectiveness variables, we must now determine whether the results reported are either artifacts of other underlying phenomena, such as interindustry differences, or whether the effects are contingent upon horizontal or vertical interdependence. We shall first discuss horizontal interdependence.

Effectiveness and Horizontal Interdependence

In Chapter Three, we saw that there are considerable differences in interlocking and board composition among various categories of firms. Are the correlations and regression coefficients presented in Tables 6 and 7 a function of these industry differences? Industries vary a great deal on performance measures expressed in terms of sales, such as return on sales and sales on assets. Return on sales has been a highly visible variable in the preceding analysis: its correlations with the interlock variables were often significant. There are vast differences, however, among various industries' turnover ratios. The interindustry differences on certain indices of effectiveness should, therefore, be held constant as we examine the effect of interlocking. In Chapter Four, we pointed out that some industries are heavily concentrated while others are fairly competitive. Concentration levels, as well as organizational effectiveness, may result in interindustry differences in interlocking. We shall first examine whether the effects of interlocking on performance hold when we control for interindustry differences. Then we will analyze the degree to which horizontal interdependence moderates the relationship between interlocking, board composition, and organizational effectiveness.

In Table 8 we present the results for the ten effectiveness variables discussed above. This table is similar to Table 7 except that thirteen industry variables were added. The industry variables are dummy variables; a firm received a score of 1 if it belonged to any of these industries and 0 if it did not. Firms that did not belong to those industries are subsumed under the intercept term. This intercept term reflects performance levels relative to the thirteen industrial categories. Table 8 shows the effects of boundary-spanning roles on effectiveness while statistically controlling for effectiveness differences among industries.

From the regression coefficients of the thirteen dummy variables, we can make inferences about the relative economic attractiveness of the various industries. The regression coefficients are raw (nonstandardized) to enable the disclosure of this information. However, the main purpose of Table 8 is to reveal the effects of the various interlock and board composition variables while holding interindustry differences constant. Table 8 should thus reveal whether the results shown in Table 7 are not attributable to interindustry variations in interlocking and performance, but rather are a function of external ties specific to the firms.

The results of Table 8 are encouraging in that they corroborate, refine, and strengthen the previous findings. The most distinct result is the importance of from-financial interlocks. Even though there are ostensible differences among industries, we notice that firms that are successful in recruiting directors from the financial institutions listed by *Fortune* are also successful economically. These cooptative interlocks are more important that the persuasive interlocks.

Although the statistical control of industry differences has diminished the size and significance level of the pertinent regression coefficients, the effects on some of the crucial effectiveness variables remain. This statement holds particularly for return on assets, which individually is strongly affected by from-financial interlocks. For many of the other effectiveness variables the significance of its effects approximated the 10 percent level of significance. It remains puzzling, however, to account for the negative effects of the number of financial interlocks that are also from-financial interlocks. Also striking, in comparison, is the disappearance of the effects of to-financial interlocks.

To fully comprehend these results and to evaluate their significance in comparison with Table 7, one has to realize that by holding industry differences constant we are applying overly strict controls. Quite naturally, financial institutions do not only associate with attractive firms but also with attractive industries. It is plausible to assume that they gravitate to better-performing industries. One might also point to the explained amount of variance (R^2) as listed in Tables 7 and 8 and realize that in spite of the explained variance being small in Table 7, it is quite substantial when contrasted with obvious predictors of effectiveness, as the industry dummy variables of Table 8

Table 8. Multiple Regression Analysis of Selected Effectiveness Variables, Controlling for Industry Differences

Independent Variables[a]	Y_1[b]	Y_2	Y_3	Y_4	Y_5	Y_6	Y_7	Y_8	Y_9	Y_{10}
	b	b	b	b	b	b	b	b	b	b
Intercept[c]	-132.36	3.59*	-3.42	.71*	-2.46	8.77	-46.50*	14.63*	-121.61	1.63
Interlocks (general)	.30	-.26	-.02	.00	.01	-.05	-.09	-.03	-5.15*	-.10*
Financial interlocks	.91	.43	-.01	.00	-.10	.13	-.26	.07	8.16	.13
To-financial interlocks	-3.96	.55	.02	.01	.40	-.43	.20	.31	-22.75	-.18
From-financial interlocks	.38	6.25*	.22*	.04	-1.98	.47	1.43	.61*	1.48	.24
Horizontal interlocks	1.71	-.43	.01	-.01	-.05	.28	.00	-.26	15.83	.25
Proportion of inside directors	-19.25*	-1.48	.06	.02	.69	.11	.38	-.10	-3.78	-.24
Number of financial directors	-2.14	-1.42	-.05	.00	.47	-.07	-1.19*	-.34	-15.16	-.39*
Retail	-7.11	7.66*	.41	.33*	2.71	-.23	4.24*	.50	-322.16*	-4.78*
Transportation	51.15*	27.25*	1.35*	.17*	7.32	2.44*	14.65*	-1.81*	45.90	2.83*
Utilities	-8.04	18.46*	1.54*	-.91*	5.68	-1.51*	16.90*	2.09*	217.43*	4.27*
Entertainment	14.31*	15.20*	-.04	.21*	-1.02	1.97*	4.95	2.34*	-46.82	-5.60*
Food	13.99	-.12	.48	.15*	-1.52	2.11*	5.30*	-.76	-55.97	-.70
Chemical	2.06	-23.25*	-.41	-.21*	-6.25	1.37*	-2.87*	-3.10*	178.54*	1.83*

	Y_1	Y_2	Y_3	Y_4	Y_5	Y_6	Y_7	Y_8	Y_9	Y_{10}
Energy	4.61	1.61	.97*	-.19*	4.28	-1.71	12.38*	-1.74*	143.05*	2.92*
Plastics, rubber	15.81	15.49*	.75	.17*	7.12	-2.65	7.12*	.64	-31.78	.97
Glass, construction	-3.63	-6.08	.68	-.06	3.58	-.67	9.22*	-2.41*	137.67	2.41*
Primary metals	31.56*	14.85*	1.00*	.02	8.81	-2.06*	11.73*	.77	-7.26	2.36*
Equipment	1.44	-8.12*	-.41	-.06	-1.60	.37	-5.16*	-1.00	127.45	.57
Electronics	.51	-10.82*	-.87*	.03	-11.35*	.92	-5.21*	-.36	141.97*	-.98
Transportation equipment	17.00*	6.59	.09	.13*	2.61	-1.29	.74	-.15	-51.81*	-1.81*
R^2	.126	.155	.158	.486	.043	.117	.219	.177	.209	.286

[a]Y_1 = Performance Forecasting Error
Y_2 = Return on Assets
Y_3 = Return on Net Plant
Y_4 = Return on Sales
Y_5 = Price-Earnings Ratio

Y_6 = Net per \$100 of Market Value
Y_7 = Net and Interest on Assets
Y_8 = Net, Deferred Taxes, and Depreciation on Assets
Y_9 = Sales per \$100 of Market Value
Y_{10} = Sales on Assets

[b]In the analysis Y_1, the performance forecasting error, was supplemented by generalized least squares to see whether the estimation improved by eliminating nonnormal variance. First, we ran ordinary least squares and saved its residual variance. We then divided the independent and dependent variables by the square root of this residual and reestimated the regression equation with a weight (1/465) included but the intercept suppressed. The results were similar to those listed in this table.

[c]See Table 7 for the number of observations for each dependent variable.

$*p \leqslant .05$

can be denoted. Interlocking is only a small component in an organization's institutional level, but these results suggest that they cannot simply be dismissed as inconsequential. From Table 8 we must conclude, consistent with Table 7, that within the set of interlock variables, from-financial interlocks count most in identifying the effectiveness correlates of interlocking.

Through these from-financial interlocks, the focal firm imports critical acumen, experience, and intelligence about both the general economy and the specific industry. Directors who are recruited from banks and insurance firms are ideal transmitters of information. Perhaps to-financial directors are less effective sources of information. As outsiders on a bank's board, they may not have an overview of their own organization's industry or they may have information that is of an inferior quality compared to that of a financial representative who has access to large amounts of information stored in his or her organization.

The effects of the last independent variable, number of financial directors, continues to be negative but the coefficients have dropped in magnitude. The relationship between this variable and sales on assets ($b = -.39$) is consistent with our earlier finding that firms with high sales turnover ratios are among the ones with the fewest ties. The negative relationship between number of financial directors and Y_7, likewise consistent with the earlier results, accentuates the differential impact of this variable relative to the frequency of from-financial interlocks, although it is not nearly as crucial as the latter variable.

The data in Table 8 unequivocally demonstrate that organizational effectiveness is not related to the more vaguely defined measures of interlocking such as interlocks whose directionality is not specified. An identical conclusion can be stated for the frequency of financial interlocking directorates. Many linkages between financial and nonfinancial organizations are formed by third parties—parties that are neutral with respect to the two interconnected firms. In the first chapter, we virtually dismissed their role in the dissemination or transmission of information. It seems that directors from third organizations are not instrumental in the dispersion of industrial economic information, because much of this information is accessible only to members of financial institutions.

We presumed that financial interlocks were instrumental in the management of vertical relationships, and we have seen that they are also important among horizontally interdependent organizations. In Chapter Four, we observed that financial interlocks are correlated with industrial concentration ratios. On the basis of that analysis, we inferred that competitively interdependent organizations rely on banks and insurance firms to obtain information specific to their industry. From Table 8, in which industry differences are held constant, we can now make the additional inference that the primary role is played by from-financial interlocking directors, who are at the apex of interfirm relationships and who are not neutral. They are committed and, although this commitment favors the financial institutions that employ them, this commitment is also favorable to the recipient organizations.

We have hypothesized that firms that face higher degrees of interdependence have a stronger incentive to coordinate their interrelated activities and to acquire superior intelligence about their competitors' actions. Indeed, we did discover a correlation between concentration and frequency of interlocking directorates. It is natural now to investigate whether firms in more concentrated industries perform better if they are well interlocked—either horizontally or with financial institutions. We performed regression analysis in which we regressed horizontal interdependence, interlocking or board composition, and their mutual interactional term on the ten effectiveness variables. We tested two variations of this model; the first analysis was:

$$Y_i = \alpha + \beta X + \beta Z_j + \beta(XZ_j) + \epsilon$$

where Y_i is any of the ten effectiveness variables, X is the adjusted concentration ratio and Z_j is an interlocking or board composition variable. If the multiplicative term has a positive and significantly incremental effect on effectiveness, one might concude that the effect of interlocking or board composition is contingent upon the magnitude of horizontal interdependence. The outcomes of this analysis were not significant.

A second model, somewhat analogous, accommodated possible nonlinear relationships and also yielded negative results. This model was similar to the above, except that the sample of firms was decomposed into four categories based on the concentration of their industry. The above X variable was replaced by three dummy variables, the fourth category corresponding to the intercept. The interlock and board composition variables were multiplied with each categorical variable. This model was tested to see whether the relationship between interlocking and effectiveness was strong and positive at very high concentration levels. The results, however, do not favor such an assumption: With a few exceptions, the relationship was equally strong or weak for each level of industrial concentration. Therefore, the relationships between interlocking and performance are not moderated by the level of horizontal interdependence.

Any examination of interdependence is predicated on the delineation of the underlying systematic variations that characterize industrial categories. Other global variables that describe industrial differences, such as the degree of maturity of an industry's products or modal patterns of financing, could effect differences in the relationships between interlocking and effectiveness. We could also examine more homogeneous sets of firms, as we did in Chapter Four when we investigated industry differences. In the present analysis, we discover interindustry differences that might likewise result from factors peculiar to a given industry. For example, if we repeat the analysis reported in Table 6 for industrial corporations only, that relationship between interlocking and return on assets (Y_2) is positive, especially for from-financial interlocking directorates. Comparing the various categories of firms within the set of industrial firms, we find strong and positive relationships among firms belonging to the food industry (SIC 20) and the energy industry (SIC 29). There are only a few significant relationships among the chemical (SIC 28), primary metals (SIC 33), and electronics industries (SIC 36). Other industries tend to show negative relationships—for example, equipment (SIC 35) and transportation equipment (SIC 37).

As with the results presented in Chapter Four, these differences are hard to explain and require ideographic research that would uncover conditions specific to an industry. Also, these summary statements are somewhat inadequate, because there are, within each industry, some exceptions. Thus, while horizontal interlocks have little relevance to effectiveness, they are strongly correlated with some effectiveness variables in such industries as primary metals, equipment, and transportation equipment. Parenthetically, we may note that these industries tend to have an intermediate concentration ratio. The ratios in our sample range from 10.0 for lumber and wood products (SIC 24) to 73.6 for tobacco (SIC 21); the concentration ratios for primary metals, equipment, and transportation equipment are 48.2, 30.5, and 59.0, respectively.

In light of our earlier discussion of intermediate concentration ratios and horizontal interdependence, these results signal some support for the hypothesis that the relationship between interlocking and effectiveness depends upon the degree of interdependence, with the relationship more pronounced at intermediate levels of concentration. The evidence, however, is too spotty to be construed as solid proof for this hypothesis. Furthermore, many of the industries for which we have concentration ratios are poorly represented in the sample; the number of firms sampled is sometimes too small to justify conclusions about the entire industry. The small sample also precludes a multivariate analysis in which the joint or individual effects of the independent variables are examined. These results, however, do justify our emphasis on the overwhelming importance of from-financial interlocks. This variable is also important as a determinant of effectiveness in most of the individual industries.

In conclusion, the analysis of horizontal relationships and industrial differences fails to favor the contention that the strength of the association between interlocking and effectiveness is contingent upon the degree of horizontal interdependence. The results are incongruent with the view that interlocking implies collusive or conspirational behavior, which is most probable in oligopolistic industries. The results do support the view that interlocking is a device for collecting and importing environmental intelligence, regardless of industry conditions. Firms are well advised to recruit officers from large financial corporations for their board, as this appears to be the most favorable correlate to effectiveness. The extent of directional interlocking, especially interlocks originating from large organizations, is a more than adequate predictor of the economic success that accrues to well-tied firms.

Effectiveness and Vertical Interdependence

In our study of effectiveness within the context of vertical interdependence, we focus on the relationship between financial and nonfinancial organizations. We are interested in exploring whether the relationship between interlocking and effectiveness varies with the degree of a firm's capital dependence. Since banks are important external constituencies that provide critical resources for some firms, we pay particular attention to financial interlocking. As we have seen in this chapter, from-financial directors are highly conducive to organizational effectiveness, and thus the current analysis acquires an extra significance.

Earlier, we discussed how directional interlocking directors can be construed as transmitters of intelligence who provide the interlocked industrial firms with the industrial information accessible to the banking community. In theory, however, such directors are understood to serve primarily as coordinators for vertically interdependent organizations: They provide nonfinancial organizations with better access to the capital market, and allow the financial organizations to participate in the nonfinancial firm's decision-making process.

Many indicators can be used to measure a firm's financial dependence. In this section, we focus primarily on the debt-equity ratio and capital intensity and examine the bivariate relationships between these factors and the interlocking and board composition variables. Linear relationships can be determined by simply incorporating a multiplicative term into the regression equation, as we have done in previous analyses in this chapter. We can detect nonlinear relationships by converting the capital dependence measure into a number of categories and multiplying each of the dummy variables with the interlocking or board composition variable. This second analysis reveals whether the relationship between interlocking and effectiveness has a different slope at different levels of capital intensity.

The statistical outcomes show considerable variation in the magnitude and sign of the relationship between interlocking and effectiveness. For current ratio, the relationships do not vary substantially with the firm's level of current assets to current liabilities. But a different finding emerges with respect to debt-equity ratio and capital intensity.

Table 9 shows the product-moment correlation between two interlock variables and six effectiveness variables for each of four levels of debt-equity ratio and capital intensity. The listing of correlation coefficients in this fashion yields information about the nonlinear relationships among the variables and is comparable to the second analytic technique mentioned above. If the size or sign of the coefficients varies among the four levels, we conclude that the effect of interlocking on effectiveness is dependent on the levels of debt-equity and capital intensity. We limit our report of the findings to the directional interlock measures, as they were singularly important in predicting effectiveness; as in our earlier analyses, the from-financial interlocks are particularly significant.

The most striking result shown in Table 9 is the asymmetrical pattern of coefficients for the debt-equity variable compared to the capital intensity variable. The results are most pronounced for the from-financial interlocks. With the exception of return on assets, all performance measures relate positively to the two interlocking measures. We have previously encountered this distinct deviation for return on assets, and we also have seen that this unexpected finding vanishes after the removal of leverage: when we use a performance measure that combines net income and interest expenses, the relationship becomes positive. Similarly, we encounter a positive relationship for the narrowly defined measure of profitability (return on assets) and for return on net plant.

The most interesting result shown in Table 9 pertains to the differences in relationships for varying levels of vertical interdependence. The signs of the coefficients pertaining to directional interlocks and return on assets are negative only for organizations that rely primarily on equity financing. If a firm is saddled with relatively large amounts of long-term debt, there is neither a positive nor a negative association for these variables; nor is there a relationship when capital intensity is low. Similarly, only if investments are substantial, relative to labor expenses, is the coefficient involving return on assets negative; otherwise, no relationship exists.

This finding stands in sharp contrast with the results for all the remaining effectiveness variables, including those that do not involve leverage. Return on net plant, return on sales, net and interest on assets, and sales on assets show generally positive relationships for firms that rely on equity financing or that are capital intensive. Except for size of coefficients, we observe similar paradoxi-

Table 9. Relationships Between Directional Financial Interlocks and Effectiveness.

Dependent Variables		Frequency of To-Financial Interlocks				Frequency of From-Financial Interlocks			
		Debt-Equity Ratio		Capital Intensity		Debt-Equity Ratio		Capital Intensity	
		Zero-Order	β	Zero-Order	β	Zero-Order	β	Zero-Order	β
Performance Forecasting Error	(1)	-.03	.048	.08	.111	-.02	-.053	.03	.081
	(2)	-.03	-.073	-.14	-.087	-.02	-.092	-.12	.013
	(3)	.15[a]	.123	.05	-.095	.18[a]	.176[b]	.10	.101
	(4)	-.05	-.183	.09	-.007	.00	.063	.15[a]	-.126
Return on Assets	(1)	-.26[a]	-.037	.00	-.038	-.36[a]	.241[a]	.18[a]	.236[a]
	(2)	-.14	.122	-.06	-.013	-.32[a]	.120[b]	-.05	.027
	(3)	-.11	.086	.07	.193[b]	-.34[a]	-.026	-.12	.172[b]
	(4)	-.08	-.133	-.34[a]	-.112	.05	.093	-.49[a]	.136
Return on Net Plant	(1)	.39[a]	.051	.01	.055	.57[a]	.148[a]	.11	.246[a]
	(2)	.10	.041	-.10	-.014	.16[a]	.062	-.09	.005
	(3)	.00	.023	.16[a]	.038	.36[a]	.035	.22[a]	.134[b]
	(4)	-.04	-.091	.61[a]	-.118	-.01	.009	.70[a]	.072

Return on Sales	(1)	.35[a]	.041	.09	-.120	.44[a]	.146[b]	.18[a]	.097
	(2)	.23[a]	.088	.07	-.033	.31[a]	.139[b]	.00	.097
	(3)	.29[a]	.135[b]	.28[a]	.202[b]	.41[a]	.005	.26[a]	.156[b]
	(4)	.12	-.032	.24[a]	-.017	.14	-.010	.28[a]	.072
Net and Interest on Assets	(1)	.52[a]	-.037	-.04	-.056	.83[a]	.101	.03	.137
	(2)	.27[a]	.024	-.06	.044	.49[a]	.080	.10	.106
	(3)	.20[a]	.036	.29[a]	-.092	.68[a]	-.023	.48[a]	.049
	(4)	-.03	-.062	.63[a]	-.092	-.08	.025	.73[a]	-.016
Sales on Assets	(1)	-.06	-.061	-.12	.025	-.04	.013	-.05	.109
	(2)	-.14	.003	-.05	.000	-.15	-.028	-.12	-.053
	(3)	-.16[a]	.007	-.13	.080	-.09	.075	-.01	.121
	(4)	-.16[a]	.004	.44[a]	-.111	-.20[a]	.005	.52[a]	-.025

Note: Each cell lists correlations for each of the four quartiles of the sample. The quartile is shown in parenthesis: (1) indicates low Debt-Equity Ratio or Capital Intensity, and (4) indicates high scores on these variables. The beta coefficients control for frequency of general interlocks, financial interlocks, horizontal interlocks, proportion of outside directors, and number of financial directors. The sample size for each cell is approximately 120 firms.

[a] $p \leqslant .05$
[b] $p \leqslant .10$

cal reversals of coefficients in Table 9 for debt-equity and capital intensity. Thus, interlocking is conducive to higher levels of effectiveness for organizations that do not have leverage and are not labor intensive.

Table 9 shows the performance forecasting error to be a striking exception. This variable is the purest measure of an organization's specific performance, because it is relatively free from macroeconomic and industry-related interference. Plotting of this variable for each of the four subsets of organizations revealed heteroskedasticity not unlike that found for the total sample. Regression analysis—using the technique of generalized least squares to adjust the variance for nonnormality—indicated that the patterns of positive relationships shown in Table 9 also held for this variable. The beta coefficients for to- and from-financial interlocks are—unexpectedly—negligible at low debt-equity levels, rather high and positive for the two intermediate levels, and again negligible for high debt-equity levels. Firms that are labor intensive also show negligible effects, but the effects are extremely strong for firms that are highly capital intensive. The beta coefficients are .27 (t=3.16) and .23 (t=2.59) for to- and from-financial interlocks, respectively. These organizations appear to flout the earnings expectations that prevail among the investment analysts if they are well tied to financial institutions.

The full meaning of all these results may never be ascertained. The striking difference between debt-equity ratio and capital intensity, however, yields definite results and merits further analysis. High levels of debt relative to stockholders' equity, which was shown to "repel" banks and insurance firms, acquires a different meaning in the present context. Our new evidence suggests that, by contrast, firms that have low debt-equity ratios augment their attractive performance outlook by establishing financial ties. These firms supply many directors to large financial institutions, and these institutions reciprocate. We seem to have uncovered a situation in which some firms have a double advantage and others are in double jeopardy. Low levels of debt-equity ratio have strong performance implications, as discussed at the end of Chapter Five. Conservative investors, averse to taking risks, invest primarily in debt-free or near debt-free firms, and financiers judge such firms to be attractive customers. The strong correlates of interlocking seem to indicate a natural desire among financiers to enhance their business relationships for their own betterment. The strong correlates of to-financial interlocks can be seen as a cooptation strategy to make such firms more captive of a particular bank or insurance firm. In contrast, firms burdened with extensive amounts of debt seem to be too risky for financial institutions, which avoid debt-laden firms even if they are superior economic performers.

The interaction effects within the context of capital intensity are equally interesting. While labor expenses, such as retirement payments, are associated with financial interlocking, no relationship exists between interlocking and effectiveness for firms that are labor intensive. (This conclusion also applies to the number of financial directors, a variable not under discussion here.) It is remarkable to see that the positive effects of effectiveness also extend to sales on assets (Y_{10}), with $r=.52$ and $p \leqslant .0001$. This coefficient suggests that firms that are capital intensive and have a relatively large sales volume are well entrenched in the financial community. This clearly is an exception to the financiers' general disinclination to interlock with firms that have high sales turnover. These firms are likely to have a strategy that emphasizes long-term growth.

Capital intensity reflects considerable amounts of financial outlay, which may or may not be financed by loans, bonds, and other types of long-term debt. As such, this measure does not connote performance, as does the debt-equity ratio. Nevertheless, firms that are capital intensive with major concern for boundary spanning with financial environments appear to enjoy higher levels of effectiveness than do capital intensive firms that have lower levels of interlocking. Perhaps effective capital intensive firms are seemingly attractive customers for banks, particularly if the referent of their effectiveness has a dynamic, long-term character.

The standardized regression coefficients shown in Table 9 are comparatively weak. The small number of observations also diminishes the likelihood of coefficients reaching a significant level.

It is instructive to consider some effectiveness measures that have a long-term referent. For example, product-moment correlations involving the interlock variables and ratios of new capital expenditures relative to net plant and new capital expenditures relative to total invested capital were high and negative. Those two ratios can be construed as measures of long-term growth. Banks and insurance firms generally do not interlock with such organizations emphasizing growth nor is their interlocking contingent upon the degree of capital dependence. There is one interesting exception to this finding: Financial institutions interlock heavily with solvent firms whose long-term strategies incorporate an emphasis on inferred growth. In other words, when the current ratio is favorable and shows a growth-oriented firm to be solvent, there is bound to be financial interlocking. The correlation for to- and from-financial interlocking with new capital expenditures relative to invested capital are .38 and .33 ($p \leqslant .01$), respectively. In comparison, the correlations are high and *negative* at lower levels of solvency. Naturally the positive and negative correlations are also significantly different from each other, confirming the existence of interaction between interlocking and solvency. The implication of this outcome is that financial organizations do not always disassociate themselves from interlocking with firms that require large amounts of external financing. On the contrary, they are eager to interlock provided the recipient firm is financially sound.

In this research we have refrained from imputing personal motives to the decisions of the directors to join or not to join a firm's board. Doing so is a matter of sheer speculation. However, we should consider that, apart from the rationale of organizations to be interlocked with others, personal considerations may affect the behavior of directors with overlapping board membership. Whether these considerations involve need for power, ingratiation, public exposure to "blue ribbon" companies, or other motives cannot be determined here. Nevertheless, to the extent that well-performing organizations are favored by the personal motives of directors, it is likely that such motives will aggravate the double advantage-double jeopardy of poorly and well-interlocked organizations.

In Chapter One we set out to investigate whether firms at higher levels of interdependence perform better if they are well interlocked. The analysis thus far has tried to answer that question. However, at the conclusion of Chapter Five we speculated that the tendency for commercial banks to disinterlock with debt-levered firms could be explained by these firms as being risky and unattractive from an investment point of view. The results of Table 9 reinforce the contention that some of the capital dependence indicators connote effectiveness. We have seen, for example, that an effectiveness variable that eliminates the effects of leverage relates differently to interlocking than does a similar measure that considers only the interests of stockholders. Finally, our statements on growth indicators suggest a reversal of our hypothesis and a need to investigate whether the relationships between interdependence and interlocking are a function of organizational effectiveness. Let us resume the examination of whether the effects of interdependence on interlocking vary with a firm's effectiveness.

Horizontal Interdependence, Interlocking, and Effectiveness

The explanatory role of horizontal interdependence, as inferred from industrial concentration, was ambivalent. On the one hand, we noted in Chapter Three the unexpected result that interlocking is most prevalent in industries that approximate a shared monopoly, in other words, in oligopolies in which a few of the largest firms dominate the market. We had expected, however, that intermediate degrees of concentration induced the highest amounts of interlocking. On the other hand, we found in this chapter spotty evidence that the correlation between interlocking and effectiveness was higher for industries with intermediate levels of concentration. This evidence was inconclusive, and significant correlations did not appear for all industries that have intermediate concentration. Now we can ask whether organizational effectiveness mediates the relationship between market structure and the measures of interlocking and board composition.

We partitioned the set of corporations displaying horizontal interdependence into ineffective and effective sets by making a split at the mean point of effectiveness. We then computed the third-order correlations between adjusted concentration ratios and interlocking, controlling for the number of employees, total sales, and size of the board. In most cases, the correlations between these variables did not change as a result of the partitioning; the resulting correlations are fairly similar to those reported in Chapter Four.

However, there appeared a rather strong moderating effect for some effectiveness variables. This effect is especially noticeable for the frequency of horizontal interlocks with the coefficients being stronger for ineffective organizations. The effectiveness variables involved include return on sales and other performance indicators related to sales. Organizations with a low return on sales show a correlation of .29 ($p \leqslant .001$) and those with a high return on sales a correlation of .02 (nonsignificant) between concentration and horizontal interlocks. Firms with higher turnover rates do not show high associations either. These findings apply primarily to the frequency of horizontal interlocks and the proportion of outside directors.

These results indicate that slow growth firms that belong to concentrated, well-established industries, in the absence of opportunities for growth, retrench into a niche with their competitors. The picture is one of a "buddy system" in which well-established, low-growth oligopolists freely share directors, a picture that contrasts sharply with oligopolies that have high turnover and growth. It seems that the more competitive oligopolies have the greatest need to establish common messengers.

This tentative interpretation is not inconsistent with the conclusions of Chapter Four. Oligopolies in which sales and growth are of a lower magnitude are among the most competitive markets. Oligopolies in which the sales volume is large show less cutthroat competition, even if they are highly concentrated. Although there are few competing organizations, the size of their combined market is expanding such that zero-sum conditions are softened or even avoided. Markets with little or no growth show severe competition, high bankruptcy rates, and stagnation. In these markets the common messenger interlock is most frequently employed. It is striking that this result applies to horizontal interlocks but not to financial interlocks. Because the above interpretation is rather tentative, we should not dismiss the role financial interlocks play in disseminating market information. It is more interesting, however, to examine this role of financial interlocks with respect to financial interdependence.

Vertical Interdependence, Interlocking, and Effectiveness

Earlier (see Table 5), we found that financial institutions tend to break or avoid interlocks with firms that are capital dependent. Now we can determine whether this tendency is contingent on the firm's level of effectiveness. An analysis of poorly performing organizations might reveal more strongly the negative effects of external financing and the corresponding positive implications of financial solvency. Organizations that perform well are expected to have partly neutralized the financial dependency that they have incurred from heavy long-term debt and capital intensity. Consistent with the discussion of Chapter Five, we therefore expect that the results of Table 5 will be stronger for poorly performing organizations and weaker for well-performing ones. Low performing firms have serious problems with coverage; their inability to cover their interest expenses renders them even more dependent on their financiers. High performance firms can offset the riskiness associated with high levels of external debt and are not as dependent on their financiers. Their financiers are less likely to attempt to protect their investments by establishing a directional interlock, and the firms themselves have less incentive to establish to-financial interlocks because they do not need such devices to persuade their financial suppliers to continue financing them.

A quite different argument, based on the concept of financial control, produces another set of hypotheses about the relationships among dependency, interlocking, and effectiveness. Let us interpret interlocking behavior as motivated by the financial firm's desire to cement a connection with an attractive client. An interlock between a financially dependent firm and a bank is then a persuasive interlock initiated by the financial institution, which is seeking a favorable borrower, rather than a cooptative interlock initiated by the firm. The bank would be attracted to firms that have comparatively little debt, enjoy a healthy solvency, and reveal a need for external financing.

According to these assumptions, the negative relationships between interlocking and capital dependence should be most prominent for effective organizations. The effect of capital dependence on interlocking is weaker for ineffective firms because such organizations are less attractive to financial institutions and, therefore, are less likely to show interlocking patterns; similarly, financial institutions are not motivated to form ties because of capital dependence. It is also relevant to reconfirm our earlier findings involving differences between directional interlocking directorates and the number of financial directors on an organization's board.

Table 10 shows the standardized regression coefficients of vertical interdependence with respect to measures of financial interlocking. We define effectiveness by the performance forecasting error; the pattern of findings listed in Table 10, however, is rather similar to results based on the other effectiveness variables. These findings are also similar to those obtained from a model that includes both the financial dependence variables and the above-mentioned industry dummy variables. Although there are interindustry variations in the ways firms finance their operations, controlling for these variations does not have any appreciable effect on the results. The results presented in Table 10 can therefore be interpreted as relatively free from interindustry variation.

Table 10 shows standardized regression coefficients for nine capital dependence variables, two measures of organizational size—which are included because some of the variables are strongly correlated with size—and the two interaction terms. As explained in Chapter Five, those interaction terms serve to isolate the effects of capital dependence for those firms for which short-term and long-term debt are critical resources. These interaction effects, in particular, should show a difference in magnitude if effectiveness does alter the nature of interdependence. In fact, if the interaction effects for the two types of organizations are different, we could infer the existence of a double interaction, that is, the interaction between effectiveness, short-term or long-term debt, and current ratio or debt-equity ratio.

Table 10 shows few significant results for the ineffective organizations. Capital intensity affects the total number of financial interlocks (β = .139, t = 2.06) and the number of from-financial interlocks (β = .154, t = 1.93). Current assets, reflecting independence from short-term debt, negatively affects the frequency of financial interlocks (β = -.619, t = -1.70) and the number of financial directors (β = -.834, t = -1.80). The frequency of financial interlocks and number of financial directors are fairly broad, however, compared with the directional financial interlocks. We notice that the amount of variance that is explained by the model is relatively small for the number of financial directors (R^2 = .155). Nevertheless, it is interesting to see that long-term debt, reflecting dependence, and current assets, reflecting independence, have the expected effects. Although these cross-sectional data permit only static conclusions, the findings suggest that local banks are indeed the financiers who bail out financially troubled organizations.

Table 10. Multiple Regression Analysis of Measures of Financial Interlocking for Ineffective and Effective Nonfinancial Organizations (N = 186 and 211, respectively).

	Ineffective Organizations				Effective Organizations			
	Number of Financial Interlocks	Number of To-Financial Interlocks	Number of From-Financial Interlocks	Number of Financial Directors	Number of Financial Interlocks	Number of To-Financial Interlocks	Number of From-Financial Interlocks	Number of Financial Directors
	β	β	β	β	β	β	β	β
Size (sales)	.212	-.788[a]	-.206	-.196	-.248	-.209	-.373	-.334
Size (employees)	.702[a]	1.069[a]	.393	.478[a]	.409	-.072	.480	.811[a]
Capital intensity	.139[a]	.060	.154	.101	.079	-.031	.011	.023
Capital expenditures	.348	.413	.300	-.143	.101	.139	-.868[a]	-.519[a]
Debt-equity ratio	-.071	-.019	-.051	.114	-.297[a]	-.290[a]	-.309[a]	-.032
Long-term debt	.097	-.196	.187	.301	1.232[a]	.814[a]	1.776[a]	1.126[a]
Current ratio	-.008	-.053	.036	-.037	-.159[a]	-.173[a]	-.079	-.048
Current debt	-.442	-.340	.205	.068	-.748[a]	.344	-.268	-.817
Current assets	-.619	.195	.049	-.834	-.265	.696	.100	-1.017
Retained earnings	-.173	.543	-.355	.331	.280	-.205	.446	.774
Pension and retirement expenses	.209[a]	-.134	.189	.105	.258	-.209	-.079	.263
Debt-equity ratio × Long-term debt (a)	-.214	-.450	.004	.183	-1.085[a]	-.546	-.969[a]	-1.070[a]
Current ratio × Current debt (b)	.608	.242	-.286	-.013	.072[a]	-.299	-.026	.774[a]
R^2 with (a) and (b)	.476	.333	.265	.155	.481	.254	.215	.147
R^2 without (a) and (b)	.465	.288	.250	.155	.402	.232	.128	.100
R^2 difference	.011	.045	.015	.000	.079[a]	.022	.087[a]	.047

[a] $p \leq .05$

The findings for directional interlocks are generally negative, particularly those involving the interaction terms. Indeed, none of the four dependent variables shows a significant interaction effect; in each case, the increase in the multiple correlation coefficients is small. In other words, the increment in the explained variance as a result of the inclusion of the interaction terms is not significant. For the directional interlocking directorates these increments are .045 and .015, respectively. Capital dependence has, therefore, little relevance in explaining interfirm ties among ineffective organizations. Financial firms seem somewhat indifferent to establishing connections with ineffective firms.

Quite a different conclusion emerges from an analysis of the results for the effective firms. As was the case in Chapter Five, the debt-equity ratio has a pronounced negative effect and, in fact, that effect is here much stronger. For the dependent variables, the coefficients are -.297 (t = -3.85), -.290 (t = -3.13), -3.09 (t = -3.25), and -.032 (t = -.32). Long-term debt, in contrast, has a very strong positive effect with respective coefficients of 1.232 (t = 4.71), .814 (t = 2.59), 1.776 (t = 5.51), and 1.126 (t = 3.35). On the one hand, organizations do not form financial ties if they are levered and risky, that is, if they have comparatively large debts in relation to their equity. On the other hand, firms that have large long-term debt are extremely well connected with financial organizations.

Current ratio has a weak negative effect, which is to be expected as a higher ratio implies lower dependence on short-term financing. Current assets has a positive effect, indicating that decreased dependence require less cooptation. While long-term debt has a very strong influence on from-financial interlocks, current assets has a very strong effect on to-financial interlocks. Long-term debt is thus associated with cooptation, and current assets with persuasion.

The negative effect of the first interaction term (debt-equity × long-term debt) is very strong, particularly for the directional interlocks and for the number of financial members on the board. It is most interesting that the differential effect for from-financial interlockings and the number of financial directors has vanished. The second interaction term (current ratio × current debt) is significant only for the frequency of financial interlocks and the number of financial directors. In fact, the significant increase in the multiple correlation coefficients due to the inclusion of the two interaction terms is primarily due to the first of these terms. As can be seen from Table 10, there is a sharp contrast between ineffective and effective organizations in the magnitude of the interaction effects. For the effective organizations, the effect of capital dependence on financial interlocking is pronounced, especially when capital supply is critical. This result supports the hypothesis that organizations will create boundary-spanning positions to manage their dependence on critical external resources.

This conclusion applies equally to the financial interlocks and to the number of from-financial interlocks on the local organization's board. Although the explained variance in the number of financial directors is relatively small (R^2 = .147), the results involving this variable are no longer inconsistent with the overall pattern.

It has been suggested that directional interlocking directorates represent a control mechanism, or boundary-spanning device, for the management of critical resources or products. In this view, a firm's dependence manifests itself by the firm's efforts to exert control, one form of which is to establish personal ties. In addition, it has been said that banks and insurance companies enjoy control over financially dependent organizations and, according to the argument, directional interlocks reinforce the financial firms' control. These assumptions rely on Emerson's (1962) view that power originates from a dependence relationship between two agents. But Emerson's reasoning cannot account for the results of Table 10. An entirely different interpretation is necessary.

Financial institutions do not attempt to reinforce their financial control by forming from-financial interlocks. They do not acquire seats on the boards of firms that have high debt-equity ratios. In short, they do not infiltrate the decision-making structure of financially levered, risky firms; nor do these levered firms actively entrench themselves in the financial community. Few interlocks exist between financial firms and nonfinancial organizations that have adopted a long-range capital strategy that is unattractive to banks and insurance firms. A considerable degree of interlocking exists, however, among financial organizations and highly effective firms that are not deemed risky.

The first hypothesis mentioned at the beginning of this section is evidently incorrect. That hypothesis assumed that financial institutions become coopted, or become the target of persuasive interlocks, by organizations that find themselves strongly dependent on debt. These firms were assumed to assure their external financing by establishing financial interlocks—presumably at the cost of the stockholders. The results shown in Table 10 show these assumptions to be incorrect. Rather, the data support the second hypothesis, which posited that financial institutions develop and maintain interlocks to enhance their competitive posture. Financial institutions regard non-levered, well-performing firms as desirable customers, and interlocks with such firms promote the financial organization's business. Indeed, financial organizations are very aggressive in their interlocking behavior with organizations that are not financially risky and are effective. They do not avoid effective firms that rely heavily on long-term debt—quite the contrary. Financial firms avoid only levered firms; they are extremely prone to interlock with firms dependent on external debt provided these firms are nonlevered high performers. They likewise encourage representatives from those organizations to join their boards, effectively coopting those firms to grant them a privileged business relationship.

The results do not alter if we use other effectiveness variables to define our two categories of ineffective and effective firms. The results shown in Table 10 hold for most of our measures of effectiveness.

Financial Interlocks and Their Price

From our discussion of these results it is obvious that we experienced a profound discrepancy between what we originally hypothesized in Chapter One and what surfaced from the analysis in this chapter. Clearly the hypothesis on interdependence and interlocking has to be discredited. Financial organizations are not coopted, it seems, to diminish or neutralize their discretionary lending behavior when capital dependence is high. Instead, financial organizations seek representation on the boards of well-performing organizations to secure their deposits and to provide other lucrative financial services. One might then ask whether financial institutions can have their cake and eat it, too.

Within the context of interorganizational exchange relationships, this question might be reworded into the question of whether well-interlocked firms enjoy preferential treatment. The reasoning based on resource exchange would be as follows: Since a financial institution has privileged access to the financial data of firms it is interlocked with and because it has sealed an advantageous transactional relationship with them, it must have reciprocated by granting comparatively lower interest rates for short- or long-term debt. The lower interest rate amounts to the "payment" for all the privileges that are inherent to financial interlocks.

There are alternative, theoretically unrelated but supplementary reasons for expecting lower interest rates for well-interlocked organizations; the reasons are related to efficient market hypotheses. Differences in interest rates as a function of interorganizational variations in interlocking would be inconsistent with the strong form of the efficient market hypothesis. With demand and supply held constant, this hypothesis would maintain that the interest rate for a firm is determined by their financial soundness, which is reflected by the capital market's assessment of its risk and return. For large corporations that assessment is common knowledge and is widely publicized, as illustrated by *Moody's* bond ratings. These ratings depend on the firm's performance outlook; the more negative this is, the higher the interest rate. The variation in interest rates ensures an ostensible optimum allocation of capital.

Although capital markets, compared with oligopolistic industrial markets, can be assumed to be rather efficient (Fama and others, 1969), it is possible that even this market has deficiencies so that the variations in the cost of capital do not always truly reflect its risk and returns. There may be such market failures as having or lacking "inside" information and the introduction of moral hazards, opportunism, and other flaws in the transactional relationship between producers and receivers of debt. As suggested in Chapter One, interlocking might be one of the remedies for removing those market failures. Financial organizations may eliminate some of the information deficiencies by establishing communication and control channels and, as a result, become comparatively well informed about the financial soundness of the interlocked firms. The inside information that accrues to interlocked financial organizations reduces uncertainty and could materialize in lower interest rates.

In order to test this hypothesis, we computed a firm's aggregate interest rate as the quotient of total interest expenses divided by long-

and short-term debt. This interest rate correlated negatively and significantly with the frequency of financial interlocks and number of financial directors on the board, but this finding is questionable on several accounts. In the first place, as we have seen, well-performing firms are better interlocked, especially when they also manifest higher capital needs, so that these negative correlations might be spurious. Better performing firms enjoy cheaper debts. Secondly, it is necessary to control for different types of financial interlocking to determine whether it is primarily the from-interlocks that determine interest rates.

To deal with these difficulties, we tested the hypothesis by estimating a regression equation for the cost of debt (CD). The independent variables are the number of financial interlocks (FI), number of to-financial interlocks (TO), number of from-financial interlocks (FROM), number of financial directors (FD), the debt-to-equity ratio (DE), the current ratio (CR), return on assets (RA), and return on sales (RS). The results of this estimation are as follows:

$$CD = -.126 \text{ FI} + .042 \text{ TO} + .021 \text{ FROM} -.058 \text{ FD} -.079 \text{ DE} -.019 \text{ CR}$$
$$+ .161 \text{RA} -.252 \text{ RS} \qquad N = 472, R^2 = .097$$

Only three of these coefficients are significant at the 5 percent level: financial interlock (FI), return on asset (RA), and return on sales (RS). The negative effect of financial interlocks is consistent with our expectation and shows that financial institutions pay a compensation for being interlocked. The findings for the directional interlocks are meager. We had expected the from-financial interlocks and number of financial directors to affect interest rates negatively. Without controlling for capital structure and effectiveness measures, the effect of the number of financial directors was strong, negative, and significant ($\beta = -.117$, $p \leq .05$), but, as the equation just stated shows, this estimate is biased upwardly. From these results we must conclude that financial interlocks do provide for preferential interest rates, but the advantages for directional interlocks do not exist. The directional interlocks have been described as the more important boundary-spanning individuals. Nevertheless, the effect of the number of financial interlocks is intriguing and warrants further study. Perhaps this result invites an alternative interpretation. The number of financial interlocks might signal the degree to which a firm is "integrated" in the financial community, which in turn might lead to a favorable discrimination among financiers. The interpretation that directionally interlocked banks charge lower interest rates because of quasi-insider status does not appear to be correct.

It is important to mention another caveat when interpreting these results. The cost of debt has been computed on the basis of a firm's total debt. A major problem that arises is the interorganizational variation in the relative size of long- and short-term debt; short-term debt is generally more expensive. The cost of long-term debt is a function of the prevailing interest rate of the period in which long-term loans were acquired in the form of bonds and loans. The interlock effects are not likely to affect the interest on bonds, which are generally proposed by investment analysts and bankers and set by the investors. Also, the time at which the long-term debt was obtained might be far removed from 1969, the year of our study. Interest rates have witnessed a continuous growth; many firms' interest rates for long-term debt were negotiated long before 1969, and possibly before ties with the financial community were forged. Short-term interest rates might therefore be more appropriate in testing the hypothesis, but unfortunately this information is not readily available and can only be approximated by tertiary sources.

This issue was explored by taking the interest rate for long-term debt as published by the *Economic Report of the President* (1979) for the year 1969, computing the inferred interest expenses for long-term debt by using that interest rate, and subtracting those inferred interest expenses from the total amount of interest expenses, as published by the COMPUSTAT archives. The remaining sum was then used for calculating the short-term debt's cost by dividing it by the firm's short-term debt. If we repeat the regression estimation for the cost of short-term debt (CSTD) we get:

$$CSTD = .113 \text{ FI} -.014 \text{ TO} -.084 \text{ FROM} -.070 \text{ FD} + .004 \text{ DE}$$
$$-.015 \text{ CR} + .099 \text{ RA} -.163 \text{ RS} \qquad N = 472, R^2 = .035$$

Compared with the first model, the amount of explained variance (R^2) is considerably less. In fact the only significant effect is for return on sales ($\beta = -.163$). The negative effects of the from-interlocks approximate the 10 percent significance level, but, in view of their small size and the somewhat tenuous procedure for computing short-term interest expenses, we ought to dismiss those results. These results are equivocal but sufficiently intriguing to justify further investigation. The quality of that investigation hinges then on the veridical information of short-term debt and its cost.

Financially well-interlocked firms tend to enjoy lower interest rates. Whether financial institutions in general and commercial banks in particular forego higher interest rates as the "price" for having its officers on the boards of their clientele remains to be seen. This issue can only be resolved when more accurate information on their financial transactions is available.

We have seen that the existence of effectiveness correlates does not depend on the choice of the effectiveness variables. Well-interlocked firms perform better, are particularly prone to have financial ties when they are effective, and have strong needs for short-and long-term debt. They tend to be compensated for their cooptation in the form of lower interest rates.

Remember that all of the effectiveness variables in this study measure economic performance. The fact that well-interlocked firms have superior economic performance suggests that they enjoy political effectiveness, having developed personal bonds with firms in their environment, but it does not necessarily mean that they are more efficient. Such firms may be inferior on measures of performance in such areas as labor relations, product safety, pollution control, and innovation. They may be corrupting the regulatory process or inflicting harm on the public interest.

Another limitation of these analyses is their exclusive reliance on cross-sectional, static comparisons. Our analyses that incorporated longitudinal measures of effectiveness were inconclusive. In some cases, we found a negative association between change in effectiveness over the period 1960–1969 and the frequency of interlocking. We found nonsignificant correlations for interlocking and performance changes over the period 1969-1975. The negative correlations were stronger and more abundant in some industries (for example, utilities) and for more insolvent firms. Those correlations were very small, however, rarely exceeding one tenth, and they often vanished when all interlock variables were considered jointly.

Such a general longitudinal analysis is deficient on several accounts. Expecting that changes in effectiveness are related to changes in interlocking, we need to examine patterns of interlocking, their stability or change, in response to fluctuations in effectiveness. We would want to examine whether firms with perennial financial interlocking show a greater constancy in profitability, whether the dissolution of a from-financial interlock is associated with a drop in earnings or sales, and whether a change in effectiveness caused by the loss of an interlock affects the organization's financial structure. We would also want to determine whether the relationship between the variables of this analysis are recursive or nonrecursive, that is, whether one variable affects a second or whether they exert mutual causation.

It is also important to combine longitudinal research with designs that treat the interdependence and effectiveness variables in their entirety. We have dealt with interdependence, effectiveness, and interlocking in a sequential fashion. However, as we alluded in Chapter Five, debt-to-equity or current ratio have different implications depending on whether a firm can meet its interest obligations over time. This ability hinges on the constancy of income streams and is particularly critical if the debt-to-equity ratio is high. We can further complicate this issue by mentioning a firm's growth. Generally most firms are motivated to expand beyond current levels of sales or assets. A firm's earnings may be considered a critical factor in disentangling the relationships that exist between capital dependence, growth, and new capital expenditures. We ought to examine a firm's sustainable growth in sales as a determinant of interlocking. Imagine a firm where it is unclear if its retained earnings are sufficient to maintain its rate of growth. Its growth in sales might require new capital expenditures. If the assets-to-sales ratio declines—if, for example, our firm relies heavily on overtime to meet increased demands, thereby stretching production capacity—the firm would be required to issue new stock or borrow from financial institutions to finance incremental production capacity. What about the firm's debt-to-equity ratio, its interest rates on debt outstanding, and its coverage as expressed by return on sales? All these variables considered together within the context of a longitudinal design might then provide a sharper delineation of the motivation to establish financial interlocks. Although the present data do not permit an analysis of such relationships, clearly an understanding of these relationships would enable us to further refine the conclusions of this study and to disprove rival explanations of the results.

More sophisticated, dynamically flavored research designs should also consider the relative importance of interlocking in enhancing a firm's effectiveness and, if possible, discern effectiveness due to interlocking from effectiveness resulting from internal efficiency. We have controlled for differences in industry when relating interlocking to effectiveness. Rival hypotheses remain possible. For example, some might say that a firm's effectiveness is not only the result of its interlocking but also because of other concomitant attempts to secure external control. We only have to point to the empirical correspondence between to-financial interlocks and investment in joint ventures. Alternative and supplementary actions to secure external control over environmental contingencies include cartels, exchange of executive manpower, self-regulation, and lobbying. Others might argue that the effectiveness correlates of interlocking are explained by the firm's management skills, specialized focus of market domains, or long-range planning. They would argue that firms that have adopted a specialized posture in their strategic orientation are likely to perform better than firms that have diversified by moving into different and unrelated markets (see Rumelt, 1974). They would interpret interlocking as indicative of shrewd, competent management. Some might suggest that interlocking is more desirable for the specialized firms that are not vertically integrated. Others would argue that financial interlocks would be particularly attractive for specialized firms that require information about areas beyond their immediate niche. Clearly these rival hypotheses merit further investigation.

Apart from mentioning the antecedents and consequences of interlocking that require further research, this chapter should also reinforce the desire for better access to the social processes that are implicit in the phenomena of that research. There is an obvious need for ideographic research with an ethnomethodological approach that would uncover the cooptation and persuasion processes that unfold when boundary-spanning persons from different organizations interact to resolve conflict and negotiate contracts and become exposed to rich, fresh, and timely information. This research will be extremely difficult because the participants involved are probably not inclined to disclose what is generally hidden. Historical documents revealing the selection and appointments of directors, minutes of critical board meetings, and other outcroppings might be more readily available and subject to content analysis. Such studies might permit a better solution to the problem of how patterns of interlocking are translated into decision-making inputs.

By now, we have seen that the metaphor of the black box is very appropriate to an explanation of interorganizational communication. Although we cannot scrutinize the communications themselves, as we cannot observe the internal mechanism of the black box, from archival data we can infer patterns of relationships. By examining the results and effects of interlocking, we can draw valid inferences about the functioning of the unseen mechanism.

❦❦❦❦❦❦ *SEVEN* ❦❦❦❦❦❦

Implications
for Public Policy

❦❦❦❦❦❦❦❦❦❦❦❦❦❦❦❦❦❦❦❦❦❦❦❦❦❦❦❦❦❦

Before discussing the implications of our findings, it is helpful to summarize the most significant results of our study. We have investigated one aspect of the 797 largest American corporations: the relationships among the organizations' strategic interdependence on firms in their environment, their economic effectiveness, and their propensity to form interlocking directorates. Our survey of these organizations showed that only 62 of them have no interlocks with the remaining 735 and that financial firms are disproportionately active in interlocking, especially in directional interlocking (Chapter Three).

　　Our analysis of interlocking behavior in various industries showed that there are considerable interindustry differences in the frequency of interlocking (Chapter Four). We studied one aspect of these industries' structure, their concentration ratio, in order to examine the effect of market structure on interlocking. We found that all measures of interlocking relate linearly to market structure: The frequency of interlocks—both horizontal and vertical—is highest in the most concentrated industries, those most nearly resembling a monopoly.

We then examined the interlocks between nonfinancial and financial organizations, a phenomenon that is interesting both because these interlocks are so prominent and also because they represent a highly visible form of interlocking between vertically interdependent organizations (Chapter Five). In analyzing the relationship between a firm's degree of capital dependence and its propensity to establish financial interlocks, we discovered that financial institutions avoid interlocks with nonfinancial firms that are saddled with debt, are capital intensive, or are not solvent. We had expected that firms that are strongly dependent on external financing would attempt to coopt financial institutions through interlocking in order to ensure their access to the capital market. Instead, we found that financial firms shun such interlocks, that they do not seek to supplement their implicit financial control over these risky firms with the control accorded by an interlock. Rather, the financial institutions promote interlocks with firms that are not risky, such as those that have a small debt-equity ratio. A comparison of various industries showed, however, that in some industries (energy, for example), financial interlocking and capital dependence are highly correlated. Our interindustrial analysis, however, was limited by the small number of firms in certain industrial categories.

We next considered the relationships among interdependence, interlocking, and effectiveness (Chapter Six). We assumed that, since interlocks grant firms access to information about the market, well-interlocked organizations would perform better on most measures of economic effectiveness. We found positive correlations between the number of interlocks and the firm's earnings, return on sales, return on fixed assets, and sales on assets. The positive effects of interlocking on financial performance are most pronounced for the directional financial interlocks that originate from the country's 100 largest financial firms.

To better understand the relationships among interlocking, interdependence, and effectiveness, we first examined the moderating influence of interdependence on the relationship between interlocking and effectiveness. Our interindustry comparison showed that the correlation between horizontal interlocks and effectiveness is high for some markets that have intermediate levels of concentration. Our analysis of financial interlocks showed that all performance indicators, except return on total assets, have a strong positive relationship with measures of interlocking for firms that have a low debt-equity ratio. In other words, firms that rely on equity financing and those that are capital intensive perform better if they are well interlocked with financial firms.

We then examined effectiveness as a moderating influence on the relationship between interdependence and interlocking. We found that effectiveness has little bearing on horizontal interdependence. Stagnant, slow growing firms showed a strong correlation between concentration and horizontal interlocking; no such correlation exists for sales-effective firms. Effectiveness, however, did influence the relationship between interlocking and financial dependence. While there is virtually no relationship between capital dependence and interlocking for ineffective organizations, there are strong and significant relationships for effective organizations. The influence of effectiveness is strongest on those financial interlocks in which a member of one of the large banks or insurance firms sits on the board of a nonfinancial firm; effectiveness does not play this differential role on the interlocks with small local firms. We found that the large financial firms avoid interlocks with poorly performing and risky firms; they do interlock with firms that are solvent and not at risk, even if such firms have considerable amounts of long-term debt.

From these findings, we hypothesized that financial interlocks in which a member of a financial firm sits on the board of a nonfinancial firm should not be construed as the nonfinancial firm's effort to coopt the financial institution. Rather, these interlocks are persuasive attempts by the financial firm to enhance its position with solvent firms that will be reliable customers for loans, bonds, and other forms of debt. Through these persuasive interlocks, the financial firm seeks to secure good customers, and the nonfinancial firms benefit from the bank's commitment and access to information about the market. An interesting by-product of this research was the discovery that firms well-interlocked with the financial community enjoy lower interest rates for their debt.

Many of these results stand in sharp contrast with findings of other investigators. (A summary of research is provided in Chapter Two.) Although the results of the present study do not necessarily nullify other researchers' findings, the comprehensiveness of our research design naturally produces results that are different than those of earlier studies. We feel our results to be more reliable because we have used specific measures of interlocking behavior and considered a number of relevant variables, including market structure, capital structure, and economic performance.

Our findings show that directional interlocking directorates are the singularly most important type of interlocks for predicting the propensity of organizations to establish interfirm ties and for understanding the relationship between interlocking and effectiveness. Measures of board composition are inferior predictors because they are defined only from the perspective of the focal organization and do not convey information on the focal organization's infiltration of other organizations' boards. In spite of this limitation, measures of board composition can be useful predictors if they are specific and delineate ties with institutionalized and well-bounded external constituencies.

Limitations of This Study

By focusing on interlocking alone, we leave open the possibility that other factors coincidental with interlocking account for the findings. Other forms of interorganizational communication include exchange of personnel, regulation (both self-imposed and public), trade associations, and private meetings (Pennings, 1980a). Several authors have indicated that contacts through quasi-public and private social clubs might facilitate the sharing of strategically relevant information (Baltzell, 1964; Braam, 1974). Apart from these personal forms of communication, strategically interdependent organizations also have access to more overt and radical methods for managing their relationships: mergers, joint ventures, diversification, and licensing agreements (Pennings, 1980a).

The relative efficacy of interlocking directorates compared with other manifestations of interfirm structure remains a question of debate and will undoubtedly continue to preoccupy many future researchers. We might say, as we did in Chapter One, that interlocking directorates could be located somewhere in the middle of the continuum between "markets" and "hierarchies" (Williamson, 1975). In Williamson's framework, hierarchies are complex organizations that are typically created to avoid market failures. Whenever a market begins to show flaws in the efficient allocation of resources, vertical integration or horizontal merger is considered. The so-called efficient capital markets discussed earlier do not show many market failures because the price of capital shows most, if not all, relevant information. Other markets are not so efficient because buyers know more than sellers, market conditions might change so that the contractual agreements in one period are inequitable in another period, or the exchange relationship between buyer and seller before the agreement is different from that after the agreement. These conditions are most prevalent in bilateral oligopolies, where the small number of firms invites opportunism, cheating, withholding of relevant information, and collusion. Williamson (1975) suggests that firms are motivated to withdraw from such markets by merging with a supplier, buyer, or competitor. In short, hierarchies are the organizational cure against market failures. Williamson sees no room for intermediate and less radical cures. For example, cartels and other forms of trust behavior are dismissed as being incapable in monitoring the behavior of the participants; they also do not allow the enforcement of norms, which is so typical of complex organizations.

Nevertheless, this book shows that interlocks are somewhere between markets and hierarchies and cannot be simply dismissed. They do not nullify market relationships of the tied firms, yet they impose some hierarchy as suggested by our discussion of boundary subsystems. Compared with cartels, trusts, joint ventures, and licensing agreements, they are highly informal, fluid, relatively invisible, and hence less amenable to public scrutiny. In combination with or as substitution for other intermediate forms—such as cartels, trade associations and private clubs and other meeting grounds—they might provide an alternative for more radical solutions, such as mergers. Interlocks might assist firms in coping with competitive conditions and in alleviating opportunism between financial institutions and their clientele. They are an alternative to vertical integration and horizontal merger, because they allow organizations to remain autonomous while permitting better intelligence and greater social control. Interlocked firms are exchange partners that are less likely to withhold information, be opportunistic, or cheat; in short, their transactional or competitive relationships are not as flawed as Williamson's discussion of market failures would imply. In all likelihood, Williamson would dismiss our claims for interlocks because interlocks do not grant firms the undisputed legitimacy to enforce interfirm norms and contractual traditions, nor do they provide the means for firms to monitor conformity as the interlocking director is comparatively ill-equipped to supervise interfirm exchanges.

Clearly, vertical integration and horizontal merger grant a firm a superior ability to control transactional deficiencies and flawed intelligence. Nevertheless, our findings indicate that interlocks are associated with organizational effectiveness. Interlocks have two advantages over mergers: the firms maintain their autonomy and they are less subject to antitrust regulation. One cannot dismiss the advantages of interlocks by asserting that their nonhierarchical influence is too limited to prevent market failures. Interlocking is most prevalent in markets where failures are most probable, and interlocking is associated with higher levels of organizational effectiveness. It would be interesting to further examine whether interlocking, as strategy for avoiding market failures, results in new transactional deficiencies, which reflect the inequality of information available to firms because of variations in interlocking.

A second limitation of this study has been our exclusive reliance on one class of variables to predict organizational effectiveness. Naturally, measures other than interlocking could be used to predict performance, including the talent of a firm's management and the degree of specialization of the firm's strategic plan. Perhaps shrewd managers realize the advantages of interlocking, but it is their business acumen, rather than the interlocks, that explains higher effectiveness. Similarly, some managers are less inclined to diversify their production if that requires entering remote and unknown markets. Ample evidence shows that specialized firms perform better than firms that have extended themselves over heterogeneous and unrelated areas (Rumelt, 1974). Accordingly, it would be interesting to investigate whether specialized firms have a greater need of sources of information, because of their limited horizons, and to determine whether their effectiveness depends on the extent of their interlocking.

A final caveat that should be observed by future researchers involves the narrow scope of our effectiveness measures. Organizational effectiveness is a multidimensional concept that can be evaluated on economic and noneconomic criteria (Pennings and Goodman, 1977). The economic measures of effectiveness used in this book do not allow us to evaluate the noneconomic consequences of interlocking. Unfortunately, a study of community support for well-tied local hospitals, the only study of interlocking and noneconomic effectiveness, is outdated and too specialized to be broadly applicable (Blankenship and Elling, 1962). The few other studies, such as the one by Bunting and Liu (1977), are subject to the same limitations as the present study.

Most unfortunately, the scope of our effectiveness measures precludes an evaluation of the consequences of interlocking for the public interest. Our study does, however, raise questions about possible harmful effects of interlocking on the public. On first view, it does not seem likely that all organizations act in concert to enhance their circumstances and to urge upon the government and its regulatory bodies a set of policies that benefits them in some undue respect. However, it seems possible that in the capital market or in particular industries interlocking might result in private or public policies that benefit some firms but contribute little to the welfare of all firms in that industry. Obviously, our study does not address these issues, but they are clearly germane to the proper assessment of the effects of interlocking. Our study does allow us to conclude by discussing whether the superior effectiveness of interlocked firms has antitrust implications.

Interlocking Directorates and Antitrust Policy

Do the effectiveness correlates of interlocking provide sufficient justification for a legislative ban on interlocking and stricter enforcement of the Clayton Act? Our answer to this question is rather unequivocal in the case of directional interlocking with large financial institutions, while the antitrust implications of general and horizontal interlocking are more difficult to delineate.

Distinct advantages accrue to a firm that has recruited a director from a large financial institution. Obviously, not all firms can enjoy these advantages because the number of such directors, especially those from the largest commercial banks, is quite limited. Furthermore, we have seen that the formation of financial interlocks is not a random process—on the contrary, market structure, financial soundness, and debt-equity position are important antecedents of interlocking directorates. Thus large financial institutions possess economic acumen and experience that they share with selected nonfinancial institutions through interlocks, and these interlocks are conducive to organizational effectiveness. Given this situation, we may ask whether such interlocks violate existing antitrust legislation and, if not, whether new legislation is needed.

Although the Clayton Act proscribes horizontal interlocks, it does not fully address the issue of vertical interlocks. Section 2 of the Clayton Act, as amended by the Robinson-Patman Act of 1936, allows a firm to quote different prices to different customers. For example, if a commercial bank charges different interest rates to different industrial firms, it does not necessarily violate the act or its amendment. In fact the Robinson-Patman amendment permits commercial banks to charge different interest rates if the cost of capital differs proportionally and if the interest rates are set "in good faith" (Stelzer, 1955). Section 3 invalidates contracts that prevent a customer from establishing agreements with competitors, where the effect may be less competition. It is Section 8 which prohibits interlocking directorates among competing organizations. Section 8 does not require the government to prove that a given horizontal interlock leads to restraint of trade; any interlock between competing organizations is a violation of the act, and the government can order its dissolution, without having to show that restraint of trade resulted.

Vertical interlocks are rather problematic under the Clayton Act. Both financial and nonfinancial vertical interlocks are obviously illegal if they violate Section 2 or Section 3 and the amendments. In such cases, however, the burden of proof rests with the Antitrust Division of the Justice Department or other antitrust agencies. They would have to be able to prove that a financial interlock permitted a bank to unfairly discriminate in favor of some organizations to the disadvantage of others. An antitrust suit that argued that the superior effectiveness of financially interlocked organizations constituted a violation of Sections 2 and 3 of the Clayton Act might find that their evidence is too circumstantial to meet the legal requirements. Lastly, we should note that the Clayton Act does not have provisions for invoking penalties on violators. When an antitrust agency detects a questionable interlock, it must notify the offending organization. If the interlock is then dissolved, the action is dismissed. Perhaps this is one of the reasons that antitrust agencies have not been more aggressive in eliminating interlocking directorates (Kalinoski, 1978).

A recent U.S. Senate report (1978) complains that the government lacks the means to monitor interlocking directorates. As shown in this study, it is even more difficult to monitor the interorganizational exchanges that must be considered in evaluating the dangers of a given vertical interlock or a general interlock. Although fewer distinct advantages are associated with general interlocks compared to financial interlocks, many of these general interlocks might represent significant ties between strategically interdependent organizations. It is impossible for researchers to determine the transactional bonds between suppliers other than those involving commercial banks and insurance companies because the information that would permit the identification of vertical, nonfinancial interlocks is considered proprietary. The U.S. Congress and the antitrust agencies have the subpoena powers to secure that information during their investigations, but as the Senate report notes, the government does not have an effective system for monitoring firms so that it can decide which firms merit investigation.

Since interlocks are difficult to monitor, one might consider the remedy to lie in legislation that would prohibit interlocking directorates. This solution seems impractical. If we were to prevent executives from serving as directors of organizations other than their own and if individuals were allowed to hold only one directorship, all interlocking would be prohibited, and all firms would be insulated. Such a measure, however, would introduce insurmountable barriers to an organization's attempts to recruit outside directors. The SEC regulations that require publicly held organizations to have outside directors inevitably result in the emergence of interlocking directorates. Furthermore, many of the existing interlocking directorates are in all likelihood irrelevant to antitrust issues. Most nonfinancial interlocking directorates may well be inconsequential, and the current required practice that individuals who hold multiple directorships disclose those memberships will indicate this.

Nevertheless, it is desirable that general and nonfinancial interlocking directors not be involved in a conflict of interests. Some vertical interlocks, for example, might be contrary to public interest. In order to prevent such abuses, firms should be required, when nominating a director, to disclose their transactional relationships with the firm associated with the potential director and to reveal their exchanges with that firm's competitors. Disclosure of interorganizational transactions that are related to the formation of a new interlock permits the identification of conflicts of interest, and the government could prohibit an interlock that interferes with the functioning of those transactions. For example, if an individual associated with a manufacturer of plastics has been invited to join the board of a rubber company, the rubber company should be required to disclose all transactions with the plastics manufacturer and, if relevant, to disclose the size of transactions with competing manufacturers.

Such mandatory disclosure of information presents a powerful means to avoid unacceptable interlocking directorates. Disclosure might be incompatible with the firm's opinion that such information is proprietary and its revelation would undermine its strategic position. Whenever this is the case, the firm might opt to declassify proprietary information or to refrain from nominating an individual affiliated with its suppliers or customers.

Several professional directors have indicated that such recommendations are obsolete. As a result of Watergate and other widely published corruption scandals, they argue, most corporations have reexamined the role and function of their boards of directors. Articles in the *Harvard Business Review*, the *Wall Street Journal*, and *Business Week* describe the new trends in corporate governance and the role of boards of directors. Bacon and Brown (1977) quote 248 executives from large U.S. corporations who emphasize the avoidance of conflict of interests when nominating new directors. Corporations may indeed now police themselves better in order to conform to the letter and spirit of the Clayton Act.

There is little doubt that the recent corporate scandals may have induced corporations to constitute new policies regarding the recruitment of executives and directors, and present practices may differ substantially from those in 1970. The extent of interlocking, however, has not changed much, as evidenced by a recent U.S. Senate

(1978) investigation. Most importantly, however, the results of this book suggest that certain forms of interlocking behavior should not be allowed. Although the excesses of interlocking behavior may have declined in the last decade, it is crucial that we understand which particular excesses appear to have been most harmful. With this knowledge we may act to prevent their recurrence in the future.

References

Adams, J. S. "The Structure and Dynamics of Behavior in Organizational Boundary Roles." In M. Dunette (Ed.), *Handbook of Organizational and Industrial Psychology.* Chicago: Rand McNally, 1976.

Aldrich, H. E. *Organizations and Environments.* Englewood Cliffs, N.J.: Prentice-Hall, 1979.

Aldrich, H. E. "Organization Sets, Action Sets, and Networks: Making the Most of Simplicity." In P. G. Nystrom and W. Starbuck (Eds.), *Handbook of Organizational Design.* Vol. 1. New York: Oxford University Press, 1980.

Allen, M. P. "The Structure of Interorganizational Elite Cooptation: Interlocking Corporate Directorates." *American Sociological Review*, 1974, *39*, 393–406.

Almond, G. A., and Verba, S. *Civic Culture*. Boston: Little, Brown, 1965.

Bacon, J., and Brown, J. *The Board of Directors: Perspectives and Practices in Nine Countries*. New York: Conference Board, 1977.

Baltzell, E.D. *The Protestant Establishment: Aristocracy and Caste in America*. New York: Random House, 1964.

Bearden, J., and others. "The Nature and Extent of Bank Centrality in Corporate Networks." Paper presented at the annual meeting of the American Sociological Association, San Francisco, September 1975.

Beaver, W. H. "The Information Content of Annual Earnings Announcements." *Journal of Accounting Research*, 1968, *6* (Supplement "Empirical Research in Accounting: Selected Studies"), 67–92.

Berkowitz, S. D., Carrington, P. J., and Corman, J. S. "Flexible Design for a Corporate Information Data Base." Paper presented at the annual meeting of the American Sociological Association, San Francisco, September 1978.

Berkowitz, S. D., and others. "The Determination of Enterprise Groupings Through Combined Ownership and Directorship Ties." Working Paper No. 7807. Institute for Policy Analysis, University of Toronto, 1978.

Blankenship, L. V., and Elling, R. H. "Organizational Support and Community Power Structure: The Hospital." *Journal of Health and Social Behavior*, 1962, *5*, 257–269.

Bonacich, P. "A Technique for Analyzing Overlapping Membership." In H. L. Costner (Ed.), *Sociological Methodology 1972*. San Francisco: Jossey-Bass, 1972.

Bonacich, P., and Domhoff, G. W. "Overlapping Membership Among Clubs and Policy Groups of the American Ruling Class: A Methodological and Empirical Contribution to the Class-Hegemony Paradigm of the Power Structure." Paper presented at the annual meeting of the American Sociological Association, Chicago, September 1977.

Braam, G. P. A. "Influence of Business Firms on the Government: New Method for Determining the Distribution of Influence, Applied in the Netherlands." *Sociologia Neerlandica*, 1974, *10*, 72–91.

Brandeis, L. D. "Breaking the Money Trusts." *Harper's Weekly*, December 6, 1913.

Breiger, R. L. "The Duality of Persons and Groups." *Social Forces*, 1974, *53*, 181–191.

Brown, C. C. *Putting the Corporate Board to Work.* New York: Macmillan, 1976.

Brown, C. C., and Smith, E. E. *The Director Looks at His Job.* New York: Columbia University Press, 1957.

Brown, P., and Kennelly, J. W. "The Information Content of Quarterly Earnings: An Extension and Some Further Evidence." *Journal of Business,* 1972, *45,* 403–415.

Bunting, D., and Liu, T-h. "Economic and Social Dimensions of Interlocking." Paper presented at the annual meeting of the American Sociological Association, Chicago, September 1977.

Burt, R. S. "A Structural Theory of Interlocking Corporate Directorates." *Social Networks,* 1979, *1,* 4.

Burt, R. S. "Cooptative Corporate Actor Networks: A Reconsideration of Interlocking Directorates Involving American Manufacturing." *Administrative Science Quarterly,* 1980, *25,* 3.

Cohen, J. "Multiple Regression as a General Data Analytic System." *Psychological Bulletin,* 1968, *70,* 426–443.

Coleman, J. *Power and the Structure of Society.* New York: Norton, 1974.

Commerce Clearing House. *Capital Changes Reporter.* Clark, N.J.: Commerce Clearing House, 1977.

Daems, H. "Invisible Concentration and Holding Companies: The Case of Belgium." Working Paper No. 77–1. Brussels: European Institute for Advanced Studies in Management, 1977.

Directory of Directors Company. *Directory of Directors in the City of New York.* New York: Directory of Directors Co., 1971.

Domhoff, G. W. *Who Rules America?* Englewood Cliffs, N.J.: Prentice-Hall, 1967.

Dooley, P. "The Interlocking Directorate." *American Economic Review,* 1969, *59,* 314–323.

Dun and Bradstreet. *Dun and Bradstreet Million Dollar Directory, 1971.* New York: Dun and Bradstret, 1970.

Dun and Bradstreet. *Reference Book of Corporate Managements.* New York: Dun and Bradstreet, 1971.

Economic Report of the President. Washington, D.C.: U.S. Government Printing Office, 1979.

Emerson, R. M. "Power-Dependence Relations." *American Sociological Review,* 1962, *27,* 31–40.

"End of the Directors' Rubber Stamp." *Business Week,* September 10, 1979, 72–83.

Erdos, P. *The Art of Counting: Selected Writings.* (J. Spencer, Ed.) Cambridge, Mass.: M.I.T. Press, 1973.

"Evading an Edict: Grumman Panel Finds Payoff Continued Despite Board's Policy." *Wall Street Journal,* February 28, 1979.

Evan, W. M. "An Organization Set Model of Inter-Organizational Relations." In R. Chisolm, M. Tuite, and M. Radnor (Eds.), *Inter-Organizational Decision Making.* Chicago: Aldine, 1973.

Fama, E. F., and others. "The Adjustment of Stock Prices to New Information." *International Economic Review,* 1969, *10,* 1–21.

Faris, G. W. "Executive Cohesiveness and Financial Performance of the Fortune 500: A Preliminary Analysis." Paper presented at the 39th annual meeting of the Academy of Management, Atlanta, August 1979.

Fennema, M. "Car Firms in the European Communities: A Study on Personal Linkages, Joint Ventures and Financial Participation." Paper presented at the conference of the European Consortium for Political Research, Strasbourg, France, March–April 1974.

"The Fortune Directory of Large Corporations." *Fortune Magazine,* 1970, *82,* 182–218.

Freitag, P. "The Cabinet and Big Business: A Study of Interlocks." *Sociological Focus,* 1975, *23,* 137–152.

"FTC Official Ruled that SCM Corp. Should be Formally Barred from Having Directors also Serve on Boards of Competing Companies." *Wall Street Journal,* July 9, 1978.

Gogel, R., Koenig, T., and Sonquist, J. A. "Corporate Control Reexamined." Santa Barbara: Department of Sociology, University of California, 1976.

Goodman, P. S., and Pennings, J. M. "Critical Issues in Assessing Organizational Effectiveness." In E. E. Lawler, D. A. Nadler, and C. Cammann (Eds.), *Organizational Assessment: Perspectives on the Measurement of Organizational Behavior and the Quality of Working Life.* New York: Wiley-Interscience, 1980.

Grabowski, H. G., and Baxter, N. D. "Rivalry in Industrial Research and Development: An Empirical Study." *Journal of Industrial Economics,* 1973, *21,* 209–235.

Granovetter, M. S. "The Strength of Weak Ties." *American Journal of Sociology,* 1973, *78,* 1360–1380.

Hannan, M. T., and Freeman, J. "The Population Ecology of Organizations." *American Journal of Sociology,* 1977a, *82,* 929–966.

Hannan, M. T., and Freeman, J. "Obstacles to Comparative Studies." In P. S. Goodman, J. M. Pennings, and Associates, *New Perspectives on Organizational Effectiveness*. San Francisco: Jossey-Bass, 1977b.

Harary, F., Norman, P., and Cartwright D. *Structural Models: An Introduction to the Theory of Directional Graphs*. New York: Wiley, 1965.

Helmers, H., and others. *Graven naar Macht* [Digging for Power]. Amsterdam: Van Gennep, 1975.

Helmich, D. "Executive Succession in the Corporate Organization: A Current Integration." *Academy of Management Review*, 1977, *2*, 252-266.

Hickson, D. J., and others. "A Strategic Contingencies Theory of Intraorganizational Powers." *Administrative Science Quarterly*, 1971, *16*, 216-229.

Hirsch, P. M. "Organizational Analysis and Industrial Sociology: An Instance of Cultural Lag." *American Sociologist*, 1975, *10*, 3-12.

"Investigating the Collapse of W. T. Grant." *Business Week*, July 19, 1978, 60-62.

Janis, I. L., and Mann, L. *Decision Making*. New York: Free Press, 1977.

Johnston, J. *Econometric Methods*. (2nd ed.) New York: McGraw-Hill, 1972.

Juran, J. M., and Louden, J. K. *The Corporate Director*. New York: American Management Association, 1966.

Kalinoski, J. O. von, *Antitrust Laws and Trade Regulation*. New York: Matthew Bender, 1978.

Kaplan, R. S., and Roll, R. "Investor Evaluation of Accounting Information: Some Empirical Evidence." *Journal of Business*, 1972, *45*, 225-257.

Katz, D., and Kahn, R. L. *The Social Psychology of Organizations*. (2nd ed.) New York: Wiley, 1978.

Kinley, J. R. *Corporate Directorship Practices*. Studies in Business Policy, No. 103. New York: National Industrial Conference Board, 1962.

Kintner, E. W. *An Antitrust Primer: A Guide to Antitrust and Trade Regulation Laws for Businessmen*. (2nd ed.) New York: Macmillan, 1973.

Knowles, J. C. *The Rockefeller Financial Group*. New York: Mss Information Corp., 1974.

Koenig, T., Gogel, R., and Sonquist, J. A. "An Investigation into the Significance of Corporate Interlocks in the American Economy." Santa Barbara: Department of Sociology, University of California, 1973.

Koenig, T., Gogel, R., and Sonquist, J. A. "Corporate Interlocking Directorates as a Social Network." Santa Barbara: Department of Sociology, University of California, 1976.

Koontz, H. *The Board of Directors and Effective Management*. New York: McGraw-Hill, 1967.

Laumann, E. O., and Pappi, F. U. "New Directions in the Study of Community Elites." *American Sociological Review*, 1973, *38*, 212–230.

Leontief, W. *Input-Output Economics*. New York: Oxford University Press, 1966.

Lev, B. *Financial Statement Analysis: A New Approach*. Englewood Cliffs, N.J.: Prentice-Hall, 1974.

Levine, J. H. "The Sphere of Influence." *American Sociological Review*, 1972, *37*, 14–27.

Levine, J. H. "The Network of Corporate Interlocks in the United States: An Overview." Paper presented at Advanced Symposium on Social Networks, Dartmouth College, September 1975.

Lieberson, S. E. "An Empirical Study of Military-Industrial Linkages." *American Journal of Sociology*, 1971, *76*, 562–584.

Lundberg, F. *The Rich and the Super-Rich*. New York: Bantam Books, 1969.

Lupton, T., and Wilson, C. S. "The Social Background and Connections of 'Top Decision Makers'." *Manchester School of Economic and Social Studies*, 1959, *27*, 30–51.

McDougal, W. J. (Ed.). *The Effective Director*. London, Ontario: School of Business Administration, University of Western Ontario, 1969.

Mace, M. *Directors: Myth and Reality*. Cambridge, Mass.: Harvard University Press, 1971.

Mansfield, E. "Entry, Gibrat's Law, Innovation and the Growth of Firms." *American Economic Review*, 1962, *52*, 296–307.

Mariolis, P. "Interlocking Directorates and Control of Corporations: The Theory of Bank Control." *Social Science Quarterly*, 1975, *56*, 425-439.

Marquis Who's Who. *Who's Who in America 1970-1971*. Chicago: Marquis Who's Who, 1970a.

Marquis Who's Who. *Who's Who in the Midwest 1970-1971*. Chicago: Marquis Who's Who, 1970b.

Marquis Who's Who. *Who's Who in Finance and Industry 1972-1973*. Chicago: Marquis Who's Who, 1971a.

Marquis Who's Who. *Who's Who in the South and Southwest 1971-1972*. Chicago: Marquis Who's Who, 1971b.

Marquis Who's Who. *Who's Who in the West 1971-1972*. Chicago: Marquis Who's Who, 1971c.

Marquis Who's Who. *Who's Who in America 1972-1973*. Chicago: Marquis Who's Who, 1972.

Marquis Who's Who. *Who's Who in the East 1972-1973*. Chicago: Marquis Who's Who, 1973.

Marx, K., and Engels, F. E. *The Marx-Engels Reader*. (R. C. Tucker, Ed.) New York: Norton, 1971.

Meyer, J. W. "Strategies for Further Research: Varieties of Environmental Variations." In M. W. Meyer (Ed.), *Environments and Organizations: Theoretical and Empirical Perspectives*. San Francisco: Jossey-Bass, 1978.

Meyer, M. W., and Associates. *Environments and Organizations: Theoretical and Empirical Perspectives*. San Francisco: Jossey-Bass, 1978.

Mills, C. W. *The Power Elite*. New York: Oxford University Press, 1965.

Mindlin, S. E., and Aldrich, H. E. "Interorganizational Dependence: A Review of the Concept and a Re-examination of the Findings of the Aston Group." *Administrative Science Quarterly*, 1975, *20*, 382-392.

"Minority Banks May Get Clearance for Interlocks." *Wall Street Journal*, October 12, 1976.

Modigliani, F., and Miller, M. H. "The Cost of Capital, Corporation Finance and the Theory of Investment." *American Economic Review*, 1958, *47*, 261-297.

Mokken, R. J., and Stokman, F. N. "Interlocking Directorates Between Large Corporations, Banks and Other Financial Companies and Institutions in the Netherlands in 1969." Paper presented at the conference of the European Consortium for Political Research, Strasbourg, France, March–April 1974.

Mokken, R. J., and Stokman, F. N. "Traces of Power III: Corporate Governmental Networks in the Netherlands." In H. J. Hummel, (Ed.), *Mathematische Ansatze Zur Analyse Sozialar Macht* [Mathematical Essays on the Analysis of Social Power]. Duisburg, West Germany: Sozial Wissen Schaftliche Kooperative, 1978.

Mueller, R. K. *New Directions for Directors.* Lexington, Mass.: Lexington Books, 1978.

Nader, R., Green, M., and Seligman, J. *Taming the Giant Corporation.* New York: Norton, 1977.

Parsons, T. *Structure and Process in Modern Societies.* New York: Free Press, 1960.

Pennings, J. M. "Strategically Interdependent Organizations." In P. G. Nystrom and W. Starbuck (Eds.), *Handbook of Organizational Design.* Vol. 1. New York: Oxford University Press, 1980a.

Pennings, J. M. "Mergers and Interlocking Directorates: Cases of Interorganizational Cooperation." In A. Edstrom, W. Goldberg, and H. Daems (Eds.), *Mergers and Interfirm Cooperation.* London: Praeger, 1980b.

Pennings, J. M., and Goodman, P. S. "Towards a Workable Framework." In P. S. Goodman, J. M. Pennings, and Associates, *New Perspectives on Organizational Effectiveness.* San Francisco: Jossey-Bass, 1977.

Perrucci, R., and Pilisuk, M. "Leaders and Ruling Elites: The Interorganizational Bases of Community Power." *American Sociological Review*, 1970, *35*, 1040–1057.

Pfeffer, J. "Size and Composition of Corporate Board of Directors: The Organization and Its Environment." *Administrative Science Quarterly*, 1972, *17*, 218–228.

Pfeffer, J. "Size, Composition and Function of Hospital Boards of Directors: A Study of Organization-Environment Linkage." *Administrative Science Quarterly*, 1973, *18*, 349–364.

Pfeffer, J. and Nowak, P. "Organizational Context and Interorganizational Linkages Among Corporations." Berkeley: University of California, 1977.

Pfeffer, J., and Salancik, G. R. *The External Control of Organizations: A Resource Dependence Perspective.* New York: Harper & Row, 1978.

Porter, J. *The Vertical Mosaic.* Toronto: University of Toronto Press, 1965.

Pugh, D. S., and others. "The Context of Organizational Structure." *Administrative Science Quarterly,* 1969, *14,* 91–114.

Rumelt, R. *Strategy, Structure and Economic Performance.* Cambridge, Mass.: Harvard University Press, 1974.

Salancik, G. R. "Commitment and the Control of Organizational Behavior and Belief." In B. M. Staw and G. R. Salancik (Eds.), *New Directions in Organizational Behavior.* Chicago: St. Clair Press, 1977.

Scherer, F. M. *Industrial Market Structure and Economic Performance.* Chicago: Rand McNally, 1970.

Schoeffler, S. "Cross-Sectional Study of Strategy, Structure and Performance." In H. B. Thorelli (Ed.), *Strategy + Structure = Performance.* Bloomington, Ind.: Indiana University Press, 1977.

Selznick, P. *TVA and the Grass Roots.* Berkeley: University of California Press, 1949.

Sonquist, J. A., and Koenig, T. "Interlocking Directorates in the Top U.S. Corporations: A Graph Theory Approach." *The Insurgent Sociologist,* Spring 1975, 5.

Standard and Poor's Corporation. *Standard and Poor's Earnings Forecaster.* New York: Standard and Poor's Corp., 1968, 1969.

Standard and Poor's Corporation. *Poor's Register of Corporations, Directors, and Executives.* New York: Standard and Poor's Corp., 1970, 1971 (yearly).

Standard and Poor's Corporation. *Security Owner's Stock Guide.* New York: Standard and Poor's Corp., 1973.

Stelzer, I. M. *Selected Antitrust Cases.* Homewood, Ill.: Irwin, 1955.

Stern, F. *Gold and Iron: Bismarck, Bleichröder and the Building of the German Empire.* New York: Knopf, 1976.

Stern W., and Morgenroth, W. M. "Concentration, Mutually Recognized Interdependence and the Allocation of Marketing Resources." *Journal of Business,* 1968, *14,* 56–67.

Stigler, G. J. "A Theory of Oligopoly." *Journal of Political Economy,* 1964, *72,* 44-61.

Stigler, G. J. *The Organization of Industry*. Homewood, Ill.: Irwin, 1968.

Thompson, J. D. *Organizations in Action*. New York: McGraw-Hill, 1967.

Treynor, J. L. "The Trouble with Earnings." *Financial Analysts Journal*, 1972, *28*, 43.

Useem, M. "The Social Organization of the American Business Elite and Participation of Corporation Directors in the Governance of American Institutions." *American Sociological Review*, 1979, *44*, 553–571.

U.S. Congress. *Control of Commercial Banks and Interlocks Among Financial Institutions*. Washington, D.C.: U.S. Government Printing Office, 1967.

U.S. Federal Trade Commission. *Report on Interlocking Directorates*. Washington, D.C.: U.S. Government Printing Office, 1951.

U.S. House of Representatives, Committee on Banking and Currency. *Investigation of Concentration of Control of Money and Credit*. Washington, D.C.: U.S. Government Printing Office, 1913.

U.S. House of Representatives, Committee on Banking and Currency, Subcommittee on Domestic Finance. *Commercial Banks and Their Trust Activities: Emerging Influences on the American Economy*. Washington, D.C.: U.S. Government Printing Office, 1968.

U.S. House of Representatives, Committee on the Judiciary, Antitrust Subcommittee. *Interlocks in Corporate Management*. Washington, D.C.: U.S. Government Printing Office, 1965.

U.S. Senate, Committee on Governmental Affairs, Subcommittee on Reports, Accounting, and Management. *Interlocking Directorates Among the Major U.S. Corporations*. Washington, D.C.: U.S. Government Printing Office, 1978.

Vance, S. C. *The Corporate Director*. Homewood, Ill.: Dow Jones–Irwin, 1968.

Wallace, C. *The Canadian Corporate Elite*. Toronto: McClelland and Stewart, 1975.

Warner, W. L., and Unwalla, D. B. "The System of Interlocking Directorates." In W. L. Warner, D. B. Unwalla, and J. H. Trimm (Eds.), *The Emergent American Society*. Vol. I: *Large Scale Organizations*. New Haven, Conn.: Yale University Press, 1967.

Weiss, W. "Average Concentration Ratios and Industrial Performance." *Journal of Industrial Economics*, 1962, *11*, 237–254.

Whitley, R. "Commonalities and Connections Among Directors of Large Financial Institutions." *Sociological Review*, 1973, *21*, 613–632.

"Who's Where in Profitability." *Forbes*, January 1970, 44.

Wilensky, H. L. *Organizational Intelligence.* New York: Basic Books, 1969.

Williamson, O. E. *Markets and Hierarchies.* New York: Free Press, 1975.

Zald, M. N. "The Power and Function of Boards of Directors: A Theoretical Synthesis." *American Journal of Sociology*, 1969, *75*, 97–111.

Zeitlin, M. "Corporate Ownership and Control: The Large Corporation and the Capitalist Class." *American Journal of Sociology*, 1974, *79*, 1073–1119.

Zeitlin, M., Neuman, W., and Ratcliff, R. E. "Class Segments: Agrarian Property and Political Leadership in the Capitalist Class of Chile." *American Sociological Review*, 1976, *41*, 1006–1029.

Zeitlin, M., Ratcliff, R. E., and Ewen, L. W. "The 'Inner Group': Interlocking Directorates and the Internal Differentiation of the Capitalist Class of Chile." Paper presented at the annual meeting of the American Sociological Association, Montreal, September 1974.

Index

211